Charles George Deuther

The Life and Times of the Rt. Rev. John Timon, D. D.

First Roman Catholic bishop of the Diocese of Buffalo

Charles George Deuther

The Life and Times of the Rt. Rev. John Timon, D. D.
First Roman Catholic bishop of the Diocese of Buffalo

ISBN/EAN: 9783744775205

Printed in Europe, USA, Canada, Australia, Japan

Cover: Foto ©Lupo / pixelio.de

More available books at **www.hansebooks.com**

Yrs. affectionately
✠ John Bp. of Buffalo

THE LIFE AND TIMES

OF THE

RT. REV. JOHN TIMON, D. D.

FIRST ROMAN CATHOLIC BISHOP

OF THE

DIOCESE OF BUFFALO.

By CHARLES G. DEUTHER.

PUBLISHED BY THE AUTHOR,
No. 184 WASHINGTON STREET, BUFFALO, N. Y.

1870.

TO THE MEMORY

OF HIS

Deceased Friend and College Companion,

REV. CHARLES B. MAGENNIS,

OF WORCESTER, MASSACHUSETTS,

AS A TRIBUTE OF FRIENDSHIP,

The pages of this volume are affectionately dedicated,

BY THE AUTHOR.

PREFACE.

Three years have transpired since I commenced to compile the pages of this present volume. Having had no time to devote to this work, beyond my evening hours and a few holidays, I have necessarily been delayed in bringing my labors to an earlier termination. In justice to myself I must state that owing to the extreme difficulty with which I obtained data, the compilation of this biography has been accomplished under no small embarrassments. When it will be considered that Bishop Timon was a man of a very retiring disposition, whose early history, until now, has been buried in obscurity owing to his reticence, and that he has left little or no record of his personal identity, the magnitude of undertaking his biography becomes at once apparent. It has been by dint of continual and repeated correspondence with Archbishops, Bishops, Priests, some Sisters of Charity, and many laymen, that bits of incident and information have been put together until they have swelled into the present sized volume. Besides this, there must also be added a heavy cash outlay, all of which combined have assisted me to defeat the embarrassments, in the beginning so threatening and dangerous to my enterprise.

My most sincere thanks are hereby tendered to the following kind friends for the generous aid they have given me:

Rt. Rev. Edward Fitzgerald, Bishop, Little Rock, Arkansas; Rt. Rev. S. V. Ryan, Bishop, Buffalo, N. Y.; Rev. B. Villiger, S. J., Conevago, Adams Co., Pa.; Rev. George Pax, Williamsville, N. Y.; Rev. Joseph Story, Brockport, N. Y.; Rev. Father Smarius, S. J., Chicago, Ill.; Col. Creed Taylor, Arkansas; Mr. Thomas Winstanley, Red Budd, Randolph Co., Ill.; Mr. Michael Hagan, Wyoming, C. W.; Geo. A. Deuther, Buffalo, N. Y.; Mother St. John, Philadelphia, Pa.; Miss Sallie Lilly, Conevago, Adams Co., Pa.

For convenience sake, I have divided my volume into two books: Book I comprises "The Early and Missionary Life of Rev. John Timon." Book II comprises "The Episcopacy of the Rt. Rev. John Timon, D. D."

Each Book is subdivided into several appropriate chapters.

In Book I, it will be noticed that Bishop Timon had several controversies with ministers of Protestant denominations, but that the names of the contending ministers are not given. These are no errata of mine. I have carefully perused such posthumous writings of the Bishop as I could command, but could find no mention any where of their names. These omissions, though odious to many readers, will therefore be pardonable on my part. For the verity of the incidents themselves, however, I have the Bishop's own handwriting.

I now consign the result of my humble efforts—this book—to the charity of the world, anxious to know the fate that will befall it. In any event, I am candid to express the pride I feel in having been the instrument of collecting together and preserving for coming time the virtues of a saintly man, whose memory, like the ivy, has been entwined with my heart's best affections since my childhood.

CHARLES G. DEUTHER.

INTRODUCTION.

PERHAPS one of the most interesting and distinguishing features in the history of the Catholic Church, either on this continent, or in Europe, has been the mysterious order of Divine Providence in elevating to the ministry men who have been peculiarly fitted, both by nature and education, to carry into operation the purposes of true revealed religion. Generally such selections have fallen on persons of humble circumstances, or obscure parentage. In the choice of His apostles and disciples, our Divine Saviour chose to ordain, as the disseminators of His heavenly doctrines, men gifted by nature with talents and great powers of discrimination, but blessed with little or no education. During the long and changing epochs of the world's history, what sublime examples have occurred of men revered for virtue, and esteemed for learning, acquired under the holy discipline of the Church. A great many of the Roman Pontiffs sprang from parentage distinguished, perhaps, only for piety, and respectability among the class to which they belonged.

These men have left after them memories that endear them to the christian and to religion. Divine Providence, as it were, seems to have delighted in making a bright example of an unknown but worthy human being, whose only credentials at the court of religion were his intelligence, his virtue, and his christian charity. Thus, age after age, new but splendid lights in the history of the Church have appeared, whose lives have been as varied as their characters. When persecution, dire and bitter, assailed the Church, and threatened to destroy, root and branch, the christian religion, how sublimely grand stood the vicegerent of heaven, aided and supported by a subordinate hierarchy of venerable men, before his enemies, as well as foes to true liberty, law and order, to fight the good fight of faith.

Nor could the lusts, the pride, and the ambition of worldly rulers, find an influence sufficiently potent to vanquish their moral courage. Banishment, proscription, tortures, and even death, had no terrors for them. Immovable in their principles, firm and unfaltering in their faith, they trembled only before a Supreme Being. Whether we admire more the courage that enabled a St. Ambrose to deny admission into the church door to a worldly potentate, until he had done penance for having unnecessarily dipped his hands in human blood, or, the meekness and forbearance of a Pontiff going into exile at Gaeta at the behest of a temporal power, our inferences, so far as the *sublimity* of Catholic doctrine is concerned, will still be the same. There is a broad scope for thought on this point. It necessarily leads us to inquire into the doctrines upon which have been predicated the moral heroisms and holy courage that have endured even death itself; that have given impulse to discovery, to invention, and the progress of the sciences and the arts; that have instituted houses of refuge, and asylums for indigence and sickness; that have saved from the corroding tooth of time the links that bind modern time to antiquity, in the vast accumulation of ancient writings and manuscripts; in fine, that have in their calendar so many illustrious heroes, martyrs, and saints, long since enrolled with the Church triumphant, ministering in eternal adoration and praise to the Creator of the universe.

However, aside from any consideration of the mysterious influence that has, does, and will enable a true Catholic to endure and to accomplish in the service of God, the question may be asked: What is the value attached to a perusal of biographies of these men, distinguished in the hierarchy of the Catholic Church?

It may not be a generally admitted fact, that biographies of any class of men, in any way, are entitled to consideration; and yet, they are one of the most interesting forms of history. Indeed, a due familiarity with the lives of great and good men may not only be instructive, but also be an incentive to imitate their example.

> "Lives of great men all remind us
> We may make our lives sublime;
> And, departing, leave behind us
> Footprints on the sands of time."—LONGFELLOW.

From the histories of men commemorated for their virtues, we may indeed gather food for reflection. We may meditate upon their peculiar traits of character, either developed by the force of necessity, or awakened into public recognition by some sudden and unforeseen circumstance. We may admire the strict integrity of the one, weep over the heroic but unfortunate fate that befell the other, and feel the sigh of sympathy in our bosoms for human weakness, as it is developed in the lives of such men as a David or a Solomon. Besides a certain interest that we feel in the lives of great men, there is also a moral intuition that moulds our thoughts and even controls our passions. With what enthusiasm do we not read the histories of men around whose names linger the memories of renowned institutions and great deeds, even as the fragrance lingers around the vase after the roses have been removed; and, as we read, how imperceptibly a spirit of emulation gradually animates us, until we almost imagine we are participating in the very circumstances of which we are reading.

Another value attached to a perusal of the lives of great and good men, is that of example. Examples, indeed, are most potent arguments either for evil or for good. If for good, expanding our hopes and dispelling our fears, or swelling every vein of principle or honor with an honest spirit of envy; at other times giving to our thoughts tints of beauty or the electric impulse of imitation. But it is not our intention to enter into any lengthy argument or disquisition on this point, to convince the reader of the truth of what we claim, excepting so far as to place in bold relief the fact that the lives of great and good men deserve the recognition of candid minds, because of the instruction we may derive from those God-like virtues, charity, religion, and truth which, when effectively applied, transcend even the most magnificent conceptions of man. Still, it is a difficult thing sometimes to understand, how certain results are brought about, and how mysterious are the wonderful workings of Providence. "Man proposes, but God disposes."

Hence, in the order of circumstances and time, there are born men possessed of talents peculiar to the various circles of life. Whilst we may observe one aspiring to reach a conspicuous position in the Parthenon of fame, either for science or for letters, we may see another, the pious yet ambitious disciple of Christianity, straining every nerve to rescue from misery or oppression the unfortunate and indigent of society. We may find him erecting, "*ad majorem Dei gloriam,*" not only elaborate and finely furnished places of Divine worship, but likewise institutions dedicated to sickness, to education, and to monastic discipline.

As an instance of this latter class of men, we may mention the name of the late Right Reverend John Timon, D. D., first Roman Catholic Bishop of the Diocese of Buffalo, N. Y.

CONTENTS.

BOOK I.

CHAPTER I.

Birth-place of Bishop Timon.—Parentage.—Date of Birth and Baptism.—Brothers and Sisters.—Incidents and Characteristics of the Elder Timon.—Removes to Baltimore, Md.—To Louisville, Ky.—To St. Louis, Mo.—Engaged in the Dry Goods Business.—John Timon as a Clerk.—His Accomplishments.—Makes Acquaintance with Miss De Gallon.—Engaged to the Young Lady, but never Married.—Death of Miss De Gallon.—Crisis of 1823.—Business Misfortunes.—Resolves to become a Lazarist... 17..25

CHAPTER II.

Joins the Community of the Lazarists.—Enters the Seminary of the Barrens, Mo.—Meets Mons. J. M. Odin there.—Early Reminiscences of the Lazarists in this Country.—The Seminary in 1824.—Incidents, &c.—Industry and Zeal of young Mr. Timon.—Promoted to Sub-deaconship.—Correspondence of Col. Creed Taylor.—Promoted to Minor Orders.—Joins the Order of St. Vincent de Paul.................. 25..31

CHAPTER III.

Surroundings of the Barrens, Mo.—Mons. Odin and Timon as Missionaries.—Hog Pen Converted into a Chapel.—Start for New Madrid, Texas.—Dangerous Traveling.—Dialogue with a Lady.—Arrive at the Port of Arkansas.—Quapaw Indians.—Their Belief.—Return to the Barrens.—Mission in Illinois... 32..37

CHAPTER IV.

Ordination of John Timon.—Called to see a Murderer condemned to Death.—Discussion with a Baptist Minister.—Defeats him.—Mission in Cape Girardeau.—Conversion of Mr. Ralph Doherty.—Cholera.—Mr. Doherty ill.—Father Timon called in too late.—Baptism of Mrs. Doherty.—A Night with a Cholera Corpse.—Baptism of Children.—Father Timon and the Irishman.—Confession on Horseback.—Happy Denouement... 38..46

CHAPTER V.

Mons. J. M. Odin.—Bishop Rosatti and the Barrens.—Embarrassments of the Seminary.—Meeting of the professed Priests.—Father Timon Speaker for the Community.—Bishop Rosatti responds.—Rev. J. B. Tornatori Chosen Superior of the Missions.—Purchase of the Doherty Estate.—The Sick Woman.—Her Conversion.—Incidents.—Condition of the Missions.—Discouraging Prospects.—Father Timon vanquishes six Ministers in a Discussion.—Interview with a condemned Man.—Mr. Odin goes to France.............................. 46..55

CHAPTER VI.

Father Timon named Visitor.—His Refusal.—Discouraging Circumstances.—His Humility.—He Accepts.—Convocation of Priests.—Remonstrance against the Suppression of the College.—Debts, Mortgage and Discontented Feelings prevail.—Improvements made.—Father Timon goes to New Orleans, La.—Goes to Cape Girardeau.—Returns to the Barrens.—Father Timon and the Bishop of St. Louis.—The Visitor goes to Paris, France.—His Arrival there.—Results.—His Return.—Nearly loses a large Sum of Money.—Reaches the Barrens in Safety.. 55..65

CHAPTER VII.

Improvements in the Mission.—The Visitor goes to Texas as an Envoy of Rome.—Meets Friends in Galveston.—Goes to Houston.—Opens a Mission.—Results.—Poor O'Brien.—Scandalous Conduct of two Mexican Priests.—Visitor returns to New Orleans.—His Report.—Arrives at Natchez, Miss.—Reads Mass in Mrs. Girardeau's House.—Preaches in the City Hall.—Enthusiasm.—Goes to St. Louis.—Religious Zeal.—Proposed for an Episcopal See.—Declines.—Refuses to Administrate the St. Louis Diocese.—Further Developments................ 65..72

CHAPTER VIII.

Mr. Tornatori and the Drawing Master.—Mission of Oauchita.—Visitor Timon appointed Prefect Apostolic of Texas.—Mons. Odin sent to Texas as vice-Prefect.—The two Mexican Priests silenced.—Visitor with Bishop Flaget visits the Missions.—Visitor quells a Parish Strife.—New Church for Cairo.—Evils at Assumption.—Visitor goes to Texas.—Subscription for a new Church.—Funeral Rites of Minister to Mexico.—Meets with General Henderson.—Preaches in the Capitol.—A Church for Houston.—Goes to Austin.—Dangerous Travel.—State of Texas.—Grand Reception by Judge Burnet.—First Mass in Austin.—Dines with the French Minister.—Table Talk............ 72..79

CHAPTER IX.

Petition to Restore Church Property.—Visitor Timon Preaches in the Senate Chamber.—Public Complimentary Dinner.—Discussion.—Visitor Timon explains.—Missionary Excursions in the Colorado River.—Oysters.—Return to Galveston.—First Convert.—Difficult Travel.—Good Results.—The Gospel in St. Augustine, Florida.—The Visitor parts with Mons. Odin.—Arrives at New Orleans.—Bishoprics Refused.—The Visitor in Paris.—His Return.—Incident on Board Ship.—Burial at Sea.—Arrival at New Orleans.—Visitor Timon.—Changes.—Appointed Bishop of Buffalo, N. Y.................... 80..90

BOOK II.

CHAPTER I.

The Diocese of Buffalo.—Troubles of St. Louis Church.—Their Origin and History.. 93..113

CHAPTER II.

Rt. Rev. John Timon as Bishop.—Rev. Bernard O'Reilly, V. G.—Their Arrival.—Reception.—Magnificent Demonstrations.—*Te Deum* at St. Louis Church.—Bishop Timon's first Consecration.—Told to Leave St. Louis Church.—Begins St. Patrick's.—Hard Work.—The Methodist and Hell.—The Irishman and Confession.—The Viaticum and the Presbyterian.—Upset from a Sleigh.—Father McEvoy taken for a Lawyer and the Bishop for a Priest.................................113..120

CHAPTER III.

History of the Troubles of St. Louis Church under Bishop Timon's administration, gathered from the Posthumous Papers of the Bishop.......120..157

CHAPTER IV.

The Bishop and the Mendicant.—Bishop Timon visits Baltimore to get Sisters for an Hospital and Asylum.—Resources.—Sisters arrive.—Hospital Opened.—Attacked by Rev. John C. Lord, a Protestant Minister.—Defended by Rev. B. O'Reilly.—The Orphan Asylum....157..168

CHAPTER V.

Bishop Timon and the Act of Incorporation.—St. Joseph's Orphan Asylum.—Correspondence.—Bishop Timon travels through Mexico, &c.—Learns Spanish.—Returns Home.—Lectures on Mexico.—Nuncio Bedini arrives.—His Dealings with St. Louis Church................169..197

CHAPTER VI.

The Church Property Bill.—Hon. Mr. Putnam and Hon. Mr. Babcock.—Bishop Timon's Reply.—The Foundling Asylum.—Ground devoted by Louis S. Lecouteulx.—Cottages secured.—Cholera—Bishop Timon carries Infants in his Arms to Places of Safety.—Buys a Farm for a Cemetery and other Uses.—Sentence of Excommunication against the Trustees of St. Louis Church.—Father Weninger Mediates and restores Order...197..212

CHAPTER VII.

Education.—Convent of the Sacred Heart.—St. Joseph's College.—Oblate Fathers arrive—St. Joseph's College.—Discouraging Circumstances. It Fails.—Christian Brothers.—Miss Nardin's Academy.—Incidents.—Sisters of the Good Shepherd.—A detailed Report.—Other Religious Orders.—Provincial Synod.—Its Results and Importance.—Bishop goes to Rome.—Dogma of Immaculate Conception................213..228

CHAPTER VIII.

Franciscan Fathers.—The "Immaculate Conception" at Rome.—Bishop Timon's Return.—Pastoral on Dogma of the Immaculate Conception.—Church Property Bill again.—Bishop Timon on Senator Putnam's Poetry.—Favors from the Pope to the Diocese of Buffalo............228..244

CHAPTER IX.

St. Patrick's and other Churches.—St. Joseph's Cathedral.—Correspondence.—Bishop Timon Travels the World for Help for his Cathedral.—Difficulties.—Corner Stone and Dedication.—First Diocesan Synod.—A Carillon of Forty-three Bells.—Episcopal Visitations.—Bishop Timon visits St. Louis, Mo.—The Alleghany College.—Election Day.—Juvenile Asylum...244..262

CHAPTER X.

Niagara Falls Seminary.—Catholic Funerals.—Bishop Timon goes to Rome.—His Journey.—His Return.—His Sermon.—Jubilee announced.—Efforts for the Roman College.—Jubilee Extended.—Catholic Funerals again.—Zeal of Bishop Timon.—William B. Lecouteulx.—St. Peregrinus..262..270

CHAPTER XI.

Public School System.—Bishop Timon's Views.—Bishop Lynch.—Provincial Council.—Its Importance.—Signification of the Blood of St. Januarius.—Peter Pence.—Providence Insane Asylum.—Bishop Timon's Sermon.—Dean Richmond...271..281

CHAPTER XII.

Fall of 1860.—War.—Bishop Timon's Position.—Lincoln.—Flag raising.—Bishop Timon's Remarks.—Second Provincial Council.—Bishop Timon's Sermons.—Evidences of declining Health.—St. Vincent's Asylum.—Bishop Timon goes to Rome again.—Japanese Martyrs.—Guest of the Archbishop of Tuam.—Arrives Home...........................281..291

CHAPTER XIII.

Public School Text Books.—Bishop Timon lectures at the Central School.—Correspondence with the Sanitary Commission.—Anonymous Correspondence.—Its Authors guilty Wretches.—Incident.—One Cause of the Bishop's Death.—Depressed Spirits.—Lectures at Dansville.—Catches the Erysipelas.—Decline of Life, but does not expect to die soon.—His last Sermon.—Confined to the House.—Predicts his Death.—Death of Bishop Timon...291..301

CHAPTER XIV.

Bishop Timon's Body Embalmed.—His Residence draped in Mourning.—Ninety thousand Persons visit his Remains.—The Funeral.—Procession.—The Body Deposited in a Vault of the Cathedral.—Bishop Timon's Characteristics.—His Habits.—Letter from Father Smarius, S. J..301..310

CHAPTER XV.

Review of the Bishop's Character.—His Spirit of Prayer.—His habitual Peace of Mind.—His Humility...310..319

APPENDIX.

Accounts of the Carillon...323..333
Extracts from Bishop Timon's Conference Sermons...................333.....

BOOK I.

THE EARLY AND MISSIONARY LIFE

OF

REV. JOHN TIMON.

LIFE AND TIMES

OF THE LATE

RIGHT REV. JOHN TIMON, D. D.,

FIRST ROMAN CATHOLIC BISHOP

OF THE DIOCESE OF BUFFALO, N. Y.

CHAPTER I.

BIRTH-PLACE OF BISHOP TIMON.—PARENTAGE.—DATE OF BIRTH AND BAPTISM.—BROTHERS AND SISTERS.—INCIDENTS AND CHARACTERISTICS OF THE ELDER TIMON.—REMOVES TO BALTIMORE, MD.—TO LOUISVILLE, KY.—TO ST. LOUIS, MO.—ENGAGED IN DRY GOODS BUSINESS.—JOHN TIMON AS CLERK.—HIS ACCOMPLISHMENTS.—MAKES ACQUAINTANCE WITH MISS DE GALLON.—ENGAGED TO THE YOUNG LADY, BUT NEVER MARRIED.—DEATH OF MISS DE GALLON.—CRISIS OF 1825.—BUSINESS MISFORTUNES.—RESOLVES TO BECOME A LAZARIST.

IN the retired but beautiful place of Conevago, Adams Co., Pa., situated at the distance of about one mile from what is known and called "Conevago Church," (under the care of the fathers of the Society of Jesus,) stood, several years ago, a log cabin, a kind of structure commonly found in the early days of American settlements. This rude and humble dwelling was the birth-place of the late lamented prelate of the Diocese of Buffalo, Rt. Rev. John Timon, D. D. It is only a few years ago that Bishop Timon paid a visit to Conevago, a place endeared to him by many recollections of his childhood, and saw for the last time the spot and log house in which he was born. Shortly afterwards the cabin, situated on a farm belonging to a Mr. Reilly, was torn down and removed, and thus the only remaining link that connected his later years with those of his youth, was entirely obliterated.

By birth, Bishop Timon was an American, although he himself, on more than one occasion, has asserted to many that he was *conceived* in Ireland, and born of Irish parents, in this country. His parents were James Timon and Margaret Leddy, and as near as can be ascertained, emigrated from the north of Ireland, from a place called Belthurbet, in Cavan Co. They were poor but pious christians, and their household observances were synonyms for virtue and charity.

Although in humble circumstances when they landed in America, by dint of economy and industry, they managed to accumulate, in a very few years, no indifferent amount of wealth, and at the same time support a large and increasing family. Their marriage was blessed with ten children, three sons and seven daughters. The sons were named James, John, and Owen; the daughters were called Ellen, Rose, Mary, Eliza, Ann, Agatha, and Catherine.

Of the sons, James died early in life. John became a Bishop, and was the only one of the family that rose to any degree of eminence. Owen, the third and surviving brother, still resides at St. Louis, is married, and is or was employed in some capacity near the person of the Archbishop of that city.

Ellen married a Mr. Kennedy, of New York city, and is now dead. Rose was married to a Mr. Daly, of St. Louis, Mo.; Mary to a Mr. Ames, of Louisville, Ky.; Eliza to a Mr. McGinnis, of St. Louis, Mo.; Ann to a Mr. Fox, also of St. Louis, Mo.; Agatha married a Mr. Douglas; and Catherine a Mr. McDonough, of St. Louis, Mo.

John, the subject of this biography, was born on the 12th of February, 1797, and baptized on the 17th of the same month and year, having for his sponsors John Kuhn and Christina Wolf.

However, before proceeding to enter upon the narrative of his subsequent remarkable life, it will not be amiss to refer to his parents again, in order to place in proper relief their virtues and characteristics, which, in part, Bishop Timon largely inherited.

James Timon, senior; was truly an exemplary christian. "Indeed," said a learned divine,[*] in his panegyric sermon at the month's mind for Bishop Timon, "Indeed, piety was the

---
[*] Rt. Rev. Bishop Lynch, of Toronto, C. W.

prevailing virtue of his father's household." By education as well as by nature, Mr. Timon was a high-toned, moral Irish gentleman. He loved his own native land well, and, from inferences drawn from pretty accurate information, we surmise that he (alas! like many others,) was obliged to leave it, and emigrate to a home of adoption, another victim of oppressive legislation and tyrannical misrule in Ireland. But he loved his religion too, and more dearly, not only because it was the faith of his forefathers, but also because it was in his estimation the only reliable pilot to that "bourne from whence no traveler e'er returns." In the government and education of his children, he had no wealth to lavish, but the little means with which Providence blessed his industry, he freely expended for the benefit of their spiritual as well as physical comforts. He was a man of generous impulses, and, like every true Irishman, he could not withhold from bestowing alms whenever charity in its many ways presented itself.

An incident, as related by a reliable correspondent, will serve to illustrate a trait in his character. At one time, Mr. Timon, having learned that there was in the city of St. Louis, Mo., a reverend gentleman, whose acquaintance he had in former years acquired in Ireland, called on him to pay his respects. After a very pleasant interview of a few hours, in which much was rehearsed that related to the past, particularly in their own native land, Mr. Timon rose to depart. As he was leaving the house, he paused to shake hands with his reverend friend, and in doing this placed in them a crumpled slip of paper. The clergyman, not anticipating what was intended by Mr. Timon, took the slip of paper, without, however, examining it at the time. Mr. Timon then left, and a few moments after his departure the clergyman opened the paper, and, to his utter astonishment, found it to contain a check on a bank for $100. He could scarcely credit his senses at the discovery, and thinking that Mr. Timon might have given him the paper by mistake, thereby embarrassing himself pecuniarily, he hastily donned his coat and hat, and set out to overtake his generous friend. It was an exciting chase, for Mr. Timon had by this time reached the upper end of the street, and besides the weather being very warm, it made the perspiration roll in profuse disorder from the face of the reverend gentleman. At last he overtook him, and, in a voice breathless from the briskness of the walk, asked him if he had not made a mistake.

Mr. Timon smiled, and turning to his friend, quietly but good-humoredly observed, "My dear friend, it was no mistake of mine. I intended it for you."

"But," replied the clergyman, "I have no need of it, as I have sufficient means of my own."

"No matter," said Mr. Timon, "if you do not need it yourself, there are others who are poor and needy. Distribute the money among those who most need it, and you will please me more than to ask me to retake it."

Mr. Timon had other traits of character besides charity and piety. In a worldly point of view he was an excellent business man, of a speculative turn of mind, ready to turn an honest penny to his own advantage. It was to these characteristics, as well as an unceasing thrift and untiring energy, that the liberal amount of wealth he acquired in a few years was mainly due.

Mr. Timon's wife, Helen, was really a pure-minded, christian woman. She was faithful to her husband in the discharge of her marital relations and household duties, and, in the education of her large family, always endeavored to impress upon her children the importance of esteeming virtue and the practice of their faith above every other consideration.

For five years subsequent to the birth of their son John, Mr. Timon remained with his family at Conevago. During this time, any occupation that the slender advantages of the country then afforded, was eagerly embraced to earn an honest livelihood. There is nothing of special moment to relate of these few years, except to state that, like every ambitious mind, Mr. Timon earnestly desired, and resolved to seek, other opportunities to better his condition in life. Prompted by these feelings, he accordingly, in the year 1802, turned his back upon Conevago, and bade farewell to the friends he had found there, and started on his journey to Baltimore, Md. As soon as the rude and imperfect advantages of travel would permit, he arrived in Baltimore, Md., where he opened a dry goods store in a street then known and called Howard street. In this new avocation Mr. Timon, however, met with no great success. He managed to save something above his actual wants, but altogether, to an ambition like his, business was not as flattering as he liked. He had been established in business a few years, when he found it necessary to take into his establishment, as a rather young clerk, his enterprising son John.

"John stood in his store as a clerk," writes a correspondent, "and by his polite and withal engaging manner, secured for his father a great deal of custom." From the year 1802 until the year 1817, a period of fifteen years, Mr. Timon continued his mercantile operations with varying success. As time flew by, his son became older, and in his dealings with customers, as well as making good bargains in trade, evinced a decided aptitude for business. Although little favored with the benefits of a good education, which in the early days of the Republic was an acquisition not so easily acquired as at the present day, he managed to acquaint himself with the first rudiments of the ordinary English branches. By nature he was physically a well developed young man, and in his bearing and manner was very polite and handsome. "When he had reached his nineteenth year," continues my correspondent,* "he had already become a toast for all aged mothers with marriageable daughters. He often told me of many eligible and grand offers of marriage that he received, but refused them all, although a star of the first magnitude, not only at Baltimore, but also in the most refined circles of Louisville and St. Louis, particularly among the French residents of the last two mentioned places."

The success in business at Baltimore, as has been remarked not being entirely satisfactory, and besides, being lured by those prospects which, even at the present day, invite the emigrant to the smiling lands of the west, Mr. Timon concluded to leave Baltimore and remove to the city of Louisville, Ky.

---
* Thomas Winstanley, Red Budd, Randolph Co., Ill.

Accordingly, in the month of October, 1818, he, in company with some friends, left Baltimore and began his tedious journey westward. Traveling at that time, in an unsettled state of the country, with all the disadvantages of unbroken tracts of lands, the want of a railroad conveyance, as well as embarrassments arising from dangers to travel, was by no means speedily accomplished. It required weeks and sometimes months to make long journeys, and hence it was nearly towards the close of the year 1818 that Mr. Timon reached Louisville, Ky. Here he resumed business, similar to the one in which he had been engaged at Baltimore, and in a very short time made for himself, by his candid and fair dealings, many new and warm friends. It seems, however, that he had again become dissatisfied with his new position, and concluding to remove still further west, we consequently find him, in the Spring of the year 1819, in the city of St. Louis, Mo., his future abode and permanent place of business. We say permanent, because he immediately devoted himself to his vocation with increased assiduity. Nor was his application to business more fervent than the energy displayed by his son John. Besides being a general favorite in society, John had gradually become very remarkable for a display of qualities that, as they widened by experience, earned for him the general impression then that he might have owned the greater part of the city of St. Louis to-day, on account of his energy and shrewdness in turning to advantage the many mercantile opportunities that bestrew his path, had not Providence, in its mysterious dispensations, seen fit to transfer him to the vineyard of religion, there to discharge duties that have since stamped him not only as an extraordinary man, but also pointed him out as a *chosen* apostle in the field of the Catholic Church in America.

To this end, that he might by experience become aware of the emptiness of worldly gains and aspirations, and at the same time realize that all labor devoted to mammon, in preference to heaven, would be to him as profitable as to gain the whole world and lose his own soul, misfortunes began to intercept his brilliant career, and made him enter into himself to meditate and reflect. In the very height of his prosperity came the crash.

This was the terrible crisis of 1823, a crisis the most severe of any the country has as yet experienced, with the exception perhaps of the crisis of 1837. So paralyzing were its consequences upon business, and so ruinous its effects to the merchant that, at that time, "a $5.00 bill of the best bank of the State of Illinois, would scarcely procure as much as an ordinary breakfast." "And," continues a correspondent,* "we may judge how severely it was felt in St. Louis, when that entire square front on Fourth street and running through to Third street, embracing with it a fine stone house, a barn and carriage house, were sold for $1,500,—and a clear title of them given to Judge Mulaphanty, (a man deserving to be remembered for his many fine and generous qualities,) the only man in St. Louis then who could raise money enough to buy them." This financial crisis brought ruin to thousands, sweeping like a torrent over the whole country, to paralyze the arteries of trade and commerce, and hurl mercilessly back to poverty many who had already accumulated a moderate share of wealth. Among many others, Mr. Timon, Sr., was not spared from the dire effects of this dreaded whirlpool. It shattered his fortunes, and pecuniarily destroyed his many brilliant prospects. His son John also lamented the turn that the tide of affairs had taken, and it made a deep impression on his mind. He began to realize how fleeting was man's prosperity, and how uncertain were the vanities and allurements of the world. His eyes, hitherto blinded by the glitter and tinsel of human joys, and deceived by the uncertainty of bright promises that hung over his footsteps, were now opened. Another and perhaps more tender circumstance served to increase the affliction he had received, and, so far as the world was concerned, to render all his efforts, all his prospects, tasteless.

It seems that during the time he had been engaged as a clerk in his father's establishment, he had made the acquaintance of a young lady, the daughter of a wealthy French Creole gentleman, Mons. De Gallon, who had fled from St. Domingo, Hayti, during the ever memorable massacre of 1823, when the blacks

---
* Thos. Winstanley.

rose in insurrection there, and massacred nearly every white inhabitant of the island not fortunate enough to escape. Mons. De Gallon with his family fortunately evaded the danger threatened them, and, after many painful delays and discouraging circumstances, succeeded finally in reaching the city of St. Louis, Mo., in safety.

As has already been stated, his daughter, Mademoiselle Louisa De Gallon, a young lady gifted with many brilliant accomplishments, both by nature and education, had formed an acquaintance with John Timon, and the favorable impressions made on the mind of each, after the first introduction, soon deepened into more tender and intimate relationship. John loved this young and guileless girl, for the sweetness of her disposition, her piety, and withal her moral worth, three characteristics in woman that tend to elevate her above the ordinary level of her sex. As in all cases of *true* courtship, they were soon *affianced* to each other, *but never married.* Divine Providence, in its mysterious dispensations, ordained otherwise, and by interposing a barrier between them, elevated one to the hierarchy of the true Church of God, and the other, a pure and virgin flower, to heaven.

Miss De Gallon, unhappily for John, but not for religion, was afflicted with "falling sickness," so seriously as to prevent the consummation of their betrothal vows, and very shortly after they had been wed in spirit, death severed their happy companionship, and transferred the flower to another and better world.

It was a bitter hour for John, and to a temperament like his, never unstrung, this was a sad blow. It may seem strange, however, to some inclined to be over scrupulous, that a circumstance like this (obtained from a reliable correspondent,)[*] should be mentioned in connection with the history of a Bishop in the Church, and no doubt there are those who may criticise it severely as a levity on the part of the author, in resuscitating apparently undeveloped frivolities in the life of a young man; but, in extenuation of the mention of this

---
[*] Thos. Winstanley.

fact, it may not be improper to observe that it is considered *necessary* to record this little incident in the life of the Bishop, in order to place in bolder relief the reasons that prompted him to abandon the world, and to devote his energies and soul to the amelioration of humanity and the service of religion. The bereavement occasioned by the death of Miss De Gallon, and the wreck of a fortune of years of labor and industry, scattered beyond a possibility of ever being able to recover it, were among the principal influences that lifted the veil from his eyes, that he might realize the folly of attaching his affections to the transitory shadows of mundane pleasures and profits. "He passed through a severe school," and the lessons he received were the instruments in the hands of Divine Providence with which his spirit was chastened and prepared for another and greater field, in which his enterprise, his zeal, and his piety might be directed towards honoring and serving his Maker.

―――o―――

CHAPTER II.

JOINS THE COMMUNITY OF THE LAZARISTS.—ENTERS THE SEMINARY OF THE BARRENS, MO.—MEETS MONS. J. M. ODIN THERE.—EARLY REMINISCENCES OF THE LAZARISTS IN THIS COUNTRY.—THE SEMINARY IN 1824.—INCIDENTS, &c.—INDUSTRY AND ZEAL OF YOUNG MR. TIMON.—PROMOTED TO SUB-DEACONSHIP.—CORRESPONDENCE OF COL. CREED TAYLOR.—PROMOTED TO MINOR ORDERS.—JOINS THE ORDER OF ST. VINCENT DE PAUL.

IN the month of April of the year 1823, at the age of twenty-six years, John Timon renounced the world with all its pomps and vanities, bade an affectionate farewell to his relatives and friends, and joined the community of the Lazarists, one of the most indefatigable and zealous in the cause of Christ in this country. He entered, as a student, the preparatory seminary of St. Mary's of the Barrens, Mo., then in its infancy, and by no means the imposing and flourishing edifice of to-day. For two years young Timon applied himself assiduously to his true vocation, enriching his mind with various studies, particularly philosophy and theology.

About this time, Mons. J. M. Odin, at present Archbishop of New Orleans, had arrived in this country, almost immediately after Mr. Timon had entered the seminary at the Barrens.

As, however, the Lazarists, at the time that Bishop Timon joined them, were just beginning their missions, which have subsequently preponderated marvelously in the progress of Catholicity in this country, it will be necessary to digress a little, and briefly give an account of this zealous order, since the deceased prelate has been for many years a prominent member of the same community. The following history is partly from the pen of the Bishop himself and from other sources equally reliable:

Bishop Dubourg, after his consecration on the 24th of September, 1815, as Bishop of the Diocese of New Orleans, obtained from Rome a colony of Lazarists. For a while a part of the colony stayed in the State of Kentucky with the saintly Bishop Flaget, and the rest proceeded to the scene of their future labors. Among these were the Rev. Joseph Rosatti, Felix D'Andreis, and Brother Blanka, who accompanied the venerated Bishop Flaget, reaching Kaskaskias, in the State of Illinois, in September, 1817. On the day after their arrival there, they went to St. Genevieve, where Bishop Flaget proposed to found a colony, but as he was not altogether satisfied with the offers he received from the people, he went to St. Louis, on the 17th of October, the month following.

At this time there was no resident priest at St. Louis. Rev. Mr. Lavine, curate at Cahokies, on the opposite side of the Mississippi river, came to St. Louis once every three weeks, to attend the congregation there. Bishop Flaget made proposals to the assembled Catholics to make St. Genevieve the centre of the mission. But it seems no encouraging offers were made in return. A proposition likewise was made by Bishop Flaget to fix the seat of the mission at St. Louis. On this proposition opinion was divided.

In this state of indecision, deputies from thirty-five Catholic families then at the Barrens came to offer six hundred and forty acres of land, requesting that the diocesan seminary should be established there, which was subsequently done. In the meantime Bishop Flaget, with Rev. M. D'Andreis and Jos. Rosatti, returned to St. Genevieve, whilst Rev. Henry Pratt, curate at St. Genevieve, went to St. Louis to attend to the building materials, repairs, &c., Revs. Jos. Rosatti, D'Andreis, and Brother Blanka taking his place to establish a provincial post at St. Genevieve. The parish embraced a large extent of country, including the "Mines and St. Michaels" with adjacent counties to a great distance. Father D'Andreis had to say two masses every Sunday, preach two or three hours, hear confessions, visit the sick, and teach catechism. His holy example, the zeal and unction of his preaching, however, made a profound impression among the inhabitants of the settlements. For many years the Catholics of that district remembered with veneration the holy man.

Late in 1817 Bishop Dubourg, in company with Bishop Flaget, went to St. Genevieve, having left his clergy (among whom were some Lazarists,) in Bardstown, Ky., to learn English. Thence the Bishop took with him to St. Louis that holy missionary Mons. D'Andreis, where they were both received with great joy.

Almost immediately Rev. Father D'Andreis commenced to discharge his functions there as curate, and whilst his sermons were listened to with avidity by the most enlightened, he continued to devote a considerable amount of time to the instruction of the poor negro slaves, and the change it wrought on their moral conduct through him, excited unanimous admiration. Soon after being installed as curate, he sent for Father Rosatti and his companion in Kentucky to come to St. Louis. The voyage of this holy priest will be found in the annals of the congregation. He himself composed a history of the beginning of the congregation. From that history it may be gathered how little human help was given to that great work, which embraced a tract of unfertile land of 640 acres, that cost the community then $800,—besides this there were promises of help to build, a few only of which were fulfilled; under continual obligations, which a capital of $100,000 would scarcely pay; nay more, for many years the congregation had to support and in great part clothe the seminarians of the diocese without receiving any pay. That the community did not sink under such responsibilities is truly a miracle.

In the meantime amidst poverty and great privations, the seminary at the Barrens continued to exist. It consisted of several small log houses. In the largest cabin, one story in height, was the university. In the north-west corner of the building was the theology department, for study and lecture; in the north-east corner was the room for philosophy and general literature; the south-west corner was used for a tailor shop, and the south-east for a shoemaker's department.

The refectory was in a small adjoining log cabin, but whenever the rain fell very heavy, the seminarians often preferred to go to bed supperless, than venture out of the university under such disadvantages as getting wet and muddy, to buy their scanty supper. Another house, magnificent for that period, and for that place, was, however, soon begun. It was a frame building, and it still remains, serving now as an out-house for servants, although it remained in an unfinished state until 1834.

Bishop Timon has often related circumstances that happened to him, as well as to others, connected with his experience at the Barrens at this time. Often, when persons reached the seminary, either to become members, or to share a night's hospitality, have they been obliged to spread their mattress on the floor, where they slept well and comfortably; but, towards morning, feeling themselves very warm, they awoke to find a heavy coat of snow on their blankets, which had gathered there through the openings and crevices of the building. Yet such was the piety and the resignation of the inmates of the seminary, under the pious government of Mons. Rosatti, that all seemed to feel happy, and advance in the way of salvation.

In connection with the seminary, a college for seculars was opened in the unfinished house. There the seminarians, on an average, taught three hours per day; the rest of the study hours were given them to prepare their own lessons, and recite them to their own professors of Latin, philosophy, or theology.

On vacation days, and even during the hours of recreation, the seminarians employed themselves in felling the trees of the primeval forests, and splitting wood either for a scanty Summer's use, or an abundant Winter's supply. At other seasons they could be seen with sacks on their backs, gathering the potatoes, beans, etc., or driving the ox and cart, well laden with the corn which they themselves had hoed. All were healthy and well, and with their beloved Superior at their head, no labor seemed hard. In the discharge of all these duties young Timon was ever a ready and willing worker, and the cheerfulness and zeal with which he sought to aid and improve the condition he had chosen for his future life, brought notice at once upon his head.

By this time, too, Mr. Timon, who had been busily engaged in improving his mind with a knowledge of Church discipline and ceremony, had made a rapid progress in his various studies, under the tutelage of his learned and talented professors, particularly under his young but beloved bosom friend, Rev. J. M. Odin, now Archbishop of New Orleans.

Mr. Timon pursued his studies diligently in the interim, not only storing his mind with knowledge necessary to glorify and preach the sufferings and goodness of his Redeemer, but also by frequent meditations, prayers and fastings, reducing to submission the appetites of his flesh and body. Mons. J. M. Odin, Archbishop of New Orleans, in a letter to the author, observes: "A sincere intimacy grew between us, which time cemented more and more, as it was grounded on a respect inspired by his sterling virtues. I was five years younger than he was, but as I had completed my studies at an early age, before leaving France, I was his teacher of logic and theology, especially when our good Superior, Bishop Rosatti, was absent from the seminary."

So thorough and rapid was his acquisition of theology and philosophy, and so familiar had he become with Church discipline and ceremony, that, continues Mons. Odin, "in the year 1824 he was ordained sub-deacon, and from this time he began to preach with great zeal and great success, and to the edification of his bearers. He accompanied me in a missionary tour through the State of Arkansas, where no priest had been seen for over thirty-five years."

Col. Creed Taylor, at the kind request of the Bishop of Little Rock, Rt. Rev. Edward Fitzgerald, furnishes the following interesting communication:

"In the Spring of the year 1825, Rev. Mr. Odin, (now Archbishop of New Orleans, La.,) passed through Arkansas on a missionary excursion, accompanied by a young gentleman a year or two my junior. The latter appeared to be a traveling companion to the other, who said mass, and preached to a French congregation in that language.

"Mr. Timon, the young gentleman referred to, served at his mass. Many children were baptized by Rev. Mr. Odin, and I was asked to have mine baptized also, but I refused, for the reason that I understood but little French, and besides, having imbibed all the prejudices of the sects against Catholicity, I could not consent to have it done.

"In about three months," continues Col. Taylor, "the Reverend gentlemen returned, and this time Mr. Timon, who had been raised to minor orders, preached the first English sermon I ever heard. I could now no longer refuse to have my children baptized; whether I attribute the dissipation of my prejudices to the winning eloquence of the young deacon, or, whether, in the mercy of God, the prayers of my wife induced me to yield; but it was done, to the gratification of my family.

"The reverend gentlemen were the guests of my father-in-law, Major Vaugine, for several days, and where I expected a kind of superstitious priestcraft, I found the greatest humility, the most profound learning, and captivating eloquence. Most of their time was spent in saying mass, making their meditations, and prayers. Mr. Timon was often found carrying wood for a poor old widow, who occupied one of Major Vaugine's cabins, on the farm. This," observes Col. Taylor, "in my state of mind then, might have been called affected charity, but, thank God, I imputed nothing of the kind to him, for he was so humble and so kind, that the impression made on me then will go with me to the grave."

From this simple reminiscence of the Bishop's early life, we may see in advance the tendency of his disposition, and the simple charity that he, in an unaffected manner, bestowed on the poor old woman, was but the foreshadowing of subsequent sublime and ever memorable virtues, that stand to-day recorded throughout the length and breadth of this diocese, in his various institutions of charity and mercy.

In the year 1825, John Timon was promoted to the priesthood, by the Right Rev. Bishop Rosatti. Now commenced the most active period of his life. As priest, he assisted in the two-fold capacity of Professor at the seminary of the Barrens, and, at the same time, as Missionary in the surrounding counties, mostly at Cape Girardeau and Jackson, Mo., where he preached occasionally in the court house.

Here his labors were crowned with great success for the good of souls, and the conversion of many Protestants to the true Church. In the discharge of his duties he was indefatigable, and never spared himself when engaged in doing good for the glory of God and the salvation of souls. He sometimes met with opposition from ill-disposed persons, and some even aimed at his life; but his patience, his gentleness, and withal his winning manner, surmounted every obstacle, and paved the way to the high position he occupies to-day in the memories of those who knew him, and could appreciate his deeds and virtues. To complete his sacrifice, he finally joined the order of St. Vincent de Paul, then in its infancy in this country.

Oh! what joy was this to his religious fervor, what a delight to his heart, surcharged with love for the cause of his Redeemer, and for the poor and imbecile sinner of society. His zeal exhibited itself in the multitudes he rescued from sin by his winning eloquence, in the spread of the Gospel, and in the general abundant harvest, reaped in a careful culture of the field of religion.

CHAPTER III.

SURROUNDINGS AT THE BARRENS, MO.—MONS. ODIN AND TIMON AS MISSIONARIES.—HOG PEN CONVERTED INTO A CHAPEL.—START FOR NEW MADRID, TEXAS.—DANGEROUS TRAVELING.—DIALOGUE WITH A LADY.—ARRIVE AT THE PORT OF ARKANSAS.—THE QUAPAW INDIANS.—THEIR BELIEF—RETURN TO THE BARRENS.—MISSION IN ILLINOIS.

The great majority of the inhabitants of the Barrens, and especially those who were rich, were Protestants, and their prejudices against Catholics were very strong. To that extent did they evince their bias, that the ministers of some of the denominations often came to the very doors of the Catholic church to challenge the priests to controversy. But how great was the change effected in a few years. The prejudices soon were dissipated; the seminary, a log cabin only twenty-five by eighteen feet, began to flourish, and seeds of christian doctrine take deep root in the hearts not only of many Catholics, but also of many converts. Mons. Odin and Timon were accustomed to go around the neighborhood in a circuit, to the distance sometimes of fifteen or twenty miles, assemble the children to Catechism, visit families far less Protestants than haters of the Pope or papists, and preach to them whenever an opportunity presented itself.

South of Apple Creek, they began a station for saying mass, but subsequently transferred it to the present site of St. Joseph's church. At Apple Creek, the station alluded to, a chapel was formed from a large pen in which swine had been kept. The missionaries themselves dug out the dung, cleaned it as well as possible, covered it with fresh branches of trees, and built in it an altar, which for its beauty became the wonder and admiration of the neighborhood. Here they celebrated mass, and performed the other functions of their divine calling.

God singularly blessed their apostolic excursions, perhaps the more so because they were made in great poverty and privations, especially at a place called Bois Brulé, where all the inhabitants were Protestants. Early in the morning after breakfast, the missionaries would leave the seminary, seek for lost sheep until dinner time, and then, wearied with their labor, would retreat to a blackberry bush or other fruit tree, and there make a dinner out of what nature gave.

In 1824, Rev. Mons. Odin and Timon (sub-deacon,) set out on a long mission, and although they traveled on horseback, yet like the apostles and disciples of old, "*sine secula et pera*," gave their first distant mission in New Madrid, Texas, afterwards remembered by the people of that place for a long time. After leaving New Madrid, they were obliged to cross large swamps, attended with great personal danger, and were necessitated to rest all night on swampy grounds, where a dry spot could not be seen, and where water fit to drink could not be found. They were accompanied by a guide, who, deeming it impossible to proceed, retraced his steps and left them; but the missionaries, nothing daunted by the adverse circumstances that surrounded them and seemed to multiply at every step, pushed boldly on, swam across a river, and late next day, in an almost starved condition, reached a log habitation, where they refreshed and rested their weary feet. They then continued their journey, which was a continual mission among a people that had never before seen a priest, although the missionaries were continually inquiring for Catholics. At length, late one sultry day, they reached a stately mansion, and being very tired, approached the house and humbly asked for a drink of water. To their astonishment, they were kindly received by the lady of the house, who directed a negro servant to bring some fresh water and other refreshments, not knowing the character of her guests.

Whilst the negro servant was complying with the order of the lady, an interesting conversation ensued, in which one subject after another was discussed. At length as one of the missionaries took advantage of a pause to inquire, "Madam, are there any Catholics in this neighborhood?" the kind and courteous manner of the lady immediately changed, and she said, "Oh, sir, I don't like Catholics."

"And why, madam," interposed the missionary, "have they ever injured you?"

"No, sir!" replied the lady, "but they are idolaters."

"Oh! madam," interrupted the missionary, "how can you think so? There are so many Catholics in the world, far more than all the sects put together, very many of whom are men and women of cultivated intellect and deep religious feeling, and how can you believe that so many good and learned men would be such fools as to adore idols?"

"Well, indeed," replied the lady, "that thought never suggested itself to me yet, and I am almost inclined to think that you are right, for, as you say, it would indeed be strange."

The missionary then pointed to a painting of Washington on the wall of the room, and observed, "Do you adore that picture, madam?"

"Why, certainly not," said the lady.

"I thought not," pursued the missionary, "you keep it merely to remind you of the hero and savior of our country. So do we keep the crucifix, pictures and other sacred things, to put us in mind of our *Divine* Hero and our ever adorable Saviour; or of those who have served Him best and whom He most loved." Then, taking a crucifix from his bosom, he continued, "Here is what those who malign us, say we adore; but God forbid the thought. This crucifix is for us a book with hieroglyphics of might and power, to enable us to read in a *second*, at one glance, what it otherwise would take us five minutes to read in the Bible. We have often instructed poor slaves who cannot read. We have told them what Jesus has done for them, and shown them the crucifix, and thus appealed to their eyes and ears in far less time than by any other method."

The lady, who had never before seen a crucifix, immediately took up another thread of conversation, which proved how difficult it is sometimes by words alone to have a clear conception of a thing, unless it is made practical, and observed: "Well, it is possible that what you say may be all very true, but, really, is that what you call a crucifix?"

"Yes, madam, it represents the Saviour of the world dying for the sins of men. See here, where his cruel enemies pierced his hands and feet and side, and thus he hung on the cross three long hours, dying for you and all mankind."

At these words the lady became deeply affected, and in a voice scarcely articulate from the vehemence of her emotion, she said: "Dear me, how much he must have suffered." She then called her children, two bright, intelligent little boys, and thus spoke to them: "Here, children, come and see how much your Saviour has done for you."

The little lads approached, and with eagerness listened to the details of the Saviour's passion, illustrated to them, then for the first time, by means of the crucifix.

When the missionaries had finished, they rose and departed, thanking the lady for the hospitality she had shown to them, and feeling confident in their hearts that ever after a missionary would be well received in that house.

All along their route to the Port of Arkansas they related this incident, and in every place they penetrated they found the same prejudices against Catholics existed. The general request, however, after hearing of the incident, was to see a crucifix; and, after gazing on it, these words would burst forth as if unbidden from the lips of many, "Well, well, I see that I was mistaken; I see that I have been deceived."

Finally, the missionaries arrived at the Port of Arkansas. Here they paid several visits to the Quapaw Indians, a tribe at that time inhabiting the south bank of the Arkansas river. The missionaries erected a rustic altar before the wigwam of Sarasin, the chief of the tribe. The Indians assisted at mass, and through the interpreter, a Mr. W. Neuismere, the Catholic doctrine was explained to them.

At night the Indian chief and medicine man were persuaded to explain the dogmas of their faith. In general, however, it is a difficult thing to get a clear detail, even of the little they pretend to know. They are generally afraid of being laughed at, although, like other Indians, they believe in a God, in subordinate gods, both good and bad. They have vague conceptions of good and bad angels, of future rewards and punishments, in which the Catholic view of a three-fold state are distinguishable. Their traditions are, that they came from the cold North, and that the first recollection their forefathers had, was of floundering on the surface of a vast lake. That a god in white from the South, one in red from the North, one in black from the East, and finally one in motley colors from the West approached them.

The god in white was the superior god. A bird had been sent out to discover land, but with no result. Then other animals followed, of which only one returned, with his feet and legs besmeared with mud. The god in white then led them towards the spot from whence the animal had returned, and there land was found. They immediately knelt down to adore and thank the god in white.

"No, children," said the god in white, "I am sent by the Great Spirit, Him you must adore."

He then predicted their victories over all the nations they should encounter, until they reached the sunny South, and that, after the lapse of ages, they should see white men, who were children of the god in white, and whom they should not injure, for the sake of their guide.

The Indian chief and medicine man, as well as the other Indians accompanied the recital of these traditions, (of which the above is only an abridgment) with strange gestures and wild noises.

From their traditions, however, it will be apparent to the reader that, besides some vague recollection of early revelation, they retained a remembrance of Noah's ark, the deluge, and of Noah's experiments to ascertain whether the waters of the deluge had subsided sufficiently to allow him to leave the ark.

During the mission much good was accomplished, both among the Catholics and the Protestants, by rehabilitating a great many marriages, baptizing many adults as well as children, hearing confessions and admitting to the Holy Sacrament, many who, for forty years before, had had no opportunity of so doing.

After such laborious and sacrificing efforts in the service of God, Father Odin and Timon returned to the Barrens to resume the discharge of their duties in the college, which included, as it formerly had done, their excursions in the neighborhood of the Barrens for twenty miles around.

By degrees, the result of such zeal began to manifest itself, so that in 1826 the extent of the missions embraced a wider tract of country. Frequently Mons. Odin and Timon could be seen together visiting as far as New Madrid, and even for a distance of 150 miles south of the Barrens. In the State of Illinois, Mr. Timon, who had already been raised to the priesthood in 1825, built churches in places known as "O'Hara's and the English settlements." At Kaskaskias, they re-established an old mission long abandoned, with such success, that in the vast and stately log church, (built there years before by the Jesuits, and which was crowned with a magnificent steeple, more than one hundred feet high,) there was soon gathered together a respectable congregation, among whom several converts might have been counted.

At a place called "St. Michael's," or "Mine la Motte," as it was then called, another mission was established. At this station Mr. Timon baptized the first persons, as the records there will show, and which are the names of Francis P. Bellenerè and P. G. Chevalier, on the 14th of May, 1827. The two Lazarists' friends then extended their zealous labors to Potosi and the "Old Mines," visiting an extent of country, reaching about 250 miles north and south.

CHAPTER IV.

ORDINATION OF JOHN TIMON.—CALLED TO SEE A MURDERER CONDEMNED TO DEATH.—DISCUSSION WITH A BAPTIST MINISTER.—DEFEATS HIM.—MISSION IN CAPE GIRARDEAU.—CONVERSION OF MR. RALPH DOHERTY.—CHOLERA.—MR. DOHERTY ILL.—FATHER TIMON CALLED IN TOO LATE.—BAPTISM OF MRS. DOHERTY.—A NIGHT WITH A CHOLERA CORPSE.—BAPTISM OF CHILDREN.—FATHER TIMON AND THE IRISHMAN.—CONFESSION ON HORSEBACK.—HAPPY DÉNOUEMENT.

RT. REV. JOS. ROSATTI, Bishop of St. Louis, in the Spring of 1825, visited the seminary of the Barrens, and whilst there raised to the priesthood among others Mr. John Timon. It was a period for which Mr. Timon had devoutly prayed, that he might be better enabled to discharge the promptings of his religious feelings, in ministering more freely to the wants of the people. It was a moment in his life when it seemed he had reached the zenith of his aspirations, and could, by the aid of Divine grace, penetrate every locality, irrespective of danger or opposition; when he felt panoplied with the truth and the power to defy the world in the service of the only true faith.

Hence, the circumstances of the preceding chapter reveal the zeal, the indifference to opposition, and the ultimate success with which he faced every obstacle. Before his eloquence, evaporated the prejudices against Catholics; before his logic and theology, fell the united strength of reasoning of anti-Catholic bigots; numbers enrolled themselves under the banner of the cross, converted by his winning manner, and edified by his holy piety. His name soon became a bulwark to the cause of Catholicity and a household word in every dwelling and log cabin for hundreds of miles around and near the Barrens. Messengers frequently came from long distances to solicit his aid. Sometimes it was to visit the bedside of a poor dying Catholic; sometimes it was in response to the wishes of a departing Protestant, who during life had been favorably disposed to religion, but deferred accepting it until the last hour; and often, it was to hasten to console an unhappy victim sentenced by the rigor of the law to be hanged on the gallows. Early in the Spring of 1828, Father Timon was summoned to a place called Jackson, at a distance of about thirty miles from the seminary, to visit a murderer under sentence of death, who, up to that time, had persistently refused to see a clergyman of any denomination whatever.

Father Timon started immediately, but it was towards nightfall before he arrived at the prison door, where, on various pretexts, permission to see the prisoner was flatly denied. It was only after the arrival of a Baptist minister named Green, who was also the editor and proprietor of the village newspaper, as well as an influential man among the town people, that Father Timon was allowed to enter the cell of the condemned man. Mr. Green also entered, accompanied by a band of anti-Catholic bigots, and when Father Timon appealed to the jailor to clear the cell and leave him alone with the prisoner, for the purpose of conversing in private on the affairs of the latter's conscience, it was inhumanly refused.

On a bed of straw, strewn over the clay floor, lay the culprit, chained to a post fastened in the wall.

Finding that he would only be allowed to converse with him in the presence of the hostile crowd, Father Timon, laying aside all reserve, resolutely stretched himself on the pallet of straw at the side of the prisoner, and, in a clear and loud tone of voice, began to expound to the poor man the great truths of religion, the Holy Trinity, the incarnation, future rewards and punishments, the redemption and the Holy Sacraments.

When he had finished, he turned towards the prisoner and found that he who, up to that moment, had laughed at religious teaching, was deeply affected, and that even tears were flowing from his eyes. This was the impression Father Timon had desired to make, and judging it to be more proper that he should now be left alone to meditate and reflect upon this his first favorable lesson, he rose to depart, already fatigued and worn out with his journey on horseback over a rough road of thirty miles, not having tasted a morsel from daybreak until nine o'clock that night. As he did so, however, he once more turned to the prisoner, and told him he would end the instructions of that night, by reciting with him the Apostles' Creed.

The condemned man, with much emotion, complied, and repeated after the priest the Apostles' Creed, word for word, until both had recited the words, "and in Jesus Christ our Lord." At these words Green, the Baptist minister, rushed forward, and in an authoritative manner exclaimed:

"Do not deceive the poor man. Do not make him lose his soul by teaching him the commandments of men."

Father Timon, thus addressed, slowly turned around, and in a calm but earnest tone of voice, replied, "Mr. Green, I am teaching him the Apostles' Creed. Do you not also hold that venerable creed?"

"Oh," answered Green, "but your Church is that idolatrous one, that worships images, and that gives to Mary the homage due only to God."

"Mr. Green," replied Father Timon, "not long since I preached in the court house of this village, on the very subject you now touch. I proved beyond a contradiction, the charges against the ancient Church to be foul calumnies. You were present. I *then* called upon any one, who could deny the truths which I announced, to come forward, and show if there was any flaw in the evidence which I brought to prove that Catholics had been cruelly and most unjustly calumniated. You were silent. Surely, then was your opportunity to discuss and disprove, and not this hour, in which I am preparing an unhappy man, who has sent for me to aid him, in meeting a death so certain and so near."

Green was at a loss what to reply, and in his confusion commenced some vague and insulting charges, challenging the priest to meet him next day in the court house, to discuss the merits of their respective beliefs. Father Timon immediately accepted the challenge.

Then Green claimed the privilege of saying night prayers, and kneeling down with his friends, made out a long and extemporaneous prayer, in which, among other insulting expressions, he prayed thus:

"And, oh! God of mercy, save this poor man from the fangs of Antichrist, who now seeks to teach him idolatry and the vain traditions of men."

Scarcely, however, had he finished, when Father Timon, at the top of his voice, cried out to the crowd that filled the dungeon:

"Gentlemen, is it right that, in a prayer to the God of charity and truth, this man should introduce a calumny against the majority of christians?"

Deep silence followed this remark, and showed that all felt the truth of the appeal.

It was now late at night, and the sheriff, wishing to close the jail, required all to leave the cell. On quitting it, however, Green renewed his challenge, and it was finally arranged that a meeting should take place in the court house next day.

But it is scarcely worth while reviewing the controversy. At the hour appointed, the disputants assembled at the place agreed upon, and the district judge was chosen moderator.

The time for speaking was limited to half an hour at a time to each disputant. After a discussion of three or four hours, Green gave up the contest, and withdrew completely outgeneraled by the superior arguments of his adversary. The indefatigable Father Timon, however, continued to speak and reviewed for half an hour longer the argument, exhorting serious and candid men to return to the old, but true religion. What was the result of this labor? When Father Timon had finished and returned to the cell of the poor prisoner, he found the latter ready to receive the Catholic faith, having already heard of the result of the controversy. At his own request he was accordingly baptized. But this was not all. The discussion served to resurrect in the hearts of many, prior to that time not known as

Catholics, the slumbering embers of their holy faith, and induced them to approach the sacraments of Penance and holy Eucharist. Several children were also baptized.

Thus under God, this circumstance was the cause of beginning the flourishing mission of Cape Girardeau.

Among those present at the controversy was a Protestant gentleman named Ralph Doherty, who was married to one of the first Protestant ladies of the neighborhood. Mr. Doherty was greatly impressed with the truths there announced, and, until then, quite new to him. Soon after this, Mr. Doherty fell sick, sent for Father Timon, and became a Catholic. In a few years afterwards, his whole family, except his wife, (who left him,) became Catholics. His conversion, followed by several members of the Sanford family, alarmed the bigotry of those inimical to the Church. Then Mr. Doherty became the object of persecution.

In the interim, Father Timon had begun a mission at Cape Girardeau. For six months, during each visit there, he said mass very privately at 6 A. M., and gave communion to a few converts. At 9 A. M. he would begin catechism for all the children he could collect together, and at 11 A. M. preached for the many Protestants who flocked to hear him. All this transpired in Mr. Doherty's house. At last, so vehement had the persecution become towards Mr. Doherty, that, to save the latter from losing his property, it was found necessary to purchase it from him. It is the most beautiful estate in that part of the country. The seminary, with its large and spacious grounds, and the handsome church of St. Vincent's, stand on a part of it. Finally, to augment the number of converts, the aged father of Mr. Doherty also became a Catholic.

Several years afterwards the cholera raged fearfully in the district of Jackson and Cape Girardeau. It so happened that at this time Father Timon was returning from New Madrid, and on his way stopped at the log cabin of the aged Mr. Doherty. It was full of company, nearly all of them Protestants; and so, inviting the priest to adjourn to the garden, Mr. Doherty there unburdened his conscience to his spiritual father.

As soon as he had finished, Father Timon bade good-bye to his aged friend, and without losing any more time, continued his journey to Jackson, a distance of ten miles. Here he stopped to refresh himself and feed his horse. About 8 P. M., just as he was again starting to ride, (as he very commonly had to do all night long,) a messenger came to tell him that Mr. Doherty, whom he had left only a few hours before, had been taken sick with the cholera, and begged for his spiritual father to return and comfort him.

Father Timon, from the depth of his charity for man, immediately turned his horse's head in the direction of Mr. Doherty's house, and through the rain, which by this time had began to fall very freely, hastened back to the cabin of the poor old man in the thick forest, where he arrived only to find that Mr. Doherty was dead.

Father Timon then recited some prayers for the dead, and gave a few words of exhortation to those present. When he had finished, the wife of the deceased man declared her intention of becoming a Catholic, and was immediately instructed. Those present were then invited to withdraw, there being but one room in the house, and as the convert knelt by the side of the bed on which her dead husband lay stretched, she, in accents of deep penitence, made her holy confession. The company were invited to enter again, and, *sub conditione*, the sacred rite of baptism was performed over the old lady, who expressed a great consolation in being made a member of the true Church.

In the meantime, the rain had been falling more heavily, and now poured in torrents. The forest became intensely dark, and it being near midnight, it was impossible for Father Timon to continue his journey further that night. As in all log cabins at that time, there was but one room, and only one bed in the corner, upon which lay the dead man. Having been invited to stay all night, however, Father Timon was not at a loss how to make the best of the situation. So, pushing the corpse up against the wall, a clean sheet was spread on the bed near it, and whilst the rest of the company disposed themselves to the best advantage upon the clay floor, the missionary was invited to share the bed with the corpse. *He did so, and slept soundly.*

Truly strange scenes frequently occurred in those missions, then so poor and wild. But to a disposition like Father Timon, whose heart knew no fear but the fear of God, these scenes as related to us and which seem so strange, were as commonplace occurrences.

He once preached near New Madrid, on the banks of the Mississippi. Six young children were offered to him for baptism by their Protestant parents, with the promise that they should be brought up as Catholics. After the ceremony was over, Father Timon mounted his horse to leave for the next station, a distance of fifteen miles, in order to meet an appointment for the following day. He had hardly left the crowd, when an old man, also on horseback, rode after him, and, in accents that showed him to be an Irishman, exclaimed:

"Ah! but my heart warmed to you as you spoke, for I too am a Catholic; but you are the first priest I have seen for forty years. Often these 'swaddlers' tried to get me to change my religion, telling me that I could never expect to see a Catholic priest here, and that it was better for me to have some religion than none at all. I, at times, almost believed them, but whenever I thought of joining them, upon my word, *it seemed as if my confirmation was about rising in my throat to choke me. And I couldn't do it.* But I married a Protestant who was never baptized. We have many children, and I have often spoken to them of my religion, and I think they can easily be made Catholics. Come with me, my wife is very sick, it may be her salvation."

Father Timon was not astonished at the poor man's history, such a scene was common to him; and, although he had to turn in a direction quite opposite to that he had intended to take, he willingly did so, entering a dark forest just as the shades of night began to fall, and the rain from the threatening black clouds overhead was making music on the leaves of the trees above them.

Father Timon, upon inquiring found, as was usual with all frontier settlers, that there was but one room in the house, and this room was occupied by the sick woman. Therefore, after a moment's reflection and prayer, he turned to his companion at his side, and said:

"But, my friend, if I go and baptize your wife, I must also marry you both."

"Sure, that's what I want," replied the man.

"Then," said Father Timon, "you should first make your confession and be prepared."

"And sure, it's willing I am," sorrowfully rejoined the poor man, "but how or when can I get confession?"

"Here," said the missionary, "even here as we ride along this solitary road."

"And will that do?"

"Why not?" answered Father Timon. "God is good. He wants us only to do the best we can, and surely, there is no other way than this for you now. So prepare yourself, by examining your conscience carefully, and when you are ready I will hear your confession."

Thus encouraged and advised, the old man devoutly took off his hat, made the sign of the cross, and then, riding on in silence, prepared himself to reconcile his long deferred account with his Maker. It was indeed an humble, but at the same time sublime scene. The forest was intensely dark, and no noise could be heard than the heavy fall of rain, as it spattered in heavy drops from the leaves of the trees, through which they were winding their way. Priest and penitent, now trotting along the night path of the forest, now leading their horses through some uncertain spots in the wood, thus journeyed on for some time in silence.

Presently the man declared himself ready to confess, and aided by the priest as they both started their horses into a gentle canter, the confession was soon finished, the priest's sacred duty performed, just a few moments before they reached the door of the log cabin, where lay the sick and anxious wife.

But the rest of the incident is soon told. Before midnight, Father Timon had instructed the whole family, and baptized the children. Just as morning began to dawn through the apertures of the cabin, the wife had been also instructed and baptized, and the happy couple re-married. By daylight, Father Timon had to leave, and at a hurried pace, ride to meet an appointment, some distance away, besides saying mass and preaching before noon.

---o---

CHAPTER V.

Mons. J. M. Odin.—Bishop Rosatti and the Barrens.—Embarrassments of the Seminary.—Meeting of the Professed Priests.—Father Timon Speaker for the Community.—Bishop Rosatti Responds.—Rev. J. B. Tornatori Chosen Superior of the Missions.—Purchase of the Doherty Estate.—The Sick Woman.—Her Conversion.—Incidents.—Condition of the Missions.—Discouraging Prospects.—Father Timon Vanquishes six Ministers in a Discussion.—Interview with a Condemned Man.—Mr. Odin goes to France.

Once had the Right Rev. Jos. Rosatti been called to the Episcopate, and feeling it painful to his humility, had respectfully refused. In 1824, however, he was forced to accept it, and in the church of the Ascension (and parish of that name in the State of Louisiana,) he was consecrated Bishop, *in partibus infidelium*, of Tenagre, and Coadjutor of New Orleans. In the meantime the few priests at the seminary were gradually dispersed, whilst the Bishop himself was often forced to be absent. Thus, for a considerable length of time, Mons. Odin was left, the sole priest at the seminary. Besides the discharge of his duties as provisional Superior, parish priest, and confessor to the brothers, seminarians, collegians, and Lorentine Nuns, he was obliged to direct the general course of teaching in the college. Nay, more, often on Saturdays particularly, he would be out until ten o'clock at night, on a sick call or other important duty, and when he came home, he found the students and brothers waiting to go to confession, and occupying him the greater part of what remained of the night. But, despite the tedium of this excessive labor, he cheerfully fulfilled his duty, with a holy zeal and peace of heart, that alone can account for his not having entirely lost his health. He suffered much, however, and sick headaches, often for days, would be the penalty for having taxed both body and mind too much. But, as has been already stated, on the 20th of May, 1824, Bishop Rosatti was named first Bishop of St. Louis, and Administrator of New Orleans. On the 1st of January previous, however, he had solemnly laid the corner stone of a new stone church, near the seminary, on the plan of the chapel of the mission near Monte Citorio, Rome.

Although Bishop Rosatti loved the calm retreat of the Barrens, and thought of making it his residence, to govern his diocese from it, he reluctantly abandoned that idea, at the instigations of a certain missionary, whose opinions on the subject were such as to show that it would not have been for the glory of God or the good of souls. Meanwhile much dissatisfaction existed among the few priests of the mission. As yet they did not possess an inch of ground; on the contrary, they were burdened with heavy debts.

Even some of the first brothers, who had been in America twelve years, murmured less at their poverty than at the prospect of spending the close of their lives in the poor house. Something had to be done to relieve the community from their embarrassing dilemma. Accordingly a meeting of the professed priests was held at the seminary of the Barrens, to which Bishop Rosatti was invited, in order to hear the complaints that were necessary to be made. Father Timon was delegated to act as speaker for the community, and in compliance with the wishes of his fellow priests, he reverently but at the same time firmly and distinctly, laid before the Bishop all the complaints and the existing feelings of dissatisfaction. Bishop Rosatti was an attentive listener to the clear and eloquent language of the young and zealous Lazarist, and as an expression of his sympathy for the community, he kindly consented, at the conclusion of the meeting, to give the congregation a deed of the property, assume some of its debts, and at the same time promised to make some provision for such of the seminarians as might not be occupied in teaching.

After Bishop Rosatti had fixed his residence at St. Louis, Rev. J. B. Tornatori, an Italian priest of great learning and piety, was sent to the Barrens, as Superior of the whole mission. In this connection it may be proper to observe that, owing to the persecution he had received from his bigoted friends and acquaintances for the abjuration of his Protestant faith, Mr. Ralph Doherty came nigh losing his valuable piece of property. It was only through the intervention of his brother-in-law, Mr. Hen. Sanford, of Jackson, Mo., that he was relieved of this persecution, by selling the property to the community of the Lazarists. This occurred during the administration of Rev. Mr. Tornatori. For this purpose Father Timon was sent to Potosi, and whilst there he negotiated with a Mr. John Casey for a loan of $2,000, (or about 10,000 francs). From Potosi he went by the way of Selma to the city of St. Louis. At Selma he was very successful in obtaining an endorsement on his loan, by a rich Protestant gentleman, Capt. J. M. White. But on his arrival at St. Louis, Father Timon found the good Bishop exceedingly displeased at hearing of the purchase of the estate. A little explanation soon followed, and, of course, when he discovered that the Doherty property had been bought without putting him under any pecuniary obligations whatever, he was again much pleased. Subsequently Father Timon bought more property at a low figure, by purchasing a number of tracts of valuable land from Congress, at about one-tenth their value.

At Cape Girardeau, a house formerly used as a store-house, and adjoining one of the principal residences, was converted into a church. At first, once in every three months, then once in a month, Father Timon rode down there from the Barrens, said mass and catechised, with very happy results in dissipating the prejudices of the Protestant people.

About two weeks after he had held his regular mission, and consequently at a time when no one expected a visit from him so soon, Father Timon was sent by his Superior to complete some arrangements about the deeds of the Doherty estate. The shades of evening had begun to gather when he arrived at the Cape. In about a half an hour after his arrival he unexpectedly received a visit from one of the most respectable persons of the place, a gentleman who subsequently became its Mayor. This gentleman called to request the priest to visit his step-mother, who was dying.

"Is she a Catholic?" inquired Father Timon.

"Oh, no, there is no Catholic in my house, sir," replied the stranger.

Father Timon, thinking (as it often before had so occurred,) that the dying Protestant lady wanted him only to pray for her, very willingly consented to accompany the gentleman, and accordingly took neither vesture nor holy oils with him, which, in administering extreme unction to a dying *Catholic*, are so necessary. He found the lady very ill, but, as far as religion was concerned, very well disposed. At her request he exposed aloud the faith of the Catholic Church, in the presence of her children and friends, to which she readily assented, and expressed the desire to become a Catholic and be baptized. Father Timon was a little surprised at this eagerness on her part to embrace the faith, but observing that she sought to become a member of the Church with earnest emotions, and with an expression of much devotional feeling, he hastened to get baptismal water and holy oils. As he was leaving the sick room, however, and entering another, the lady of the house and wife of the gentleman who had called him to visit his sick step-mother, followed him, and in an earnest tone of voice said:

"Sir, there is something very extraordinary in all this. My mother has never yet been in a Catholic church. Only once in her life time has she heard a Catholic sermon, and yet she has for months thought that she heard a voice saying almost continually to her, '*If you want to be saved, you must become a Catholic.*' She has often related this to us, and begged us to send for you; but we thought it only the wild freak of a wandering mind, and

(4)

of course we refused to comply with her wishes. A few days ago, she thought she had a vision of a man dressed like you, who *gave her a crucifix to kiss,* and at the same instant the voice said, '*Do what this priest will tell you, and you shall be saved.*'

"She started from her sleep, told us of the vision, and begged us to send for you. But we refused, as it was a long journey to the Barrens, and we thought it seemed only a wild frenzy on her part. Just as we were debating the matter with her, a neighbor came in and told us you had already arrived, and then it was that we determined to send for you."

The lady here ceased, and altogether the circumstances of the case seemed very strange, and at the same time marvelous to Father Timon. It only served to give greater zeal to the haste he made to obtain the necessary articles with which to prepare her for her reception into the Church, and to bestrew her path to eternity with the roses of devotion and piety. In a very short time he returned, and approaching the bedside of the sick woman, he *presented the crucifix to her to be kissed,* and as he did so, he remarked that she pressed it with eager emotion to her lips. He then baptized her, *sub conditione,* heard her confession, and administered to her the holy Sacraments of the altar, and extreme unction. It was near midnight before all the religious ceremonies were finished. In a few hours afterwards the happy woman, her countenance lit up with the radiance of an inward serenity of heart, and the consolation of having embraced the true faith, lay back on the pillow and gave her soul to her Maker.

This circumstance seemed strange to Father Timon, and accordingly he inquired of her relatives what were the antecedents of the deceased lady, and discovered that during life she had been particularly distinguished for her *charity* to the poor and the sick. It was this no doubt, he concluded, that drew down upon her a special mercy from heaven in her last hour. Soon one after another of the rest of the family became Catholics, and many years afterwards, when a fine stone church, dedicated to St. Vincent, had been erected on that very spot, Mons. L'Eveque de Forbin Janson confirmed the last convert of that family.

In 1829, Mr. De Neckere was named Bishop of New Orleans. At first he hesitated much, and consulted his friends as to the feasibility of his accepting of it. Among others, he solicited the opinion of his friend, Father Timon, who advised him to refuse the Episcopacy, alleging that his character and constitution were such as would cause him to sink under its burdens in a very few years. In effect, the saintly Bishop died about three years after his consecration.

From 1829 to 1835, the priests of the congregation of the missions continued to labor and make the sacrifices which had marked their early career. Several priests fell victims to their zeal. Mr. Cellini, Mr. Borgna, Mr. Rosti, Mr. Pernoli, and others, were engaged separately in different missions in Louisiana. Mr. Dahmen was laboring with great zeal at St. Genevieve, and the adjacent country. At the Barrens, the college suffered much from sickness. Many of the pupils neglected to pay their bills; that of one family, amounting to six thousand francs, was never paid. Several other bills, still unpaid, approached nearly to that amount. Debts against the seminary began to accumulate. The house was still in an unfinished state; the building of the new church had been stopped after the saintly death of brother Oliva, who, fortunately, had finished the stone work of the building before he had been called away. On every side circumstances conspired to cast a gloom over the prospects of the mission. Protestant ministers again began to preach in the vicinity of the seminary. One of the missionaries (Father Timon,) was sent to meet a minister at the court house at Perryville, Mo.; there the minister endeavored to rally his logic and theology in defence of his religious opinions, but to no purpose. He was put to shame, and forced to avow himself vanquished; but he intimated that on a certain day, at a place the distance of six leagues from there, his Bishop and several of his brother ministers would assemble for a general conference and prayer meeting, and that if the priest wished to go there he would meet his match, and have the error of his ways pointed out to him. Father Timon asked him if he meant what he said as a challenge.

"No," said the minister, "I don't invite you; I only say that you may go there if you choose." This, of course, under the circumstances of the case, Father Timon refused to promise. He soon publicly declared that he would not go, and that he would not have been there (Perrysville) then, if it had not been for the calumnies and public insulting attacks of the baffled Protestant minister.

In the meantime, for the distance of four or five leagues around the seminary, the minister, counting on impunity, spread the report that the Catholic priest had *pledged* himself to meet the ministers in the intended public discussion.

By accident, however, the night preceding the day appointed for the conference, Father Timon heard of this artifice, and accordingly early next morning, he saddled his horse, and hastily rode to the scene of action, where his maligners hoped to gain a bloodless victory. Here he found the crowd to be very large, and in order to be able to accommodate all, the church had been abandoned, and benches hastily constructed under the shade of the trees of a neighboring wood. Just as Father Timon had reached the ground, a minister was finishing his last prayer. In the meantime, some of the bystanders whispered into the ear of Father Timon that one of the ministers had been endeavoring to show the folly of the "Real Presence," and the wickedness of "Transubstantiation." He had said, also, that there was "a Romish priest" present who, "if he dared to come forward, would have the error of his ways pointed out to him," and, said the informant, "we all thought he spoke of you."

When the minister had finally concluded his prayer, Father Timon, mounting the stump of a tree, in a loud tone of voice announced that he would, in a quarter of an hour, preach on the Real Presence and Transubstantiation. Six preachers immediately surrounded him with violent gestures, as if they intended to strike him, declaring that he would not or should not preach in that place. But Father Timon, nothing daunted, appealed to the people, and to their credit be it said, they resolutely consented to hear him.

Father Timon first showed the unworthy trick that had been attempted to be practiced at the expense of his name, but which by God's Providence he had been enabled to defeat. He then took a Protestant Bible from the hands of one of the ministers, and read fourteen texts from it, and explained them. He showed the meaning of Transubstantiation, by its entering in a slow yet real manner into the economy of God for the growth and existence of all that lives. He continued at some further length, advancing undeniable proofs of his thesis, and appealed to either of the six ministers present, or their Bishop, to produce a single text from the Bible that would disprove his argument, and that would be as strong and conclusive as any one of the fourteen he had advanced.

In their turn the opposing ministers rose to respond, not, however, confining themselves to the subject in question, and quoting the texts called for; but, as invariably is the case with many, by showing that Catholics worshiped the Virgin Mary and adored images. This was the sum and substance of their remarks. When the ministers had finished their argument, Father Timon again arose, and turning to the attentive crowd, asked if they could believe that the God of truth would, on so important a subject, leave fourteen texts in the Bible to say clearly and strongly a damnable falsehood, and yet without a single one to say plainly the truth. For half an hour he continued to review the subject, supporting his position from the Bible, from writings of men who have handed down their testimonies, age after age, on the doctrine of Transubstantiation, and by appealing to the standard of intelligence with which man then was wont to accept the truth, if consistently presented. His appeal was irresistible, for he won the sympathies of his audience, and won their minds as well as their hearts. Before such eloquence and logic the ministers could not stay, and in their confusion they left the grounds abashed and confounded.

The indefatigable missionary continued to address the crowd, and to exhort them to profit by this evidence of truth, which

God in his mercy had vouchsafed to give them, and to return to the Church where *alone* truth in its holy fullness is taught.

This splendid triumph of Father Timon had its desired effect. After this controversy the preachers, by degrees, avoided the neighborhood of the seminary. Little by little, the inhabitants renounced their prejudices and errors, and became Catholics.

The recital of the missionary adventures which thus far have been the principal points of interest in this biography, is nothing more or less than the history of Father Timon, and curious or strange as they may appear to the reader, still no better indices could be given to point out as clearly the true character of the distinguished missionary and prelate. To enter into an analysis of his character, his disposition and his religious opinions, would form a subject of elaborate length. This we will avoid as far as it will be possible, preferring to reserve for the closing chapter of this book, a careful analysis of his character and spirit.

In 1831, Father Timon, returning late one evening from Cape Girardeau to the Barrens, was told that a man was under sentence of death for murder, and would be hung the following day. Thus far he had refused all spiritual aid and succor. Father Timon immediately went to the dungeon of the hardened criminal to see him, and by his zeal and interest in the poor man's fate, gradually softened his heart before the truth. He ordered the liquor, which had been allowed him, to be removed, and besides exacting a promise from the prisoner not to drink any more, stationed friends near the prison door, to prevent any access on his part to the fatal draught. Early in the morning, the prisoner ate a good breakfast, and recommenced his instruction. About ten o'clock A. M., the culprit was baptized, his tears during the ceremony proving how deeply his heart had been touched. In a few hours afterwards the condemned man was launched into eternity.

A number of zealous and talented priests had in the interim joined the congregation, and made their vows, eminent among whom were Mr. Boullier, Mr. Paquin, Mr. Vergani and others, who, alas, for the perpetuation and progress of the Church militant, have already passed to their reward. Others still labor zealously in the different missions. In September 1833, Mr. Odin, who had labored so much, and who was generally so venerated and beloved, started for France.

---o---

CHAPTER VI.

FATHER TIMON NAMED VISITOR.—HIS REFUSAL.—DISCOURAGING CIRCUMSTANCES.—HIS HUMILITY.—HE ACCEPTS.—CONVOCATION OF PRIESTS.—REMONSTRANCE AGAINST THE SUPPRESSION OF THE COLLEGE.—DEBTS, MORTGAGE, AND DISCONTENTED FEELINGS PREVAIL.—IMPROVEMENTS MADE.—FATHER TIMON GOES TO NEW ORLEANS, LA.—GOES TO CAPE GIRARDEAU.—RETURNS TO THE BARRENS.—FATHER TIMON AND THE BISHOP OF ST. LOUIS.—THE VISITOR GOES TO PARIS, FRANCE.—HIS ARRIVAL THERE.—RESULTS.—HIS RETURN.—NEARLY LOSES A LARGE SUM OF MONEY.—REACHES THE BARRENS IN SAFETY.

THE age of the venerated Mr. Tornatori not permitting him to learn English, it was decreed at a general assembly of the congregation, held at Paris, at which Mr. Odin assisted, that Father Timon should be made Visitor, thus, for the first time, establishing the American mission into a province. Whilst the decrees appointing Father Timon were on their way to the Barrens, Mr. Tornatori and Timon were traveling together to view the state of the mission and property at Cape Girardeau. On the 16th of November, 1835, they returned to the seminary, and on their arrival, letters were handed to them, appointing Father Timon as Visitor of the congregation of missions, and ordaining the suppression of the college, and the expulsion of one of the priests, besides requiring as a condition, *sine qua non*, that the Bishop should pay six hundred francs annually for each seminarian. Father Timon at first determined on refusing to accept the office of *Visitor*, as he foresaw difficulties of every kind in the way, and, in his humility, thought he was not capable of undertaking such a charge, particularly under the circumstances. He therefore requested Father Tornatori to keep the contents of the letters secret, at least until a meeting of the priests of the mission could be convened. To this proposition, however, Father Tornatori would not acquiesce, but assembled the entire community, and informed them of the change that had been made. Although the announcement of this news was entirely satisfactory, still Father Timon persisted in refusing to accept the position. He accordingly paid a visit to St. Genevieve to see his friends, Mr. Dahmen and Borgna, and to the "Old Mines," to confer with his confrère, Mr. Boullier. Even these united to condemn his unwillingness to don the robe of office, and finally, in obedience to the unanimous wish of the community and friends, he bowed his humble head, and accepted to discharge the obligations for which he felt himself incapacitated. His first step was to convoke a meeting of the priests, who unanimously requested the new Visitor to suspend all action on the college until the Superior General had been informed of the almost impossibility of its suppression then, as well as the apparent or real necessity of continuing the college for years, perhaps for time to come. Father Odin, who had returned from France, was one of the most firm in protesting against the suppression of the college. Letters breathing this spirit on the subject were written to Paris, and consultations held, at which it was found that the congregation owed about sixty thousand francs, whilst it possessed nothing excepting the newly acquired property at the Cape. Even this estate was mortgaged for the purchase money. Great and general discontent at the unfavorable state of things prevailed to a greater or less degree in the community. Mr. Raho had left for Louisiana, without asking for permission, whilst Mr. Rosti and others already there were unwilling to return.

The prospects indeed were gloomy before the new Visitor. No wonder, then, that it was with feelings of reluctance, owing to a diffidence in his own ability, that Father Timon hesitated to comply with the wishes of his Superior and the community. But when he once had accepted, it was no longer for him a subject of regret. He applied himself zealously and diligently to the work before him. He dissipated, by the native resources of his intellect and energy of purpose, the gradual discontent that had been gathering, like a cloud on the horizon, among the members of the community. He traveled far and wide, infusing into others the spirit of sacrifice and piety that animated him; rescued the college from annihilation, lessened the burdens of debt and expense; brought new hands into the vineyard of the Lord, to labor and improve; and proved by his zeal, his piety, and above all, by his charity, that he had been the chosen of God, and had been called to his true vocation for the time being. Finally, after nearly two months' labor at and around the Barrens, Visitor Timon went to New Orleans. Here God blessed his efforts, for he succeeded in inducing Mr. Raho, Mr. Rosti, and others, to return to community life at the Barrens. In the meantime, letters from the Superior General had been received, permitting the college to continue. Gradually this institution, over which the unexecuted sentence of suppression had so long hung suspended, was relieved from its dilemma, and lost its character for sickliness, which a few years of epidemic and several deaths had acquired for it. Payments became more regular, and the mortgages on the old property were consequently paid, whilst new property, since very valuable, was acquired in the city of St Louis.

Whilst Visitor Timon was at New Orleans, however, preparing for his return to the Barrens, an interesting incident occurred, that will be worth the while relating. He was called upon by a Rev. Mr. Kendalon, to aid in converting a young man, connected with one of the first families of the city, who was under sentence of death for murder. This young man was to be executed in ten days, and thus far had refused to see any clergyman of the different denominations in the city. Much to the surprise of many, however, he at once consented to admit Father Timon and Kendalon, who found him to be a highly educated young man, and who listened with eager avidity to all that his reverend friends had to impart. Each day the priests continued, one after the other, to instruct and prepare him. Finally he consented to be baptized, and once, when both of his reverend friends were present together, he told the following history of his life:

"In my early youth, in company with several other Protestant boys, I was sent to an excellent Catholic college. Whilst there I made rapid progress in my studies, and soon became a general favorite among my college mates. On my part I venerated the Catholic priests, who were my teachers also, and very soon perceived in the conduct of the Catholic boys something which I judged to be an almost unearthly firmness in virtue, so that I began to wish I was a Catholic. My parents heard of this tendency of mine, and being very much prejudiced against the Catholic religion, immediately removed me from the college. I was next placed under the care of a Baptist minister, who became my tutor and teacher. But what I learned from him, and what I observed in his house, only served to make me an infidel. At times the bright dream of my youth in that Catholic college would rise before me, and for the moment check the reckless life that I had commenced to lead. As soon, however, as the memory of that vision would leave me, I again plunged more deeply into my former wild habits until, at last, I soon succeeded in checking its too frequent return. Oh! how vividly the recollection of those hours I spent under the roof of that Catholic institution, once more passes in bright review before me, which, alas, by contrast with the life that I have since led, seems like a dream of happiness I shall never more realize.

"I lost all restraint over my passions; I followed one career of crime to another; I could do any thing, so blunted and indifferent had my sense of modesty and conscience become, until, finally, I now find myself here in this dungeon, a victim for the scaffold. Now, must *I* expiate by a shameful death the bigotry that tore me from the influence of the only religion that could have restrained my passions, and have saved me."

Here the prisoner ceased speaking, overcome by the violence of his grief and emotions, and bursting into tears, he buried his head between the palms of his hands, and gave way to his sorrowful feelings.

In the meantime the priests had determined on the day before his execution for his baptism, and for administering the holy

Sacrament of the Altar. But a few days prior to the one on which he was to have been baptized, some of his friends called on him, and said:

"Our efforts have been useless. The Governor refuses a pardon, and the alternative for you is death. Here," they continued, "is a weapon. Take it, and with it save your family the disgrace of having one of their number hung."

The culprit, however, answered: "A few days ago, had you called on me, I might have accepted the remedy you propose, but lately I have seen a Catholic priest, who has given me quite different views of duty and of the life beyond the grave. I therefore cannot now, consistently with my deep conviction of what is right and proper, lay hands on my own life."

This conversation, and the determination of the prisoner to continue in the change of life he had begun, were soon noised through the city, and all rejoiced in the evidence of a sincere conversion.

But on the morning of the day fixed for baptism, both priests were with the prisoner in his cell. The poor man seemed in the best of dispositions. About 11 o'clock, the jailor came to request the priests to withdraw, as the mother and sisters of the prisoner wished to take their last farewell of their son and brother. Father Timon and Kendalon, of course, retired, and went to the Episcopal residence, at that time only a short distance from the jail. They had been gone perhaps an hour, when they noticed, from the windows of the room in which they were, a great commotion in the street below. Father Timon hurriedly went out to ascertain the cause, and to his great sorrow was told that the prisoner had killed himself. He hastened to the prison, and although access was forbidden to the crowd, the jailor readily admitted him within the prison door. Here, he found in the cell the body of the young man, still warm but lifeless. The jailor averred that, prior to the arrival of his relatives, the young man had had no weapon about him, as he had been carefully searched when they first placed him in the jail. But at his side was found a costly dagger, with which the sad deed had been committed. All surmised, however, when and by whom the dagger had been given; the sad circumstance forming another sad chapter on the consequence of anti-Catholic bigotry.

On the 24th of March, 1836, Visitor Timon returned to the Barrens, and on the 9th of April following, started with Rev. Mr. Odin, Robert, and servants, to begin a permanent establishment at Cape Girardeau. Heavy rains, however, had made the creeks so high as to render swimming necessary. It was attended with much difficulty. Visitor Timon, on horseback, swam the river, examined for a more fordable place, then recrossed and brought over Mr. Odin and the rest of the company. Then all had to remain over night at Jackson, ten leagues from the seminary. Early in the morning, Visitor Timon started to say mass, according to appointment, at Cape Girardeau. The others, who were much fatigued, remained at Jackson to take breakfast. They reached the Cape, however, twelve miles distant, at 11 A. M., just as Father Timon was saying mass. After mass, Visitor Timon introduced Mr. Odin to the congregation, as their future pastor, and alluded, as far as the well-known humility of Mr. Odin permitted, to the virtues, learning and zeal of the pastor whom God then gave them, and to the great services he had already rendered to religion, with the hope that Providence prepared for Cape Girardeau, through him, still greater blessings.

After this, Visitor Timon returned to the Barrens. On Sunday, April 17th, he preached on the zeal for building God's Temple, and took his text from I Parali. xxixth chapter, and read of the zeal with which, in olden time, God's people had contributed towards building a Temple to the Lord. He exhorted his audience to come forward and contribute generously, so that their new church, beautiful even in its unfinished state, might be prepared more decently for celebrating Divine worship. To their credit be it said, the congregation replied liberally to his appeal; a large collection was made, and more money promised. Under such encouragement, the work of finishing the church soon began.

Although Visitor Timon had a special affection and veneration for the Bishop of St. Louis, and although the Bishop also esteemed the Visitor much, still there transpired some painful and trying scenes between the two, on account of an order which the Bishop tried to execute, to restore to community life priests who were then living apart as mere parish priests. A large and painful correspondence was kept up regarding Rev. Mr. Douterlounge, then stationed at Cahokias, near St. Louis. It required some years to enable the Visitor to effect an understanding and final settlement. On the 11th May, 1836, the Bishop of St. Louis wrote to the Visitor to remonstrate again against the departure of Mr. Douterlounge from the parish of Cahokias. The letter said:

"I must observe to you to do every thing *secundum ordinem;* hence, with regard to the parishes, or missions entrusted to the priests of the congregation of the missions, the Superior has not only to make choice of the subject of the congregation of the missions, who is to perform the functions of pastor of the parish or mission, but he must apprise the Bishop of it, and propose to him the successor. However, when no change is made, the missionary may leave his parish for a time, for instance to go and make his retreat, and the Superior may send in his place some priest to attend to the congregation during his temporary absence. This being well understood and exactly observed, there will be no occasion for any misunderstanding."

Against some details of the above rule, however, the Visitor felt himself impelled to protest, and consequently refused several parishes, which the good Bishop pressed him to accept. Finally, he did consent to take a few of them under a rule which left him more free to act. Visitor Timon continued to develop the missions on every hand, and make such improvements in his undertakings that were necessary, among other things raising and completing the columns required for the gallery of the new church and house at the Barrens, thereby making them more comfortable, and giving them a much better appearance.

At this time, too, several seminarians were raised to the tonsure, subdeacon, and deaconship by the Rt. Rev. Bishop Rosatti, who had been invited to the seminary for the purpose.

In the meantime, the Visitor deemed it necessary to pay a visit to the mother house at Paris, and therefore, with the advice of his brother priests of the mission, he started for Europe. On his way from the Barrens to Baltimore, he made the acquaintance of several persons, afterwards valuable to the congregation. At Baltimore, Md., Archbishop Eccleson offered him the College of Emmittsburg, Mount St. Mary, and the care of the Sisters of Charity in America. Without, however, accepting this offer, the Visitor promised to present this request to the Superior General at Paris for consideration, but which subsequently was not accepted. On his way to New York, he stopped at Philadelphia, where he was requested by the Rev. Rich. P. Kenrick, now Archbishop of St. Louis, to give a retreat to the seminarians, which he did, and then started for the city of New York, whence he sailed for France on the 24th August, 1837. Nothing of special mention transpired during the voyage, excepting that he edified all on board by his engaging manner and his pious deportment, and after a favorable voyage of twenty-three days, reached the mother house in Paris, on the 16th September, 1837, where he was received most kindly by Mr. Aladel, Superior General, and where, before the blessed Sacrament and the sacred shrine of St. Vincent, the missionary, a native of the New World, poured out his heart in indescribable feelings of gratitude and oblation.

This visit to Paris by the Visitor, proved to be of great benefit to the congregation. The Superior General allowed ten thousand francs to the congregation, to aid in paying off the debt on the seminary. Several indefatigable and zealous priests accompanied the Visitor on his return to America, among whom were Rev. Mr. Armangal, Alabou, Domenec, Brother Sticca, and other brothers. They sailed from Havre, France, in the ship Georgia, for New Orleans, on the 15th October, 1837, thereby rendering the stay of the Visitor at Paris, comparatively speaking, not very long. The voyage was a long and stormy one, but not altogether useless, nor without consolation. The missionaries busied themselves on board the ship in a variety of useful ways. Visitor Timon, who was the centre of the zeal and devotion, was a continual pattern for all. In a part of the ship occupied by them they built an altar, on which, when the sea was calm, the holy sacrifice of the mass was said. Each morning they made their meditations together, as well as the exercises of the community, nearly as regular as if they had been in a convent. Besides these pious practices, the Visitor busied himself in giving lessons in the English language to the Spanish priests, who were accompanying him to the New World. At length, after a long and tedious voyage, they reached New Orleans in safety, late in the month of December, having been nearly ten weeks on their voyage from France to America.

Prior to leaving France, religious charitable communities, through the Superior General, had requested Visitor Timon to invest about two hundred thousand francs in stock of the United States Bank. Accordingly, from Paris the Visitor sent a portion of this money to a trusty friend in the city of New York, whose acquaintance he had formed on his outward voyage. The balance of the entrusted sum the Visitor took with him in letters of credit. Consequently, when he arrived in New Orleans, he applied to a very rich and intelligent friend to invest this fund he had with him in United States Bank stock, which, at this time, was selling at twenty per cent. above par. In the most confidential earnestness, the friend thus applied to besought the Visitor not to take this stock, as the bank was *rotten*. In a frame of mind not quite decided what to do, the Visitor, for the present, deferred any further action in the matter, but hastened to the city of St. Louis, anxious to return to his beloved retreat at the Barrens, and to meet with his dear priests and friends. On his arrival in St. Louis, he found there several letters, among which was one from his friend in New York, to whom he had sent ten thousand francs to be invested in United States stock. In the letter the kind friend advised him that he would invest as directed, if again commanded to do so, but, at the same time, he requested the Visitor not to touch the stock of this bank; for, although its credit was very high, and the stock above par, still the "knowing ones" considered it dangerous. Accordingly, acting under the precautions of his friends, he determined to abandon the idea of risking his means to the care of the United States Bank, although the appearances were so very attractive and apparently lucrative. He, therefore, invested all his funds in the State Bank of Missouri, of whose solvency he had the surest guarantees. In less than a year afterwards, the Visitor had occasion to thank the foresight and precautionary judgment of his friends, for the United States Bank failed; its stock became worth nothing, and has remained so ever since. The failure of this bank entailed ruin on almost all the banks of the Union. All suspended specie payment, except the State Bank of Missouri, although, indeed, for a few years it would declare no dividend, in order that it might keep itself strong amidst the frightful crisis of 1837. Afterwards, however, it gave very large dividends, and thus all the invested funds of the religious charitable societies which, through the Visitor, had been entrusted to this bank, were saved, and brought good revenue.

On his arrival in New Orleans, the Visitor had placed his little colony of missionaries in the houses of different clergymen, and, at the request of Bishop Blanc, gave a retreat to the Sisters of Charity in New Orleans, as well as retreats to other religious institutions, until the Mississippi river would be free of ice and become navigable. During this time, the Bishop of New Orleans offered his seminary to the Lazarists, which the Visitor accepted, subject to the approbation of the mother house at Paris. The Bishop likewise pressed the Visitor to accept of Donaldsonville as an almost necessary port of entry. The latter did so, *ad tempus*, but subject also to the will of the Superior General.

Finally, when navigation had opened, Visitor Timon embarked with his little colony of missionaries, and on the 10th of February, 1838, reached the seminary of the Barrens in safety. It may be well imagined that great were the rejoicings of the community for the help vouchsafed, and for the evidences of interest which the mother house took in that distant infant province. Indeed, the *personnel* of the congregation was greatly augmented by the security which the Visitor had obtained. From Paris, Italy, and Spain came the disciples of Christ, among whom were Mr. Domenec, Alabon, Pasqual, Amat, Cercox, Calvo, Estany, Burlando, D'Marchi, Bagliloli, Gustiniani, Parodi, and several lay brothers. Some were called in a few years to their eternal reward, others were sent to Mexico or recalled to Europe, whilst the rest still remain, laboring most zealously in the holy ministry.

---o---

CHAPTER VII.

IMPROVEMENTS IN THE MISSION.—THE VISITOR GOES TO TEXAS AS AN ENVOY OF ROME.—MEETS FRIENDS IN GALVESTON.—GOES TO HOUSTON.—OPENS A MISSION.—RESULTS.—POOR O'BRIEN.—SCANDALOUS CONDUCT OF TWO MEXICAN PRIESTS.—VISITOR RETURNS TO NEW ORLEANS.—HIS REPORT.—ARRIVES AT NATCHEZ, MISS.—READS MASS IN MRS. GIRARDEAU'S HOUSE.—PREACHES IN THE CITY HALL.—ENTHUSIASM.—GOES TO ST. LOUIS.—RELIGIOUS ZEAL.—PROPOSED FOR AN EPISCOPAL SEE.—DECLINES.—REFUSES TO ADMINISTRATE THE ST. LOUIS DIOCESE.—FURTHER DEVELOPMENTS.

In March, 1838, the Visitor contracted with Messrs. Fiena and Taylor, for finishing the towers of the church at the Barrens, they indemnifying him in work for neglects in a previous contract, effected during his absence in Europe. The college was now in a prosperous condition, the number of pupils having been augmented by recruits from Louisiana. The missions also took a new impulse. In the new church, which had so far been finished as to permit the celebration of Divine worship, Mr. Burlando played the organ, whilst the other reverend gentlemen sang the Gregorian Chant in the choir. The church was always crowded, as well by Protestants as by Catholics, anxious to listen to a kind of music which until then had never reached their ears. In consequence of all this, conversions became more frequent. Early in December of 1838, Bishop Rosatti offered the missions of Peru to the Visitor, which the latter referred to his council. On the 12th December, 1838, the Visitor with Mr. Armangol, Boullier, Amat, Tiernan, Gustiniani, and two lay brothers, met Bishop Blanc at the Church of the Assumption, and began the intended new seminary. The Visitor wrote for a patent, and knowing the disposition of Mr. Armangol, he also requested that certain restrictions should be imposed on him as the new Superior. The advice, however, was not followed. He also established Mr. Boullier, Superior of the Church of the Ascension in Donaldsonville.

In the month of June, 1838, Bishop Blanc had written to Bishop Rosatti and to Visitor Timon, relating the sad condition of Texas, and stating that it was the wish of the Holy See that a trusty person should be sent there to examine into the condition of religion in that country, then independent, and to report to Rome. This duty the Bishop of New Orleans wished the Visitor to undertake, which, by the advice and wish of Bishop Rosatti, he consented to perform. Accordingly, on the 24th December, 1838, accompanied by Mr. L'Eberia, the Visitor set sail for Galveston, Texas. Here the missionaries expected to meet with none but strangers, yet, by a providence of God, almost the first man the Visitor met at Galveston, was Col. Michael Menard, a man distinguished in that part of the country, and who had been one of the convention for forming the State constitution. Other faces, some of them formerly pupils at the Barrens, soon made the missionaries quite at home in Galveston. On the feast of the Holy Innocents, the Visitor said what was considered there the first mass ever said in that place. During the few days' sojourn, waiting for the steamer, Visitor Timon preached often, baptized several, heard many confessions, and ratified several marriages. On the 31st December, the missionaries started in the steamer Rufus Putnam to ascend the river up to Houston, then the seat of government. There, too, the Visitor had the consolation of meeting some senators and members of Congress, whose acquaintance he had made on his extensive missions. He preached in the hall of Congress, senators and representatives being present.

He also rented a convenient room, put up an altar in it, and held regular service. Many came to confession and communion. It would indeed be difficult to estimate the sad and dangerous condition of a Catholic at that time in Texas.

' The following reminiscences, from the pen of the Bishop, will reveal a state of things altogether deplorable, but which was the result of his investigating missionary visit to Texas. For instance, the Visitor was one day passing along in the suburbs of the city, making inquiries and taking notes of the condition of the people, with regard to their spiritual wants. It was a chilly, drizzly day, and as he walked along, he found lying upon the ground a poor Irishman, named O'Brien, very sick, but by no means intoxicated or in liquor. The Visitor got a few men to assist him in lifting up the sufferer, and bringing him to the nearest house. Whilst there and striving to relieve him, the priest revealed his sacred character. Words can hardly express the joy that beamed from the countenance of the poor, unfortunate man. He immediately forgot all his sorrows and sufferings, in the thought that he, a dying man, who believed himself to have been hundreds of miles from a priest of God, had one then standing by his side, prepared and ready to aid and console him. With joy he, therefore, made his confession, and really, the emotions and sentiments with which he received the blessed sacrament of the Altar and the holy Viaticum, were very touching. Hearing that there was a kind of hospital in the place, Father Timon engaged some persons to bring the sick man thither, and in a few hours followed after, to aid still more the penitent on the long journey he was about to take. The missionary found the hospital to consist of a log hut, through the crevices and openings of which a chill wind was blowing upon ten or twelve sick persons, whose straw beds rested on the clay floor. In the middle of the hut there was a hole in the clay floor, in which a fire had been made, and over the fire hung a pot of boiling soup. There being no chimney or stove-pipe, the smoke found its way out through the crevices or openings, according to its whim or the caprice of the wind. In the meantime, whilst the priest was urging the keeper of the hospital to take some precaution to keep the wind from the sick and dying, and whilst he was giving him some aid to do so, the poor sick man, O'Brien, in his agony, groaned much and painfully. The keeper hallooed to him several times to "be silent." Alas! poor man, he could not be silent ; *death had already seized him*. Then the keeper, in his anger, stepped up to the dying O'Brien, shook his fist in the latter's face, and said: "If you don't be silent, I'll make you," &c. Here Father Timon rushed forward to intercede for the poor man, and save him from the threats of the infuriated keeper, but when he had drawn near, poor O'Brien had just breathed his last, and was no more.

> "No timely hand was here to save ;
> In death he calmly sleeps ;
> Let Charity the stone engrave,
> As Pity turns and weeps."

From senators and men of extensive information, the Visitor got full details of the most scandalous lives led by the only priests then in Texas. They were two priests from Mexico, living at San Antonio de Bexar, in the West of Texas. Both publicly cohabited with women whom they themselves called their wives, and the children by such cohabitation these wretched men acknowledged to be their own. They said mass daily because they were supported by the people, and derived their support by it. But they gave no instructions, heard no confessions, and taught no catechism. The poor Mexicans were willing to die for their religion, yet they hardly knew what their religion was; how could they? Their faith seemed rather a Divine instinct that grew from their baptism, than a faith of knowledge.

Such was a part of the condition of Texas at that time, sufficient, at least, to show the utter destitution of spiritual comfort, and the low degradation in which the people lived, but for whom God in his mercy was about to provide, and properly elevate to the true standard of enlightened christians. On the 9th of January, 1839, the Visitor returned to Galveston. Before leaving this place on his tour through the State, he had appointed a committee to see about getting a lot for a church. On his return, these gentlemen met him, and showed him that there would be every facility for raising money to pay for a lot and build a church, if a priest could be sent to take charge of it. Holding this answer under consideration, the Visitor, on the 12th of January, returned to New Orleans, and made an official report of his investigations in the State of Texas, to Bishop Blanc, who sent it on to Rome.

The Visitor delayed several days in New Orleans, on various business, among other things preaching at a retreat for a religious community, during the duration of which, at the urgent request of Bishop Blanc, he accepted an invitation to establish a mission at Natchez, Miss., on his way home to the Barrens. On his way thither he stopped at the new Seminary of the Assumption, where he found the affairs of the seminary in such a disordered and extravagant state, that he censured the Superior, Mr. Armangol, who, it will be remembered, was reluctantly appointed for that position by the Visitor, on account of the misgivings the latter had of Mr. Armangol's administrative qualities. He, however, set the matter aright there as well as at Donaldsonville, where he also delayed on his way up the river, and, after an uninterrupted journey of a few days, arrived in Natchez, on the 25th of January, 1839.

At this place, it was but a renewal of the zeal and missionary devotion, which he had exhibited on other occasions and in other places. The usual difficulty occurred of obtaining a proper and fit place in which to celebrate the sacrifice of the holy mass. But Providence, ever ready to assist the indefatigable labor of this zealous Lazarist, soon enabled him to obtain a place for Divine worship; and at length, under the roof of an old lady, the good and pious Mrs. Girardeau, who offered the missionary a large room in her house, an altar was erected, mass celebrated on it, and a mission started that was productive of great benefit to that poor community. By invitation, also, he preached sermons of controversy in the City Hall of Natchez, that redounded greatly to the glory and honor of God. Many marriages were adjusted, and numbers flocked to their duties in holy confession and communion.

Besides all this good accomplished, the people of the place submitted to the Visitor plans for building a church in Gothic style, so enthusiastic were they for establishing in the beginning a proper edifice in which to celebrate the mysteries of their holy faith. The Visitor, however, recommended them not to begin so extravagantly at first, as by so doing they might incur debts which afterwards would prove to be a burden, rather than a pleasure to them. He, therefore, advised them to begin a plain, large, but substantial building, which, (as soon as circumstances would admit of building a handsome church,) might serve for other uses. The Visitor then left them apparently determined to follow his advice. But, alas, like all human hopes, it was not regarded as faithfully as promised, and years afterwards, the first Bishop named for that place had reason to regret that it had not been followed.

On his return to Missouri the Visitor, having received instructions to invest other funds in proper stock, went to St. Louis for this purpose.

Here, at the request of the good Bishop Rosatti, he gave a retreat or mission to the people, which lasted two weeks, and during which time he also conducted a special retreat of eight days for the Sisters of Charity. Measures were likewise taken for a mission to La Salle, where Mr. Raho had been appointed Superior. After this laborious work in the cause of religion, the Visitor proceeded to Kaskaskias, where he commenced another mission for the people of that place, and one also for the Sisters of Visitation, then established there. During the mission, by special request of influential Protestants, he gave lectures at night, in the Court House, on Catholic doctrines, through which several were converted to the faith; many fervent communions also were the fruits of this mission.

On the 5th of May, 1839, Bishop Rosatti laid the corner stone of a church, under the title of the "Most Holy Trinity," to be the church of the seminary at St. Louis, under charge of the Lazarists, whom, it seems, he was determined to bring to that place. Visitor Timon preached the dedication sermon.

The Visitor continued in the exercise of this good labor until June following, when, on the eleventh of this month, it was announced by letters received from Mr. Etienne, Superior General of the Lazarist order in Paris, that Visitor Timon and Mons. Odin had been proposed at Rome for Episcopal Sees. This news was very embarrassing to the wishes and humility of both these reverend gentlemen, and caused them great uneasiness.

On the 30th of August following, the Visitor sent Mr. Estany and Escoffier to the mission of La Salle.

In the meantime, Bishop Rosatti, on the 7th September following, paid a visit to the Barrens, and handed the Visitor a papal bull, constituting the latter Bishop of Venesi, and Coadjutor of St. Louis, with the right of succession. But the zealous Lazarist would not accept of these honors, painful to his christian feelings, and returned them next day to Rome with his refusal, preferring to remain in the position he then held; and, in order to console Bishop Rosatti, who seemed very sad at the result, he pointed out the Rev. Rich. Kenrick, as one eminently qualified for the position. Bishop Rosatti, satisfied that he could not change the resolution of Mr. Timon, immediately wrote to Rome to have Mr. Kenrick appointed, which was accordingly done. The Visitor, likewise, respectfully refused to assume the duties of administration of the diocese during the impending absence of Bishop Rosatti, on business of importance for the Holy See. He feared that, by complying, he might indirectly come too near having a mitre placed upon his head without being aware of it. As his ambition was only to do all the good he could, and as his position then afforded a wide field for a display of christian charity, he was entirely content, until Providence manifestly ordered otherwise.

Meanwhile the mission at the Cape had become very important, and a convent for Lorentine Sisters was established there. On the 21st July, 1839, Bishop Rosatti had consecrated a new stone church, under the title of St. Vincent. On the 6th of October, the Visitor, in company with the Lazarists stationed there, made a very successful mission at La Salle. On the 21st of October, the Visitor began a retreat at the seminary, for the members of the congregation who were not too far away in the missions to prevent their attendance. At this retreat twenty priests, three students, and nine brothers of the congregation were present.

On the 1st of November, 1839, he began another retreat for the parish at the Barrens. This retreat lasted two weeks, during which the Visitor and Mons. Odin preached in their turn. God greatly blessed this mission.

---o---

CHAPTER VIII.

Mr. Tornatori and the Drawing Master.—Mission of Ouachita.—Visitor Timon appointed Prefect Apostolic of Texas.—Mons. Odin sent to Texas as Vice-Prefect.—The Two Mexican Priests Silenced.—Visitor with Bishop Flaget visits the Missions.—Visitor quells a Parish Strife.—New Church for Cairo.—Evils at Assumption.—Visitor goes to Texas.—Subscription for a new Church.—Funeral Rites of Minister to Mexico.—Meets with General Henderson.—Preaches in the Capitol.—A Church for Houston.—Goes to Austin.—Dangerous Travel.—State of Texas.—Grand Reception by Judge Burnet.—First Mass in Austin.—Dines with the French Minister.—Table Talk.

During all this lapse of time, the internal affairs of the seminary and college prospered, and augured bright hopes for the future.

A circumstance, however, occurred, that served by no means to interrupt the course of study, or impede the efforts of the teachers in the discharge of their duties, but which (leaving it to the inference of the unbiased reader to determine,) was a theme of conversation at the time; and since it is found in the memoirs of the Bishop, it may not be improper to repeat it here:

It seems some opposition was made by the truly pious and venerable Mr. Tornatori, to what, in his estimation, were considered innovations. For instance, from the very beginning the new Visitor, who had great confidence in the theological knowledge and unbending severity of Mr. Tornatori, had chosen the latter for his confessor. But on the 29th of January, when the Visitor had called on him to make his weekly confession, Mr. Tornatori refused to hear him, alledging as a reason that Mr. Timon had introduced into the college a drawing master, *(maitre de dessin,)* and yet Mr. Tornatori considered "*les arts d' agreement pernicieux.*" The Visitor of course referred the matter to his council, in which it was decided that "*les arts d' agreement,*" music and drawing, should continue.

The Visitor next turned his attention to the State of Louisiana, and whilst visiting some of the posts established there, commenced a mission on the Ouachita. Here he found a people, all descendants of Frenchmen, on a branch of the Ouachita river, who were even more abandoned, as to religious help, than those whom he had once found in Arkansas. The mission here was productive of much good; all that was needed was a priest.

During the continuance of this mission the Visitor, on the 26th of March, 1840, received Mr. Andrieu in the novitiate. At this time there were many Lazarists in the community who could not yet speak English, and accordingly, with the advice of his council, the Visitor resolved to place several of them in missions where, in conjunction with the exercise of their ministerial functions, they could also have an opportunity to learn to speak the English language. Besides, the Bishop of St. Louis stood greatly in need of priests in his diocese, and in order to contribute to the holy zeal of this good prelate, he consented, on the 1st April, 1840, to take, *ad tempus*, the church, house, and parish of Natchitoches, on the Red River, this place being at that time, on the land side, the key of Texas, which, by advice to the Visitor from Mr. Etienne, was to be assigned to the congregation of missions.

On the 12th of April, the Visitor returned to the college at the Barrens, accompanied by a number of boys, sons of highly respectable families of Louisiana. On his arrival he found letters there, appointing him Prefect Apostolic of Texas, with power to administer confirmation. At first the honor seemed threatening to his humility, but after consulting with his council, he accepted the appointment, and immediately despatched Mons. Odin to Texas, as Vice Prefect, and Mr. Douterlounge as an assistant. On his way thither, Mons. Odin and his companion were miraculously saved from a violent tornado, as he descended the Mississippi river. All joined to pray for their safety, which, in the providence of God, was realized, much to the joy of their friends.

Before they left the Barrens the Visitor, as Prefect Apostolic, had entrusted to Mons. Odin a letter to the two priests at San Antonio, taking from them all faculties as priests, requiring them, under pain of suspension, to desist from the discharge of all ministerial functions. This letter had the good effect of checking the enormous scandal occasioned by these two men, of whom we have already written as having lived in concubinage with women, and who discharged no other duty than merely offering up the sacrifice of the mass.

"But," pleaded these unhappy men, "at least, Mons. Odin, permit us to say mass, the *honorarium* of which is the only support we have for our families."

"I cannot," said Mons. Odin; "here are my orders. But I will do for you whatever is in my power. Receive the masses which your friends offer you, keep the *honorarium*, and *I* will say, or *have* said, the masses for you."

The generous and prudent offer of Mons. Odin was accepted for a period of about three months, Mons. Odin doing as he promised, until finally these unfortunate priests began to be ashamed of themselves and the example they afforded, and accordingly withdrew into Mexico.

On the 22d June, 1840, Mr. Paquin was appointed Superior of the seminary by the Visitor, who assembled all the priests of the community, and urged upon them a cheerful obedience to their new Superior. He then briefly alluded to the state of the congregation at the time he had been appointed its Visitor, without house or funds; no property except the Cape property, which, besides being burdened with debt, was mortgaged for the purchase money. Then he contrasted the condition of the community affairs, by showing the debts reduced, the mortgage liquidated, and more property, worth at least two hundred and fifty thousand francs, acquired. In the college, every department was well furnished with books and philosophical apparatus. Every one present seemed pleased at the happy contrast, and to echo the words, "To God the glory, to God the praise." On the 5th July, the Visitor began an interesting mission in the extensive hospital of the Sisters of Charity at the Barrens. It was a touching sight to note the fervor of those poor people, and to see the lame conducting the blind, who in turn supported their conductors, as they gave each other mutual help to reach the communion table.

St. Genevieve had long been served by a priest of the congregation. It was now offered to the Visitor as a permanent mission, and as it would have been difficult to abandon it, by the advice of his council, the Visitor accepted of it and the "Old Mines," and established there two regular houses.

In August, 1840, the venerable Bishop Flaget sent for the Visitor, and both together paid a visit to the mother house of the Lorentine Nuns in Kentucky. Here he was delayed several days, revising the rules and regulations of that congregation. In the meantime, whilst giving retreats, making other missions, and visiting the newly established houses, he received reports from Texas of the prudent course pursued by Mons. Odin, and immediately wrote to Rome, to obtain for this most worthy and saintly deputy, the power of conferring the sacrament of confirmation. In the summer of 1840, Mons. de Forbin Janson visited the mission. He was much pleased with the seminary of the Barrens. He then went to Cape Girardeau, where he rejoiced at the great change effected there, and confirmed some of the late converts. Besides visiting St. Genevieve, the zealous Bishop of Nancy accompanied the Visitor to Kaskaskias, to calm the strife that grew out of a division of sentiment either for or against their priest. But the just and strong language of the good Bishop only served to increase the irritation. Circumstances boded ill, and remained in an unsettled condition. At length a happy thought induced some one to propose leaving the whole dispute with the Visitor, who had formerly been their missionary priest. This offer was accepted by all, and, through the blessing of God, peace was once more restored to the agitated community.

From Cape Girardeau the missionaries had gone several times on a mission to Cairo, where a post had been established with vestments and other sacred things, necessary for the holy sacrifice of the mass. But at this time, in the providence of God, the Visitor was so fortunate as to obtain from the Hon. E. K. Kane, and Col. P. Menard, through Mr. Holbrook, their agent, a lot for a Catholic church. Mr. Holbrook, at his own expense, commenced to build the church, which was a neat frame building. In the Autumn months following, the Visitor, in his visits to the various houses, found that at every point much good had been done. Occasionally, however, neglects rather in the temporal than in the spiritual order were apparent. Thus at the Cape he found horses, wagons, and other farming utensils, purchased at great expense, but which had been quite idle for several months, because there were no persons able to drive the wagons. These wagons could earn twenty francs per day by hauling wood from the farm, and as a first-class driver would cost less than five francs per day, the neglect to take advantage of this circumstance was certainly very reprehensible. This oversight as well as others was corrected.

At Assumption the evil was of greater magnitude. Mr. Armangol, who in the presence of the Visitor was most obsequious in his politeness, but who often, in the absence of the latter, went directly contrary to his advice, had built a new church and house, within a short distance of the church and seminary of the Assumption. Of course, this conduct occasioned disputes between two sections of the mission, that could not be healed except by a total separation, which the Visitor was obliged to make. Still the work of God was going bravely on, and the congregation increasing in numbers and in general estimation.

On the 1st December, 1840, the Visitor, with a missionary destined to aid Mons. Odin, started for Texas. They reached Galveston on the 5th December. Mons. Odin at this time was in Austin, then the seat of government. Again the Visitor experienced the same difficulty in getting a proper place for Divine worship. But against his zeal the impossibility of obtaining a place suitable for mass could not stand. He succeeded, and as early as the 6th of December, said mass for a large audience, and preached at the Gospel. After vespers he began a subscription for building a church; two thousand francs were at once subscribed. He also explained to the people the necessity of properly supporting their priest. This all promised to do.

At this time a Mr. Treat, who once had been minister from Texas to Mexico, had died on his passage homewards, and his body was landed at the wharf just as the Visitor was about leaving for Houston. The Mayor called on Mr. Timon, and respectfully asked him to perform the funeral rites over the body of the deceased man. But he politely informed that gentleman that his Church forbade him to celebrate any but Catholic rites, and explained further that she did not wish her rites to be forced upon Protestants, and perhaps that, even could he reanimate the corpse, Mr. Treat would repel as an insult the holy water he must necessarily sprinkle over the body. The Mayor was satisfied with this explanation. As the Visitor proceeded up the river to Houston, on board the steamer, he met with General Henderson, who had lately returned from Paris, whither he had been sent as ambassador from Texas. This gentleman, who had been present at the conversation between the Visitor and the Mayor of Galveston relative to Mr. Treat, introduced himself to the Visitor, and said that, though a Protestant, he highly approved of the principle which induced the priest to refuse his ministry.

Soon afterwards they landed at Houston, where the Visitor preached in the capitol, as he had done on a former occasion, and where he convoked an assembly of Catholics, for the purpose of taking means of building a church.

For an enterprise of this nature, he found prompt and zealous friends in Mr. Neill and Donellan, who voluntarily made a donation of the land on which to build the contemplated temple of worship. A committee was immediately appointed to solicit subscriptions for the new building, and leaving the good people to push forward the noble undertaking, the Visitor started for the city of Austin, a distance of several hundred miles from Houston. His journey was somewhat hazardous, as he had to travel through a country then infested with Indians, and although, as a general rule, a missionary stands in high respect with an Indian, being familiar to them under the *sobriquet* of "Black Gown," still there are some who, as an exception to this rule, would not hesitate to harm even a missionary. But, ever watched over by the guiding hand of Providence, Visitor Timon bravely surmounted every difficulty, and finally, on the 9th of December, 1840, reached his place of destination (Austin,) in perfect safety.

Texas at this time was a republic by itself, having gained its independence from Mexico in 1835. Mr. Walker, of Mississippi, in the senate of the United States, introduced a proposition to recognize Texas as an independent nation on 5th December, of the same year. Accordingly, as an independent republic, under a few Presidents, she continued to exist until the time that Visitor Timon landed at Austin, Mr. Lamar was acting President. To this gentleman the Visitor brought letters from Cardinal Fransonicus, Cardinal of the Propaganda at Rome, which were also a virtual recognition of the independence of the Republic of Texas. As such they were hailed with joy. When the Visitor had arrived at Austin, the President had, on account of ill health, just started for the United States; but, as the Prefect Apostolic had informed him in advance of his approaching visit, the President had left a letter with the Vice President for Mons. Timon. Accordingly Judge Burnet, the Vice President, received the Visitor most courteously indeed, read to him the President's letter, and in turn requested him to translate what the Cardinal had written, since the letter was in the Latin language. Every one in Austin combined to render the visit of the Prefect Apostolic very agreeable. Mr. De Salignes, the French Minister to the republic, was also very kind, and earnestly pressed the Visitor to become his guest.

But the Visitor, ever mindful of his sacred calling, as soon as his public business had been completed, turned his first thoughts towards obtaining a suitable chapel in which to enable the few Catholics there to hear mass. As usual he had much difficulty in obtaining his wishes, but finally, on the 23d of December, 1840, succeeded, and with a heart overflowing with gratitude to God, said the first mass ever celebrated in Austin. The next day Mons. Odin also said mass.

In compliance with the kind invitation of the French Minister, both the Visitor and Mons. Odin visited his house, and took dinner there with him, the Vice President, Judge Burnet, and a few prominent members of the congress of the republic. The visit was a very interesting one. The conversation at table turned much on a sermon which the Visitor had preached the day previous in the hall of the capitol, in their presence as well as of other prominent men of the republic. In this discourse, which lasted two hours, the missionary had given a general view of the Body of Christ, and the faithful members of that living, mystic body. He had also explained the sacraments, showing how they are the *veins*, Divinely instituted, to bring a life Divine to every member of that vast and venerable body. The company at table were deeply interested in this subject, and so earnestly had the Vice President entered into it, that he exclaimed:

"Why, if those are the real doctrines of the Catholic Church, I can easily subscribe to them."

"Yes," continued a prominent senator, "the Catholic Church has been greatly calumniated. We have heard of this before; but now we know it."

CHAPTER IX.

Petition to Restore Church Property.—Visitor Timon Preaches in the Senate Chamber.—Public Complimentary Dinner.—Discussion.—Visitor Timon explains.—Missionary Excursions in the Colorado River.—Oysters.—Return to Galveston.—First Convert.—Difficult Travel.—Good Results.—The Gospel in St. Augustine, Florida.—The Visitor parts with Mons. Odin.—Arrives at New Orleans.—Bishoprics Refused.—The Visitor in Paris.—His Return.—Incident on Board Ship.—Burial at Sea.—Arrival at New Orleans.—Visitor Timon,—Changes.—Appointed Bishop of Buffalo, N. Y.

In the meantime Mons. Odin had prepared a petition or bill which, in substance, was the restoration of church lands to the Catholic Church, of which it had been, at that time, to a great extent deprived on account of the troubles between Texas and Mexico. This petition, after having been duly read, was spontaneously endorsed by the several prominent gentlemen present, all of whom declared that justice ought to be done to the Catholic Church. They even agreed to support the measure, as well as any other that tended to do justice in the matter. On the 27th, the Visitor again preached in the senate chamber, where a subscription was started for building a church. Among those particularly zealous in this step were Col. Porter and Col. Floyd.

The following day the missionaries were once more invited to a public complimentary dinner, at which the acting President, Judge Burnet, as well as several leading senators and representatives, were present. At dinner the conversation became quite animated; many topics were alluded to, particularly that of religion, out of regard to the character and presence of their guests, the Catholic missionaries. Col. Porter took occasion to renew the expression of his esteem for the Roman Catholic Church. This remark provoked a rejoinder on the part of the acting President, that the Mexicans had not been saved by it, (the Catholic Church,) and in substantiation of his assertion, referred to the great degradation of the priests and people of that unhappily distracted country.

Visitor Timon, whose extensive information and profound learning were ever ready to defend the truth, chafed at this observation of the gentleman, for if he construed it into an insult personal to himself and his reverend friend, he may not be blamed, owing to the source from whence it sprung, since Judge Burnet was a man of ability, of letters, much experience, and might have entertained other deductions on the subject; on the contrary, with the dignity and self-possession so characteristic of the man, and whilst all were profoundly attentive, he recounted how the American hero and scholar, General Pike, in 1808, had traveled through Mexico, and although a Protestant, had given a glowing account of the high standing and holy life led by the priests of that country, of their blessed influence upon the people, as well as the general happiness and morality of the population. But civil war began in 1810. Its evil consequences were soon felt. After ten or twelve years of civil war, and even absolute anarchy, independence was declared. Demagogues banished all the bishops and priests. The poor people were left with very few pastors; and to increase the evil, each Indian family that had received a farm from the Spanish government, whilst it was exempt from taxation, enjoyed only a *perpetual use* of their lands without the privilege of being able to sell them. After the independence, however, the possessor was permitted to sell.

Speculators then prowled through the country. Almost every farm was bought for a mere nothing; and, as soon as the legal robbery had been consummated, the Indians were driven from their homes, or forced to toil for a miserable pittance, in a worse condition than slaves, on lands once their own. Many were even driven to the highest slopes of the mountains, near the line of the perennial snows. Here they could get no spiritual advice, and thus dispirited and broken-hearted, they soon became utterly demoralized, and sank far below the cheerful innocence and sound morality which, twenty years before, General Pike had so justly praised.

Visitor Timon continued at some length in a strain of logic and eloquence that was really irresistible. He demonstrated that the

Church had been unjustly condemned for crimes and injustice that owed their origin to other sources. It was very easy to raise a calumny and make its weight find some minds or brain weak enough to support it, and thus, impressions once made upon such people became contaminating. The evil seed once sown begins to grow, and brings forth its fruit. It was only when an enlightened community had tasted of the fruit, or seen its evil effects, that reason once more resumed its former sway, and made man reflect and, to the credit of many good men be it said, obliterated the injustice they otherwise would unwillingly have done.

From Austin the Prefect, (Timon,) and vice-Prefect, (Odin,) started on the 31st of December, to visit Mr. Van Namme, then stationed on the Colorado river. They reached him on the 1st January, 1841, where they said mass, and then continued their journey down along the west bank of the river, on a high bluff, four miles from the river, and about five hundred feet above the level of the sea, near the Gulf of Mexico. In that vicinity the Visitor discovered a rock projecting about three or four feet above the prairie, on which they found a reef of oysters, apparently as fresh as if the sea had receded but the day before. He broke off some of the oysters and took them with him, as an incontestible evidence that the sea had once swept over high lands now two hundred miles from it.

This missionary journey of the Visitor, in company with Mons. Odin, perhaps was one of the most interesting we have had to record. All the way down to Houston it was a continual mission, and when they arrived at the latter place they again renewed, with great spiritual fruit, their pious vocation, so that on the lot which the reader will remember had been given for a church, a deed was drawn up and recorded, seven hundred dollars (equal to three thousand five hundred francs,) having been subscribed for this purpose.

The missionaries did not delay long at Houston, but continued their journey towards Galveston, where they arrived on the 12th January, 1841. Here they found the altar (erected on a former visit,) still remaining in the same large room in which they offered up the oblation of the Body and Blood of Christ. On the 15th January following, the first convert of Galveston, (a Mrs. De Lacy,) was baptized, and on the 18th confirmed. The Visitor next contracted with Dr. Labodié and Col. Menard, for building the first church in Galveston.

From Galveston, it became necessary for the missionaries to return to Houston. Accordingly, leaving the former place on the 20th of January, they set out on their difficult and perilous journey Whilst they were continually doing good in the spiritual order, such as reconciling a family to God, baptizing children, ratifying marriages, and reconciling many in the sacred tribunal of confession, they suffered greatly for conveniences with which to travel properly. Torrents of rain inundated the country, swelling the river to an extent dangerous beyond precedent. They were forced to abandon the frail boat in which, by rowing, they tried to ascend the river. It was only by hiring horses, and occasionally swimming the creeks that intercepted their way, that they at length reached Houston. From Houston, they continued their course to Nacogdoches, through a wild and unbroken tract of country, never before trodden by priests, making their journey a continual mission. They were constantly obliged to cross rivers or creeks, that the rainy season had swollen into torrents, by the aid of little canoes, at the same time swimming their horses alongside, or they sought for some logs, or branches of trees that intertwined from both sides of the river, thus admitting of a passage from bank to bank across the stream, over which Mons. Odin, who could not swim, would pass; whilst Visitor Timon, invariably, swam the river with the horses, however dangerous the ford or pass.

On the 30th of January, the Visitor having reached Nacogdoches, as usual, sought for a place for Divine worship, and in an old stone house, built over a hundred years ago, he erected an altar, on which he said mass and preached. January 31st, in the afternoon, he preached again, when the little chapel was literally packed with audience. After mass, February 1st, a Mr. Chevalier very generously came forward, and gave a lot for a church, at the same time offering his own dwelling as a shelter to the priest that might be sent there. At this place much good was done. Hundreds went to communion, who, for years before, had had no opportunity of so doing. On the 2d of February, the solemn blessing of the candles took place, and with great liberality the people subscribed for beginning the erection of a new Catholic church

Leaving this mission in the hands and promises of the people to continue to it faithfully, the missionaries then started for St. Augustine. They were received with unbounded expressions of welcome by the inhabitants of this place. At first they were told that no Catholics lived there, but before they left, they found a great many. Protestants even, who had known the Visitor and Mons. Odin on other missions, crowded around them, and at the mass, which Mons. Odin celebrated, the Visitor was forced to preach for over two hours, in which he explained Catholic doctrine to those who never before heard aught but the rankest calumny against the Church. For several days the Visitor preached to a willing people, many of whom were the principal men of the place. God blessed the holy zeal of the zealous Lazarists, for by their piety, their eloquence, and withal their sincere zeal, manifested in the cause of the poor sinner, such men as Mr. Thomas, Mr. Cansfield, Judge Hanks, Dr. Griffen, Mr. Donald, Mr. Border, Mr. Frames, and many others, all leading minds of St. Augustine, Florida, at that time came forward and declared themselves Catholics. So enthusiastic was their zeal, that a Mr. Nixon offered a half a league of land, on which to build a church, whilst five or six others also offered lots on which to begin Catholic institutions. A subscription was then begun for raising funds, with which to carry into effect the new projects.

At St. Augustine, it became necessary for the Visitor to part with Mons. Odin, as business of importance required his time elsewhere; besides he had to finish his official visit, already too long delayed. Before leaving, however, he left with this good missionary and bosom friend all his shirts and clothing, as those of Mons. Odin were badly worn and almost useless. That same evening he had crossed the Sabine river, and the very next night after, found himself at Natchitoches in the United States, where he was most kindly received by Mr. Gustiniani, Superior of the mission, and by Messrs. Pasqual and Alabou, his assistants. The Visitor then resumed his official visit, and found much good had been done, and great edification given by the Lazarist community. But he had to reprimand Mr. Gustiniani, (son of an Italian nobleman, and allied to some of the first houses of Europe,) for denying himself even of many of the necessaries of life, in order to economize, in finishing and beautifying the church.

The Visitor reached New Orleans on the 10th of February following. Here he paid a debt of about six thousand francs, which Mons. Odin had incurred with Mr. Benoit, of New Orleans. After a visit to the Seminary of the Assumption, sufficient to reëstablish the order which Mr. Armangol, through an excess of zeal, had deranged, he set out for the Barrens. Some difficulties had occurred there during his absence, but he soon succeeded in restoring peace and order.

When the Visitor was parting with Mons. Odin in Texas, he had requested him to repair in May, 1841, to the Barrens, in order to perfect arrangements for the Texan mission. Mr. Odin, accordingly, reached New Orleans at the time appointed, where he was most kindly received by Bishop Blanc, who, after scolding the good missionary for appearing almost in rags, handed him papal bulls, by which he was appointed Coadjutor Bishop of Detroit, and insisted even on keeping him at New Orleans until he should consecrate him. Mons. Odin replied, that he could take no step without first consulting the Visitor. He then started for the Barrens, where, on the night of the 5th of May, he gave his bulls and urgent letters from Cardinal Fransonicus to Visitor Timon, leaving the subject to his decision.

The Visitor said: "No, Odin, I beg of you to say the mass of to-morrow morning for my intention, that God may guide me to the fitting answer, and I, in turn, will offer the holy sacrifice for the same intention."

After mass, next morning, the Visitor gave his decision: "Mons. Odin, good men can easily be found for the bishopric of Detroit, when things are already in a prosperous way; but it would be difficult to find a competent person now to take so poor and difficult a post as your's in Texas; hence, I think it more for the glory of God and the good of souls, that you send back the bulls and return to your post."

In compliance with the decision of the Visitor, for whom Mons. Odin always cherished a special affection, he refused to accept the sacred office in Detroit, and returned to Texas. In the meantime the Visitor, without letting Monsieur Odin know of his intention, wrote to Rome and to Paris, urging the nomination of Mons. Odin as Vicar Apostolic and Bishop *in partibus infidelium*. This was soon effected, to the great benefit of that country.

In June of the year 1841, the Visitor was called to Paris by the mother house, where he was greatly edified by the fervor of the inmates, as he had been on his former visit. By permission of the Superior General, he visited many other religious houses, taking notes to imitate, as far as possible, the holy works which so much edified him. His stay in Paris was somewhat protracted, though pleasant. He made many new acquaintances, who, in turn, were highly delighted with the missionary of the New World, already so famous for his exertions in the field of religion.

Finally, on the 20th of November, he left Paris for Marseilles, where he was to take shipping for New Orleans. On his way to the diligence he was kindly accompanied by Mons. Etienne, since the worthy and much honored Superior General of the community of the Lazarists. After arriving in Marseilles, he was delayed there by circumstances until the 2d December, 1841, when he finally set sail for America, accompanied by nineteen companions, priests, students and brothers. The voyage was an interesting one. Part of the ship was allotted for the sole use of the little band of missionaries. On board ship an altar was erected, on which, each morning when the sea was not too rough, mass was said. In fact, the missionary quarter of the vessel was "a convent at sea." Meditations were made in common each morning, and conferences held. Classes for instruction were also instituted, Visitor Timon acting as teacher of English for all. Each Sunday too, after mass in the chapel, the Visitor preached on deck for the crew as well as the community; whilst at night, on the poop of the vessel, the missionaries would sing some sacred melody or hymn to the Virgin, as the Protestant portion of the crew and passengers gathered around them, evidently feeling the influence of Catholic devotion. The reader may readily infer the happiness that dwelt in the midst of that little community, hourly winging its eager way towards scenes in the New World, of which their minds, inexperienced in missionary life of the New World, could only draw a picture. The journey over the ocean, besides being pleasant, was also a continual mission. Carolo Testa, a sailor, whose brother, Casari Testa, lived in Alexandria, Piedmont, had long neglected his religion. The Visitor began to instruct him, for he was sickly, and though obliged each day to work, he seemed as if he might at any moment be called to his account. On the 14th, the Visitor was called up at midnight for the poor man. He did what he could for him and then left him, apparently as well as usual. In the morning, at 7 A. M., he said mass, which he had scarcely finished, when he was called again, and found that the poor man had been struck with death after he had eaten about one-half of his breakfast. There was hardly time to repeat the absolution and give Extreme Unction, when he expired. Towards evening, the missionaries saw, for the first time in their lives, the sad sight of a "burial at sea," though made more consoling by all the sacred rites of the Church. The body was enclosed in a coarse sack, the opening of which was sewed together, and the whole placed upon a large plank. This plank was then mournfully raised by the sailor crew, carried to the side of the vessel, and as it was raised from a horizontal to an inclined position, with the feet foremost, down went the body into the depths of the ocean. In an instant, all traces of the grave were obliterated, and poor Carolo Testa consigned to his watery tomb. After a voyage of forty-five days the vessel, at length, touched at New Orleans, where the missionaries disembarked on the 17th January, 1842. Bishop Blanc received most kindly the little colony, whom he subsequently distributed in different houses of the congregation, where they continued with zeal and fervor the hard and meritorious penance of learning English.

It is now the year 1842, and as we gradually draw near the period when, by the disposition of Providence, Mr. Timon was called to the Episcopate of Buffalo, we find few prominent facts to record, with the exception, perhaps, of his regular official visits to the different houses of the mission, and the discharge of such other missionary labor as we have had frequently occasion to recite in his various visits and travels through the States of Missouri, Kentucky, Arkansas, Indiana, Louisiana, Mississippi, and particularly Texas. The same zeal, rendered more vigilant by service in the cause of Christ, ever manifested itself in his conduct. Nor were his personal pious devotions less austere than the interest he evinced in his public missionary life. As a communicant of the congregation to which he belonged, and even over which he had been for such a length of time its Visitor, he was a strict disciplinarian and true Churchman. When he entered the congregation, we have seen how scattered, how discontented, nay, almost disbanded were its communicants, without property and loaded with heavy debts. When he left them, their numbers were increased, and possessed a large amount of property quite unencumbered, and less in debt than at its commencement. When he assumed the control of the affairs of the community, and for several years prior to that time, there had been no repetition on Sunday, no office of little hours on any day, and no lecture for brothers on Sundays and holidays. There were neither any "humiliations," no asking to be warmed in chapter, no missions and no cases of conscience. But how like magic were all these omissions and neglects corrected, and how wonderful the change. The record of his life, thus far, will speak for itself.

But in the interim, between the years 1842 and 1847, it seems that the Bishops of Cincinnati, Louisville, Philadelphia, of New York of that time, urged the Visitor to take charge of their respective seminaries, to which, by advice of his council, he complied. These seminaries continued under the charge of the Lazarists for a few years, with happy results to the students.

But circumstances of various kinds necessitated changes, and thus the seminary of New York was discontinued under the form it had assumed as a seminary separate from the college, and again re-united to the college. That of Bardstown, Ky., was suppressed. The Superior General ordered the priests away from Cincinnati, because they were not duly furnished. That of Philadelphia was given up by the Lazarists, when its Superior, Rev. T. Amat, was named Bishop of Monterey, in California. The Bishops of Philadelphia and Cincinnati were greatly grieved at the departure of the missionaries. The seminary of Vincennes as well as others was afterwards offered to the Lazarists, but they declined to take it. During these years, the Visitor and others of his congregation had given many missions in Philadelphia and in other cities, and in many country places, and also many retreats for the clergy and for religious houses in different dioceses.

At length, on the 5th of September, 1847, Mr. John Timon, Visitor of the Congregation of Missions and Prefect Apostolic of Texas, received his bulls as Bishop of the new Diocese of Buffalo, Erie County, N. Y. The nomination somewhat surprised him, as thus far no one thought of a See for that part of the country. At first, his humility forbade him to accept the proffered honor, and consequently he refused to take the bulls from the Archbishop of St. Louis. But, after consulting with his counselors and other clergymen, who advised him to overcome his pious scruples, he reluctantly consented to take the crook and mitre. We say reluctantly, but by this remark we would not have the reader infer that we mean reluctance for commencing another field of missionary labor, but a reluctance based upon unwillingness to be invested with titles and position, damaging to his humility and saintly character. Another motive, too, which, at the time, the Visitor kept in his own bosom, added strength to the influence of his counselors and clergymen. For some time he had been soliciting to be relieved from office. Several members, almost all of whom have since left the congregation, had greatly misrepresented affairs to the mother house, the consequences of which were that the priests of the congregation were ordered from the seminary of Cincinnati against his wishes, whilst he, however, had to keep silent and bear with the reproaches of his former friend, the Bishop of that diocese, (Cincinnati.) It seemed, therefore, that a change was needed, and since it could not be done in the way he wished, it was well to let it be done in the way that Providence decreed.

After his retreat, the Visitor took several days in making deeds and conveyances of property held in his name, and after he had completed all his arrangements and settled all his affairs, he found himself upon the world, perhaps the poorest priest in the Church, without one dollar in money, and with a small trunk not half full of clothes, and these indeed were not enough to keep him warm. These were all his possessions in the world. He applied to the Bishop of St. Louis for a loan of money, enough to bring him to his destination. This was readily promised for the next day. But in the interim some friends learned of his deep poverty, and in the course of the day, they handed him a purse of two thousand francs and a trunk well filled with clothing. These he accepted with thanks, and started on his journey, rejoicing in the holy Providence that provides for the poor of Christ.

BOOK II.

THE EPISCOPACY

OF THE

RT. REV. JOHN TIMON, D. D.

THE EPISCOPACY

OF

RIGHT REV. JOHN TIMON, D. D.

CHAPTER I.

THE DIOCESE OF BUFFALO.—TROUBLES OF ST. LOUIS CHURCH.—THEIR ORIGIN AND HISTORY.

* "The Divinely constituted Hierarchy of the Church, completed in each district by the consecration of a Bishop, with the appointment and approbation of the successor of St. Peter, always brings special blessings of progress in the spiritual, often, too, in the temporal order.

"This has been exemplified in Buffalo, and in the wide district of which Buffalo then became the centre. The diocese was established on the 22d of April, 1847, by our Venerable and Saintly Pope Pius IX, with the following limits: All that part of the State of New York which lies west of the eastern limits of Cayuga, Tompkins, and Tioga counties. The Very Rev. John Timon, then Visitor of the Congregation of the Missions in this country, was named first Bishop. It was known that his nomination was before the Holy See for other Bishoprics; but neither had he nor the public ever guessed that he would be appointed to Buffalo. He was consecrated on the 17th of October, 1847, (Sunday,) in the Cathedral in New York, by Bishop Hughes, assisted by Dr. Walsh, Bishop of Halifax, and Dr. McCloskey, Bishop of Albany. Dr. F. P. Kenrick, Bishop of Baltimore, preached the consecration sermon."

---

* "Missions of Western New York," by the Bishop of Buffalo.

We are approaching an eventful period in the life of Bishop Timon. It was a period fraught with marvelous results for the spread of Catholic faith, for the advancement of morality and education, and for the amelioration of the human race, in the many institutions dedicated to the sick, the orphan, the abandoned, and old age. But it was likewise fraught with troubles and anxieties, both in a temporal and spiritual point of view. It was a period the most important and interesting of his whole life, and during which were developed those noble energies of mind and heart with which nature had endowed him. The difficulties that arose during his administration of the diocese, some of which had already been impregnated in the soil under the Episcopal authority of Bishop Hughes, were great embarrassments to his zeal and to his sense of christian duty as well as Church discipline. But he surmounted all of them by his indomitable will, although always ready to extend a charitable and helping hand to a truly repentant sinner.

It will be obvious to the reader that, to consign the memory of Bishop Timon to history merely in outline, by simply giving a general narration of the prominent circumstances during his administration, would not be doing justice to a great and distinguished prelate. Opinion upon many an administrative act of the good Bishop has been greatly diversified, and whilst we are no apologist for the seeming defects of his many administrative acts, which, in our humble estimation, may be characterized as having been the result either of misinterpreted zeal or misplaced confidence in those whom he had chosen as counselors and friends, we will still endeavor to depict, in proper light, the events that have made his life so prominent. For this purpose, our first attention will be called to the difficulties and troubles with the trustees of St. Louis church. Since Bishop Timon, on being named Bishop of Buffalo, inherited, as it were, the opposition to Church discipline and Episcopal authority upon the part of that congregation through its trustees, who had, prior to his consecration, and have ever since, been impressed with the dread that the Bishop aimed to dispossess them of their church property, their title to which will presently be shown to be fabulous, as well as their idle fears of being deprived of their rights; and since his designs and charitable motives in regard to St. Louis church have not only been misrepresented, whether through ignorance or malice, but even exaggerated, it is high time, in writing his biography, to correct these errors; and for this purpose we propose not only to deal with facts, but also to go back to the very beginning of the difficulty and, step by step, unveil its true history.

We write from no partisan motives, nor from personal high esteem of Bishop Timon merely, whose character we always admired and loved, but we write from a disinterested standpoint of view, excepting only so far as the requirements of justice and truth are concerned. Not only will our assertions be based upon written records and papers, gathered from various sources, but also upon the testimony of eye witnesses, who, as early as 1842, were members of St. Louis church.

Prior to 1843, during which year Bishop Hughes issued his pastoral letter in conformity to the statutes of the diocese, the congregation of St. Louis church was an order-loving, pious, christian people, and although history must record a conduct that impeaches this reputation for piety and religion to a certain degree, still the majority of the congregation, even to the present day, continues to deserve the encomium which, in a letter written to a gentleman[*] once a member of this church, Archbishop Hughes so deservingly expresses:

"Of course, I always knew that there were a great many true and faithful Catholics in the congregation of St. Louis, in Buffalo. Indeed, on my visitation of the diocese that congregation was, by its *piety*, my joy and consolation. It was my pride and my boast, on my return to New York."

* * * * * * * * * *

"They say the congregation supported them (the trustees,) in their proceedings. If this be so, *which I cannot believe, unless they deceived the congregation by false statements*, then *so be it*."

---
[*] George A. Deuther.

Nor was this opinion of the good Archbishop misplaced. There are those still living who were communicants of St. Louis church at that time, who corroborate this writing of the Bishop, and who further state on personal knowledge that the people of St. Louis church fully conducted themselves as *true* Catholics, in doing precisely that which the pastoral letter required of them and other congregations, under the authority of Bishop Hughes. They did nothing without consulting with their pastor, whether it was to make improvements in their church, or concerned the employment of secular help, such as teachers, organist or singers for the choir. The greatest harmony prevailed between the priest and the people. Only a few "ambitious, designing, intriguing, and irreligious minds" ventured indirectly to murmur and to oppose; but this was all. Hence, in issuing his pastoral letter for that year, the Bishop by no means intended it *particularly* for St. Louis church. It was issued for the purpose of regulating the conduct of other congregations throughout the diocese, who, unfortunately, had deviated from the requirements of Church discipline. But as it was a *pastoral letter*, it was read from the pulpit of every Catholic congregation, as was required by the statutes of the diocese. The Bishop never intended, directly or indirectly, to dispossess the people of St. Louis church of their *title* to their church property. Their fears on this point were entirely groundless, and, in our humble judgment, but for a miscalculated as well as unfortunate circumstance, these fears might never have been awakened.

We are disposed to deal charitably with this subject, and by no means desire to revive the unpleasant memories of the past. We deal with facts, and facts only, albeit facts sometimes are stubborn things.

However, before entering into the consideration of these stubborn things, it will be necessary to go back to an earlier period in the history of the diocese. On the 29th of August, 1841, Bishop Hughes convoked the first synod ever held in the diocese. After a week spent in spiritual exercises at St. John's College, the clergy assembled at the Cathedral in New York, and in the synod, which lasted three days, several important regulations, proposed by the Bishop for the purpose of *"assimilating the discipline and custom of the Church to the decrees of the Council of Trent," were enacted. The Bishop frankly told his brethern of the clergy "that these statutes were such as it was competent for the Bishop to enact by his own sacred office, from which, in fact, their force was exclusively derived;" but he felt bound "to avail himself of their experience and knowledge of the different congregations over which they were placed, before he should enact any disciplinary statutes, that might be in violent conflict with those circumstances, or might be premature and too difficult to be executed."

Among the many statutes enacted by the synod, was that which related to the trustee system, and which in substance was as follows:

†"That thenceforward no body of lay trustees should appoint, retain or dismiss any person connected with the church, such as sexton, organist, singers, teachers, &c., *against the will* of the pastor; that the money necessary for the maintenance of the pastors and the support of religion, should in no case be withheld, if the congregation were able to afford them; that no board of trustees or other lay persons should use the church, chapel, basement, or other portion of grounds or edifices consecrated to religion, for any meeting having a secular, or even an ecclesiastical object, without the approval of the pastor; that no board of trustees should vote, or expend, or appropriate for contracts any portion of the property they were appointed to administer, (except the ordinary current expenses,) without the approval of the pastor; nor, in case the sums to be thus expended should exceed one hundred dollars in any one year, without the approval of the Bishop also. The clergy were required to keep an inventory of church property, and to exhibit annually to the Bishop a synopsis of the financial condition of the church. For this purpose they were to have access whenever necessary to the books of the

---

* Life of Archbishop Hughes Hazard.
† Life of Archbishop Hughes Hazard.

treasurer and the minutes of all official proceedings of the board of trustees. Should any board of trustees refuse to comply with these statutes, the Bishop declared that he 'should adopt such measures as the circumstances of the case might require,' but in no event should he 'tolerate the presence of a clergyman in any church or congregation in which such refusal should be persevered in.'"

These statutes were published in a pastoral letter, dated September 8th, 1841, and were hailed with joy by all true Catholics at large; nay, the trustees of several churches offered to surrender their trust into the Bishop's hands, if he wished them to do so, a proposition which he declined; but the secular press assailed the Bishop severely, and waxed warm with indignation at what they deemed a violation of the rights of the Catholic laity, who themselves were unconscious of their injuries, and by no means grateful to their self-chosen champions, the secular press.

All the boards of trustees in the diocese acquiesced, except that of St. Louis church, in Buffalo.

On page 219 of the "Missions of Western New York," we read:

"In Buffalo, the very small number who, perhaps unconsciously, tried to sow discord in St. Louis church, had been frustrated in their first attempt. Yet they only awaited a more favorable time; and in the year 1838, some of them having gone through the legal forms, incorporated under the above named general law of 1784, which *Protestants* rejected. The Bishop was grieved, for in sending the Rev. Mr. Pax, he said: 'The usurpations of the trustees are not to be feared, for the ground belongs to me.' The residuary heir of the donor, P. A. Lecoutenlx, Esq., a man of great honor and probity, also declares that his father never wished *such* an incorporation. This was an event productive of evil to the pious members of the congregation, of annoyance and grief to ecclesiastical superiors; and, until lately, of almost incessant discord and embarrassments to the church. The Rev. J. N. Mertz, their pastor, left that church and removed to Eden. The Rev. Alex. Pax, by the wish of the

Right Rev. Bishop Dubois, undertook pastoral charge. This worthy clergyman, finding the church too small, and being assured by the Bishop that, as the ground belonged to him, no annoyance was to be dreaded from trustees, began to build the present spacious edifice, with the hearty coöperation of the people."

One Sunday, in the year 1843, Father Pax read from the pulpit of St. Louis church the pastoral letter of Bishop Hughes. An eye-witness says that, "in reading the pastoral letter, Father Pax did so without much comment, taking it for granted that the people already knew their duty full well, relying upon their well-known piety and Catholic faith to accept it." But the unfortunate circumstance already alluded to, occurred just at this time. Father Pax concluded his remarks by saying, that the *sum* and *substance* of the pastoral letter was "that the Bishop desired to obtain the *Verwaltung** of the church," meaning that the discharge of the temporal affairs of the church, and the discipline that should govern it, would be under the surveillance and coöperation of the pastor with the congregation, through its trustees. As to the fears awakened among the people of St. Louis church, that the Bishop aimed at depriving them of their church property, these were entirely unfounded, both in act and in the spirit of the pastoral letter; since, so far as the title and right to the property were concerned, it is necessary merely to inform the reader, that a copy of the deed of St. Louis church property, given by Louis Stephen Lecouteulx de Chaumont, Esq., † to Bishop Dubois and his successors, is recorded in the county clerk's office, and can be seen there at any time.

But had Father Pax expressly stated that Bishop Hughes, in obedience to the statutes of the diocese, desired merely to com-

---

* Administration.

† In 1829, when deeds of trust were valid, Louis Lecouteulx executed one to Bishop Dubois, for the property of the St. Louis church, in words as follows: "This indenture, made this fifth day of January, 1829, between Louis Lecouteulx, &c., of the one part, and the Right Rev. Father in God, John Dubois, Roman Catholic Bishop of New York, of the other part, witnesseth.—That for and in consideration of their love of God and the veneration of the said Louis, for the Holy Catholic Religion, have given, granted, aliened, enfeoffed and confirmed, and by these presents do give, grant, alien, enfeoff and confirm unto the said party of the second part and his successors in the holy office of Bishop, (in trust for the uses and purposes hereinafter

municate the information that the discipline and custom of the congregation of St. Louis church, which thus far governed them under their beloved pastor, with regard to the discharge of the temporal affairs of the church, had been enacted in the form of diocesan laws, and that *no innovation of their rights*, which they so much feared, was at all contemplated, perhaps, in the providence of God, the scandal of a congregation refusing to obey its Bishop, might have been spared from the pages of this work.

Still, though we cannot depart from truth and justice in the relation of these unpleasant facts, there is one circumstance in extenuation of the conduct of a great many of the people of St. Louis church, which may perhaps serve to soften the rigor of opinion that the reader may entertain in perusing this history. The people of St. Louis church, considered collectively, and composed of French and Germans, were a class of people simple-minded in their views, honestly disposed to do what was right with regard to every obligation in life, religious or secular, but at the same time not endowed with that educated intelligence and knowledge of Church custom and discipline, which from time immemorial has governed the Church of Christ.

It is true, they loved their religion. They were frequent and pious partakers of the sacrament. They supported their pastor generously, and contributed, according to their means freely, for beautifying and improving their church. Nay, their liberality in this regard is, even to this day, their distinguishing characteristic. With reference to the temporal affairs of the church, they enjoyed the exercise of an opinion and a voice through their trustees. As has been already stated, nothing was done without first agreeing and consulting with Father Pax; apparently every thing seemed peaceful, all was quiet.

---

named,) all that certain piece or parcel of land, &c., for the sole and only use and purposes of a Roman Catholic church and cemetery, and to the intent that a house of worship for that denomination of christians may hereafter be erected thereon, together with all and singular the hereditaments and appurtenances and revisions, rents, issues and profits, and all the estate, right, title, interest, claim and demand whatsoever, either in land or equity, to have and to hold, &c., unto the said party of the second part and to his successors in said office forever.

(Signed.)   "LOUIS LECOUTEULX,
                                                             "ANNA ELIZA LECOUTEULX."

But suddenly, as if a bombshell had been thrown in their midst, their serenity was disturbed, and the expression, *Verwaltung*, not sufficiently explained by Father Pax, suggested ideas to their simple minds that seemed dangerous to them as a congregation, and threatened a serious inroad upon rights and titles to which they had no legal claim, and which, fostered and encouraged by designing irreligious men among them, and in whom they unwisely placed too much credence and trust, led them into the unfortunate belief that they were to be deprived of their church and their property. Revolve the matter in their minds, as they might, "it seemed," says an eye-witness, "as if they were so *intoxicated* with this idea, that no argument, however potent, no assurance, however sincerely given or endorsed, could dislodge it. And this idea remains in the heads of many of the congregation even to the present day.

This fear of being deprived of their title and right to their church property, (a title which we have said was fabulous,) was fostered by the board of trustees and one man, through whose persistent spirit and course of opposition against lawful church authority, the trouble assumed greater and more gigantic proportions, then perhaps it otherwise might have done, until it finally burst into open rebellion. We have said that to the trustees was mainly due the vehemence of the trouble, and it is consistent to say further, that their spirit of opposition derived its origin from the restrictions placed upon their conduct and government of the temporal affairs of the church, by the discipline and requirements of canon law, then for the first time promulgated as diocesan laws. They desired to be rid of this incumbrance upon their actions, and to be considered as *sine qua non* in their official capacity. They even presumptuously declared their conduct to express the will of a *majority* of the congregation. We insert the following from the files of the Buffalo *Daily Gazette*, Thursday A. M., October 19th, 1843:

"St. Louis Church, Buffalo.—An election of trustees for this church was held on Sunday last. Mr. —— and Mr. —— were elected. These gentlemen are understood to be decidedly in favor of the course adopted by the former board of trustees, in retaining in their own hands the management of the temporal affairs of their own church.

"A candidate of opposite opinion was run, who received four votes against two hundred and ninety-two, the lowest on the ticket elected. A hundred more votes were polled than ever before, notwithstanding the weather was very boisterous.

"This decisive action on the part of the congregation of St. Louis, should admonish the clergy, that the unusual measures to which they have resorted for the purpose of constraining the trustees into an acquiescence in their recent pretensions, may produce consequences the very opposite of those that they were intended to effect. The line dividing *temporal* from *spiritual* power is, we are glad to see, clearly distinguished by the congregation; and in the firm position they have taken in defending it, they have shown that they merit the privileges of American citizens, because they understand one of the first principles of American liberty."

This article was intended to express the will as well as the sentiments of the *majority* of the congregation. But W. B. Lecoutenlx, in an article published in the *Daily Gazette*, April 7th, 1843, relates:

"It is perfectly well known to every one here, that the congregation of St. Louis church consists of German and French population, amounting to several thousands, many of whom reside several miles from the city, and that it would be utterly impossible for St. Patrick's church to contain them."

Now, out of this immense congregation, numbering thousands, only two hundred and ninety-two votes were cast for the election of trustees of the church, according to the article above quoted, and which, as the reader will observe, was either written or caused to be written by the trustees themselves. We leave to the reader the inference as to whether or not this was an expression of the will of a *majority* of the congregation.

Page 221, "Missions of Western New York," we read:

"Scarcely had the new church of St. Louis been built by the Rev. Alex. Pax, when the trustees of the congregation broke out in opposition to Church discipline, by refusing to comply with the statutes of the diocese, and the faction so harrassed their clergyman that his health became impaired, and he was obliged to return to his native country, to endeavor to recover it.

"His letter at this period to Bishop Hughes, breathes of nothing but grief and despondency. In that of December 26th, 1842, he says: 'This time I write to you with a broken heart. * * * I read your pastoral letter; that part of it which treats of the administration of ecclesiastical property, occupied me two Sundays, because I was obliged to correct the most malicious interpretations spread among the people. W. B. Lecouteulx is the head of the opposition party. Misrepresentations of the worst kind, and lies of every description, were resorted to. This continued agitation produced a frightful excitement.' &c."

A meeting of the congregation was called by some of the trustees of St. Louis church, prominent among whom was W. B. Lecouteulx, son of Louis Lecouteulx, the donor of the property to the church. This gentleman was chairman of the meeting, and in common with a few others, had drawn up a lengthy set of resolutions in the English language, in which a decided opposition was expressed against what was styled the "usurpations" of Bishop Hughes. In these resolutions was set forth a determination to resist all the requirements of the pastoral letter, promulgated purely for Church discipline, but erroneously interpreted through the press, and otherwise, to threaten their rights and title to the property.

"These resolutions," relates a gentleman who was present at the meeting, "were subscribed to and signed by a committee of forty names, *of whom six*, at the utmost, *understood*, and, with the exception of *one*, NONE COULD READ ENGLISH, the language in which they were drawn up." Comment is unnecessary. In the meantime the impression made upon the minds of the people of St. Louis congregation, to the effect that their interests and rights were threatened, took deep root, and accordingly they were influenced to support their trustees "resolved" to oppose the imagined inroad upon their rights.

Many ineffectual efforts were made to induce the trustees to submit to the discipline of the Church, until finally the persistent spirit of rebellion, particularly upon the part of the trustees, obliged Bishop Hughes to interpose his authority to save the Church laws, by interdicting St. Louis church.

The trustees had "respectfully declined" to submit to the proposed change, and "most sincerely regretted not to be able to comply with the Bishop's *request*."

Bishop Hughes, in reply, said: " I read your letter with surprise. My pastoral letter was an intimation of an ecclesiastical law which is to be general throughout the diocese. It is not yet in force; but, when it will be, I trust it will be of the greatest advantage to the peace of the congregation. * * * Should it prove otherwise, however, in your judgment, you will have it in your power to resist its execution; and when you do, it will be time enough for me to ascertain what shall be my duty in the case. Should you determine that your church shall not be governed by the general law of the diocese, then we shall claim the privilege of retiring from its walls in peace, and leave you to govern it as you will. Indeed, we must keep peace, peace at all events, and charity also."

On page 221, "Missions in Western New York," we read further

" It is well known that on weak minds, whilst reading history, a deep impression will be made that almost all in life is evil, there being so much said of war; whilst what regards peace and prosperity may be discussed in a few brief lines. But the attentive reader knows that many years of peace, with all its blessings, may be sufficiently expressed in the two words of the cheering cry, 'All's well;' whilst, to render history what it should be, a lesson of experience and wisdom, pages must be employed to point out the causes, the actions, and the consequences of a month's war; so also must be this history, whilst briefly narrating the onward struggle of God's Church militant, in this diocese. But we will now say, once for all, that, generally, the pastors and the flocks, amidst dangers and difficulties, of which extreme poverty was not the least, displayed deep piety, disinterested zeal, a generous spirit of self sacrifice, the christian virtues which always accompany it, and, even in poverty, charity like that of the poor widow, whom the Saviour praised for casting her last mite into the treasury of God's house. Even the strife, which history to be useful must record, was, in every instance, caused by some twenty or thirty (often fewer,) leading men. These men, too, were generally good men, but men deceived in their estimate both of the importance of Church discipline, of the extent of their powers, and of the propriety of pushing to their utmost meaning the words of a church incorporation law, which almost all Protestants refused to use. A very few of the leaders, Catholics but in name, were men who never approached the sacraments; men to whom the words of Bishop Hughes might well apply: 'In such cases, only let one enlightened, talented, intriguing and irreligious mind get among them, and then, whatever *he* concocts in his infidel mind, he induces them, under specious pretexts, to adopt; and then *he* gives it out as the act of the board; and *this* again as the act of the congregation.'— Letter of Bishop Hughes, in the *Commercial*, of New York, April 4th, 1845.

"After many useless efforts to induce the trustees to submit to the discipline of the Church, the Right Rev. Bishop Hughes was obliged to interpose his authority, to save the Church laws, by interdicting the church of St. Louis.

"Men who never approached the sacraments exclaimed against the cruelty of depriving the congregation of holy sacramental helps. W. B. Lecouteulx, Esq., who seems to have been the master-spirit in opposition to Bishop Hughes, wrote several letters to his Bishop, assuredly in no Catholic spirit. In one, dated August 4th, 1841, he says to the Bishop: 'In case that, contrary to our expectations, you should have given your consent to the above propositions, I feel bound to inform you that it would be a derogation to the clauses specified in his (his father's) act of donation, and would therefore put me under the obligation to claim the property back again.' It is a sacred duty to say the truth in giving this history to the public, but to say it in such a manner as to give the least possible pain to the living, or to the friends of the dead. The subject of St. Louis church would have been passed over, truthfully, yet only in general, hasty views; but this mode of treating it can now no longer be just to the worthy dead, to the living, or to posterity. The worldly-wise and very cunning sometimes overact their part; thus the enemies of the Catholic Church have already forced into history false and injurious statements on this subject. In the New York *Gazetteer* for 1860, published by J. H. French, page 287, we read: 'There are fourteen Roman Catholic churches in the city of Buffalo. * * * The Roman Catholic church of St. Louis, in that city, has been prominently before the public, from the refusal of its trustees to *convey* their church property to the Bishop, and the extraordinary but ineffectual efforts made by the Roman Pontiff to induce obedience *to this order*. In 1853, Cardinal Bedini visited America, having this as a prominent object of his mission; but the trustees were inflexible, and still continue the owners of the property.' No priest or Bishop ever asked the trustees to *convey* the lot to them, nor has there ever been a dispute about *the deed;* the dispute, from first to last, was solely about Church discipline.

"On the 5th of January, 1829, nearly ten years before any trustees' church existed, the deed of that property was made to the Bishop, *and he holds it still.* On the 3d of August, 1850, when Bishop Timon forgave the first series of resistance to Church discipline under his administration, the trustees, pledging themselves to abide for the future by the discipline of the Church, said: 'On our part we acknowledge that, according to the laws of the State, the titles of the temporalities of the Church are vested in the Bishop and his successors in office, in trust for the sole use and only purpose of the congregation.' With Bishop Hughes and Bishop Timon, the sole contest has been about the discipline of the Church. Bishop Hughes, no doubt, has said in substance to the trustees what Bishop Timon often did, that no pay they could give would induce him to accept the administration of their revenues. On seeking reconciliation, the trustees granted all that Bishops Hughes or Timon ever asked. Bishop Timon wished to have the revenues administered, and church affairs conducted, according to law and discipline; the people heartily agreed to this. As matters of history, it is now a duty simply to state facts and justify the vast majority, who always were deeply and sincerely Catholic, while the chief agent in discord was a member of a secret society, who never approached the sacraments. His example drew some after him, and they were his best helpers. Immediately after the publication of the interdict, some of the most respectable Germans sent a petition, through George A. Deuther, Esq. Bishop Hughes answered it as follows:

"'New York, April 5, 1843.

"'Mr. George A. Deuther,

"'*Dear Sir:* I have received your petition and letter yesterday, and lose no time in forwarding my reply. Of course, I always knew, that there were a great many true and faithful Catholics in the congregation of St. Louis, in Buffalo. Indeed, on my visitation of the diocese, that congregation was, by its piety, my joy and my consolation. It was my pride and my boast on my return to New York.

"'But when a congregation, through its officers, allows its pastors to be thwarted in doing good, to be harrassed, and be made miserable, then I cannot expect that any priest will stay with them. The trustees of a congregation are only its servants, and when these servants undertake to reject ecclesiastical laws of the diocese, and to make laws themselves, as if they were Bishops in God's Church, then it is time for those who are Bishops and priests to withdraw in peace, and leave them also in peace, to govern those who are satisfied to be governed by them. They say the congregation supported them in their proceedings; if this be so, which I cannot believe, unless they deceived the congregation by false statements, then *so be it.*

"'Much as I feel for the good, pious people, I cannot allow any priest to officiate in the church of St. Louis, until I am assured that the congregation, in its trustees as well as in its members, are *Catholics, true Catholics, in their soul,* as well as by their outward profession. If they choose to have it otherwise, I shall not quarrel with them. But, in the meantime, I have no priest to send them; and if I had, I should not expose him in such a situation. Our priests are for Catholic congregations, and no other. Now there are many other good German congregations without a pastor, and until I have German priests enough for them all, it will be my duty to provide for those congregations who make it their pride to be governed by their pastors, instead of attempting to govern them.

"'When I had written thus far, one of our city papers was brought to me containing an article from the Buffalo *Gazette,* which is false in almost every particular, and which I have answered here. I hope the editor of the Buffalo *Gazette* will publish my answer, in order that the good and pious people of the congregation, may see how much they have been imposed upon by means of falsehood.

"'The people must *oblige their trustees to do right,* or else they must be prepared to suffer for what their *trustees do,* in their name, wrongfully. I shall have no dispute with any congregation, but whenever a congregation allows its trustees to behave so badly that the pastor must leave, I will allow them no other.

"'With the same kind feeling towards all, as your true friend and father in Christ, I remain, sincerely,

"'✠ JOHN, *Bishop, New York.*'

"The trustee party made other false statements, through the public prints. Bishop Hughes answered in the following letter to the New York *Commercial Advertiser,* of April 4th, 1843, which was copied from it into the Buffalo *Gazette:*

"'*Messrs. Editors:* In your *Commercial* of Monday you published from the Buffalo *Gazette* an article purporting to be a statement of the difference between the congregation of St. Louis church and myself. It stated that I claimed to have 'the property of the church vested in my hands, and that the claim was resisted by the congregation.' This is entirely untrue. I never advanced such a claim, and of course it could not be refused. It is stated that in consequence of this refusal I 'called away the Rev. Alexander Pax and left the congregation destitute.' This is equally untrue. On the contrary, nothing but my persuasion was able to prevail on him to stay for the last eighteen months or two years, under the ill treatment of a few worthless men who call themselves the congregation. It is stated that the congregation of St. Patrick's, in Buffalo, have 'complied with my requisition.' This again is untrue. The trustees and congregation of St. Patrick's* will bear me witness that I never made any such requisition. I advised them, as a means of putting an end to quarrels among themselves, to dispense with trustees, and to avoid the rock on which St. Louis is now splitting. These are the principal statements; and the honorable confidence of the editor of the Buffalo *Gazette* has been sadly abused by those who have employed his authority for statements which they knew to be unfounded in truth. He should demand proof of them, and if they cannot furnish it, to which I challenge them, he should publish their names, and vindicate his own. He has been deceived. I attach no blame to him. If his deceivers can furnish no proof that I ever made such a demand, I can furnish proof, in their own writing, that I never did.

"'It is surmised,' says the statement, 'that the Bishop has gone so far as to forbid any priest from performing Divine service in St. Louis church until its congregation shall fully comply with his demands.' I forbade only one clergyman, whose inexperience might have been taken advantage of by the same artifice which trifled so foully with the good faith of the editor of the *Gazette*. And secondly, what are called my 'demands,' in the statement, never had any existence in reality.

---

* Corner of Batavia and Ellicott streets.

"'Surely, the editors of the Buffalo *Gazette* will feel a glow of virtuous indignation when they discover how much they have been imposed on.

"'The only difference between the congregation of St. Louis and myself is, that its trustees have thought proper not to be governed by the ecclesiastical discipline of the diocese, and expect me to supply them with priests who shall be governed by a different discipline, of which they shall be the authors. The congregation of that church are pious and exemplary Catholics, to whom their holy faith is dearer than life. Even this may be said of a large number of the trustees.

"'But it sometimes happens that our trustees may be honest and upright in their intentions, and yet men of simple understanding, and without education. In such cases, only let an enlightened, talented, intriguing and irreligious mind get among them, and then, whatever he concocts in his infidel mind, he induces them, under specious pretences, to adopt; and then he gives out the depraved purposes of his own heart as the act of the board, and this again as the act of the congregation! From the moment this arrives, wo to the flock, and wo to the pastor, who are at once divided from each other, and yet kept together by such a link of iniquity.

"'The pious and amiable Mr. Pax was not called away by me, but I left him at liberty to leave whenever he felt that he could stand it no longer. It appears to me that the time has arrived. I have no German pastor to send in his place. But if I had, it would be with instructions to rent a barn, get up an altar in it, and administer the sacraments of religion with that freedom from restraint and guidance of unauthorized laymen with which God made the ministers of His Church free, but which is not to be enjoyed, it appears, in the church of St. Louis.

"'The neighboring clergymen could not officiate in it without neglecting their own congregations, which have the first claim on their ministry. Besides, I deem it my duty now to forbid all clergymen of this diocese to officiate in that church, until it shall be determined whether it is to be governed by the ecclesiastical regulations of the diocese, or by 'the *resolves*' of its trustees. I trust, Messrs. Editors, that you will publish the above in your valuable paper, as an act of reparation which I may claim on the score of justice. I ask an insertion in the Buffalo *Gazette*, which, I am sure, the editor will not refuse. I appeal to the honor of such other editors as may have copied the false and injurious statement first published in the Buffalo *Gazette*, for a similar favor.

"'✠JOHN HUGHES, *Bishop of New York*.

"'NEW YORK, April 4th, 1843.'

"The pious portion of the German Catholics now met for worship in the basement of St. Patrick's* church, having a Redemptorist, Father Allick, for their pastor. Bishop Hughes gave the order† a deed for a lot on Batavia street, where they at once erected a temporary church, residence and school house.

"The interdict on St. Louis church, in Buffalo, continued from 4th April, 1843, to 10th August, 1844. During that epoch, many of the peace-loving, pious Catholics of St. Louis church, had attached themselves to the rising congregation of St. Mary's. The trustees became alarmed, asked forgiveness of the Bishop, and published, in English, in the *Commercial Advertiser* of August 10th, 1844, the following.

"'A CARD.—We, the undersigned, trustees of the church of St. Louis, Buffalo, having had the honor of an interview with the Rt. Rev. Dr. Hughes, Bishop of New York, in relation to the difficulties which have existed between the congregation and the Bishop for some time past, and having received from him a true explanation of certain parts of the pastoral letter, and finding thereby that we have been laboring hitherto under a misunderstanding of the same, hereby express our willingness that the church and congregation of St. Louis be regulated according to the provisions of the said pastoral letter, and the true explanation received from the Rt. Rev. author; and we promise, in our own name, and (so far as we can) in the name

---

* Corner of Ellicott and Batavia streets.
† Redemptorist.

of our successors, that the administration of temporal affairs of our church and congregation shall be conducted conformably to the same.

"'We further take occasion to say, that if our course in this matter has given any scandal or offence to our Catholic brethren, we regret it; adding, merely, that our action proceeded from mistaken impressions, and that we should be the last to oppose the authority of our religion, either intentionally or deliberately.

    "'T. DINGENS, *President Board Trustees,*
    "'JOSEPH HABERSTRO,
    "'BARTHOLOMY RINK,
    "'JOSEPH STEFAN,
    "'NICHOLAS HAAS,
    "'MARTIN FISHER,
    "'CHARLES ESSLINGER. *Secretary.*'

"The Bishop, next day, Sunday, went to their church, preached, gave absolution and his blessing.

"As few of the Germans then read English newspapers, some who still adhered to uncatholic usurpations, spread a report that the Bishop had been forced to give up, and acknowledge himself in the wrong. Several who had been deceived by such reports, mentioned it to George A. Deuther, Esq., who most prudently said nothing until he could produce documents. In a few days he found them. He had the English translated into German, and published in the German newspaper, cut out the *card* and posted it up conspicuously at the door of St. Mary's church. This had the good effect of silencing the lovers of discord."

Such was the origin and the settlement of the first difficulty that broke out in St. Louis church, prior to the consecration of Rev. John Timon as Bishop of the Buffalo diocese.

It is to be regretted that these unfavorable circumstances ever happened to mar an otherwise brilliant progress in the Church militant in this diocese. Nor is it with pleasure that we record them on these pages. Having therefore briefly narrated them, we will resume the thread of our narrative, and commencing from a period when there were not as now such splendid edifices of religious worship, so many religious orders and convents, as well as institutions of charity, (in comparison with which many an institution, not predicated on the *true revealed* religion of Christ, dwindle into insignificance;) at a period when "there were but sixteen priests and sixteen churches, though most of those churches might more properly have been denominated huts or shanties, many of which have since been replaced by brick or stone churches, in various tastes and styles;" at a period when, having accepted the mitre, Bishop Timon had scarcely a dollar to his name, nor a house in which to take shelter or rest; at a period when troubles and dissatisfactions were ripe; and contrasting the present marvelous progress, all developed by brain work, by genius, by untiring zeal and unflagging industry on the part of the good Bishop, whose life and services were instruments in the hands of Divine Providence, with which He has accomplished His mysterious will in every age throughout all time; contrasting all these circumstances, what a sublime subject of contemplation suggests itself for the philosopher and christian to digest.

---o---

CHAPTER II.

Rt. Rev. John Timon as Bishop.—Rev. Bernard O'Reilly, V. G.—Their Arrival.—Reception.—Magnificent Demonstrations.—Te Deum at St. Louis Church.—Bishop Timon's First Consecration.—Told to Leave St. Louis Church.—Begins St. Patrick's.—Hard Work.—The Methodist and Hell.—The Irishman and Confession.—The Viaticum and the Presbyterian.—Upset from a Sleigh.—Father McEvoy taken for a Lawyer and the Bishop for a Priest.

Almost immediately after his consecration, Bishop Timon named the Rev. Bernard O'Reilly his Vicar General, and wrote to the Rev. F. Guth, then parish priest in Buffalo, that he would be with him on the 22d of that month, (October, 1847). Accordingly, accompanied by Bishops Hughes, Walsh, and McCloskey, and by the Rev. B. O'Reilly, he started, on the 20th inst., for Buffalo. At that time traveling, whether by rail or water, was not as commodious or quick as it is at the present day, with all the improvements that science has since then made in locomotion by steam. Consequently, it was not until in the morning of the 22d that they reached Rochester, where, amid a large assemblage, gathered upon short notice to welcome their Bishop, in St. Patrick's church,* Bishop Timon said his first mass in the diocese, preached, and gave his Episcopal blessing to the large congregation. As Bishop Timon had written to Father Guth that he would be in Buffalo on the 22d, and as he was always a man of honor and word, he desired to continue his journey to Buffalo immediately, in hopes to reach there early in the afternoon. His Right Rev. friends, already fatigued by a night's journey, wished to remain until next morning, particularly as the weather was decidedly unpleasant. But, although Bishop Timon thought their request reasonable, and invited them to remain, when they might rejoin him on the next day, they generally agreed to overcome their disposition to do so, and accompany him on his journey. As has been said, trains moved slowly; an accident further retarded them, so that it was already after sunset before they reached Buffalo.

What must have been the emotions of Bishop Timon as he neared this city, which was to become, by the blessing of God, the centre and Episcopal seat of the diocese. What thoughts, rapid and many, must have filled his mind as regarded the future; what hopes illumined his visionary path; what fears hung like clouds, dark and uncertain, over his plans and his views with regard to a proper disposition of the circumstances and materials with which he had to deal in the discharge of his arduous duties. He was a Bishop; he had been elevated one step higher in rank, and indeed, to a heart or soul governed only by worldly motives, indifferent to all else except pecuniary reward, and ambitious for titles, for honors, and emolument, the elevation to a Bishopric was a recompense sufficient for the most ambitious, especially after the discharge of years of arduous labor, after toils and privations in the service of religion, at last to reach the goal of his wishes, the crook and mitre. But in a

* Rochester.

man like Bishop Timon, particularly in a soul filled as his was with zeal and love in the service of Christ, no such sordid element existed. On the contrary, he accepted with humility, with resignation and with joy the new field of ministerial labor assigned him, panoplied with the same earnestness with which he had penetrated forests, crossed swollen torrents, on horse or in frail canoes, every where planting the flag of faith in the very centre of infidelity and Protestantism, and in spite of the opposition of anti-Catholic bigots, who had often threatened to take his life. What a harvest he has reaped, golden with the vintage of success! But *how* successfully he has done, let facts speak for themselves.

Bishop Timon reached Buffalo at 7 P. M. the same day he had left Rochester. It was already dark, and a slight, drizzling rain fell from the murky clouds over head. As the train neared the depot, its occupants could distinguish a vast crowd, estimated at that time to have been about ten thousand persons. These were the Catholics of the city, assembled together irrespective of nationality, to welcome and do honor to their new Bishop. Torches and transparencies blazed with brilliant light, and made the sombre clouds above them more solemn and threatening. Rich and swelling strains of music from the bands enlivened the occasion, the whole forming a scene at once indescribable yet magnificent. The daily press at that time spoke in warm and flattering terms of the reception thus given to the Bishop. The *Daily Courier* said:

"At eight o'clock, our German and Irish citizens had assembled in great numbers, and formed a procession on each side of Main street, reaching from Exchange to some distance above Seneca street. Every man bore a flambeau, and at a given signal from the marshal, a line of light ran along the vast column. Some little delay was experienced before the committee appointed to conduct the Bishops appeared, but at last the rich swelling notes of distant music greeted the ears of the multitude; the din and confusion of preparation subsided, and all became hushed into a respectful silence.

"The music approached, and after a few minutes had elapsed, the carriage containing the Bishops, their attendants, and the committee, advanced about midway through the lines of fire, and then stopped. The carriage in which rode* the Bishop was drawn by four beautiful white chargers, and was the most conspicuous object in the procession. At a signal made for that purpose, the illuminated human mass moved on, and as it advanced up Main street towards St. Louis church, (its place of destination,) beneath a canopy of blazing light, it produced an indescribably beautiful effect. It far surpassed our expectations, and reflected honor upon the distinguished individuals who were the occasion of it. * * * We trust Bishop Timon will never have occasion to repent that he has come to reside among us."

It was ten o'clock P. M. when the procession reached St. Louis church. Here the Bishops, clergy and laity in silence adored the blessed Sacrament. It was near eleven o'clock when the crowd had dispersed. Bishop Timon himself, relating his experience at that time, writes thus in the "Missions in Western New York":

"The Bishop had no church to which he could safely assert a right, nor had he a house to lodge in. He agreed to board, at a certain fixed price, with the pastor of St. Louis church, and betook himself to understand the condition of the new diocese. He named Rev. Francis Guth Vicar General for the Germans.

"In a few days, the trustees of St. Louis church called on him and requested him to consecrate their church. He complimented them on the fine appearance the church presented, and that it was well worthy of being consecrated; but that he was bound by Church discipline, as decreed in the Council of Baltimore, not to consecrate any church unless the title was in the Bishop. The trustees assured him that the church had been deeded to the Bishop, and belonged to him, in trust for the congregation; and, to remove all his scruples they brought him, in a few days after, an authenticated copy of the deed of Louis Lecouteulx de Chamont, Esq., to the Bishop. This was sufficient."

---

* This is contradicted - some say he walked, carpet-bag in hand.

After several days of labor and preparation, the Bishop, having to do almost all himself for a ceremony so new to those who assisted at it, on the 21st December, 1847, consecrated the church **of St.** Louis, preached at the consecration, and, after vespers, preached again and confirmed two hundred and twenty-seven persons. Shortly after the consecration, the Rev. pastor of St. Louis church informed the Bishop that " the trustees wished him **to find other** lodgings, as they did not like to see the Bishop there." **The** Bishop felt sad; after twenty **years** of arduous ministerial labor, he found himself poor, advanced in age, and without **a shelter on** earth. He told the good priest to say to **the** trustees that " he never intended to remain permanently at St. **Louis church, for** he wished to go and labor where his beloved flock were in greatest want; that at St. Louis church the faithful had nearly sufficient help, but that the Irish congregation was greatly in need of **help; and** that he had already determined to make St. Patrick's church* his home." Although this discouraging circumstance **occurred** seemingly to shadow the brilliant ovation he had received, still it **by no means** served to dampen the **zeal which,** under sterner difficulties, had so often been put to the test, and under which he had never flinched.

He said himself that he felt sad; but it was the sadness that **sometimes** results from uncharitable and deceitful treatment, **rather than** from dispirited and discouraged feelings. For " he wished to go and labor where his beloved flock were in greatest **want;** * * * * and " had already *determined* to make St. Patrick's **church** his home." Indeed, to be *discouraged* is to fail. **Does the record of** his subsequent life show that he was discouraged? **Does it show that he** failed?

On the contrary, we find **him,** on the 28th of November, **giving a retreat at** St. Mary's, **Rochester,** at which there were nine hundred communicants. **On the 6th** of December, he confirmed in St. Peter's church, and **on the 12th he** gave another **retreat in Java. On** the 20th, he began one in St. Patrick's, **Buffalo,** preaching three times **a day, making two** meditations

---
* Corner of Batavia and Ellicott streets.

daily, and, with the exception of a few hours required for food and sleep, passing all the rest of his time in the confessional. What was the result of this zeal? It induced him to continue the retreat three weeks longer, at the end of which time the congregation, which only counted three hundred souls at first, saw fifteen hundred approach the holy table. From this circumstance we may learn what results flow from interested zeal, and what a fruitful parent of wealth and happiness is application, if it is properly employed.

The first year was thus passed in giving retreats, and in visiting the diocese; four thousand six hundred and seventeen persons, of whom one half were adults, were confirmed. On the 29th, the Bishop preached at Jefferson, at 7 P. M.; on the 30th, he confirmed twelve persons, among whom was a convert from Methodism, who had been terrified by a sermon on hell, and whose terrors had been aggravated by her dreams. The Bishop told her to "do penance and you shall be saved." In vain she read the Protestant Bible. At last she found a Catholic Bible; she read, became converted, and was baptized. At Corning there was no place to say mass in, excepting the Methodist church, in which the Bishop also preached. After the sermon an Irishman approached and said: "God bless you, but och, how good it would have been if you had said more about confession; they do mock us so much about it." The Bishop immediately cried out at the top of his voice: "To-morrow morning at ten o'clock, I will say mass here, and preach on confession and the pardon of sin." Next morning, whilst being shaved at a barber's shop, a couple of gentlemen entered, and not knowing the Bishop, observed to each other, "Well, Tom, ain't you coming to hear that Bishop, and to get your sins pardoned? better bring plenty of money with you." The conversation went on awhile like this, none suspecting the Bishop was present. As the Bishop began his sermon, however, and was just finishing the relation of this anecdote that occurred at the barber's shop, the two gentlemen entered. He explained very clearly and satisfactorily to his audience the sacrament of penance, and erased from the minds of many the error they entertained regarding confession, and satisfied them that Catholics had been wronged on this point.

At Bath, he was called to administer Extreme Unction to a dying man. An ex-Presbyterian minister, who was present, observing the devotion and sincerity with which the Bishop heard the dying man's confession, and administered the holy Viaticum, was deeply moved, and as the Bishop was about to depart, he approached him, took him by the hand, and said: "God bless you, that was very touching."

Bishop Timon visited every part of his diocese. At every station we find his presence attracting many to Divine worship, whilst his eloquence and touching sermons penetrated the hearts of his audience, some of whom were of Protestant faith. The inconveniences of travel at that time were no embarrassments to his zeal. If he reached a village where there was no church, he instinctively provided for his wants, by obtaining the court house or other public building, and with his own hands assisted in erecting altars, and preparing for the sacrifice of the mass.

Indeed, such was his zeal, such his indifference to the extremities of the weather, and the violence done to him personally by accidents and mishaps, that once, when leaving Owego for Elmira in a sleigh, accompanied by the Rev. Mr. Sheridan, he says, in his "Missions":

"The sleighing was good for a few miles, then gradually failed. Whilst seeking the roadside, where some snow remained, the sleigh upset, the Bishop was thrown on the hard frozen ground, much stunned and cut; but after a few moments he strove to continue his route; then the sleigh broke down, and though they hired a wagon, the horse gave out; and thus, after great fatigue, they were forced to stop at Factoryville." Nothing daunted by his misfortunes, the Bishop heard confession till late that night, and, as if nothing had happened, next morning was on his way again for Elmira.

At Scio, N. Y., the Bishop confirmed forty-two persons. In the evening, accompanied by Rev. Thomas McEvoy, (since dead,) he drove to the next station, Hornby House; but losing their way, they stopped at a tavern on the road, and whilst taking dinner there, the aged host and hostess told them frankly all the bad that they believed of Catholics. The Bishop kindly corrected their statements; Mr. McEvoy took their part, and pressed the Protestant arguments strongly on the Bishop, who thus had an opportunity, which he did not expect, of removing many prejudices from the minds of these good people. When the time came for starting, the Bishop asked them to say frankly whom they thought their guests to be. They answered that they thought Mr. McEvoy to be "a lawyer, and the other a Catholic priest."

---o---

CHAPTER III.

HISTORY OF THE TROUBLES OF ST. LOUIS CHURCH UNDER BISHOP TIMON'S ADMINISTRATION, GATHERED FROM THE POSTHUMOUS PAPERS OF THE BISHOP.

"*Humanum est errare!*" It is human for man to err. Hence this would be a strange world, indeed, if there were none who deviated from principle or law; if there were none who, from different motives, opposed Church authority, and by a direct spirit of disobedience strove to accomplish their own purposes, as if it were to spite the authority that had interdicted them. Nay, that there are sometimes found men who thus obstinately persist to force their plans and wishes upon the acceptance of law or authority, however at variance with propriety and right, is, in itself, a very mysterious circumstance.

One can easily understand *why* it is that men disobey, if, after disobedience, there follows true repentance; but when men disobey, and under the cloak of pretended reparation seek to add another crime to the catalogue of their errors, by continuing not only to disobey but to rebel, why then the circumstance assumes a more heinous phase, and renders such individuals unworthy of merit.

Whether this will apply to the conduct of some of the congregation of St. Louis church, particularly of the trustees, will be evident from what follows:

On page 240, "Missions in Western New York," the Bishop himself says:

"The trustees of St. Louis church asked his permission to enlarge their church, so as to prevent streets being run through their lot. *He refused*, thinking that it would spoil the church, which was already the largest in the United States, and showed them how they could build tower, priest's house, etc., to suit them better."

This was in the Fall of 1848, and almost immediately afterwards we find him making an Episcopal visit over his extensive diocese, which occupied nearly a month.

"On the 19th February, the Bishop returned to Buffalo from his visit of more than a month through parts of the diocese. On the way to his lodgings, he met W. B. Lecouteulx, Esq., in the street, who immediately accosted him thus: 'I am glad to see you. I rejoice to be able to tell you that we have begun our addition to St. Louis church, and that the work is already far advanced. I am now engaged about another important business for the good of the church. Here is a petition I am going to present to the Common Council, to request them to deed to St. Louis church the grave yard that was given for it. I have searched all the records, and I find that the deed was never made out, so that it might be taken from us. I went to your house to show you the petition before it should be presented, but you were not home.' The Bishop smiled, as he knew that his absence on the visit was well known in the city. He read the petition, and then told Mr. Lecouteulx that the petition contained things most untrue and most offensive to the congregations of St. Mary's and of St. Patrick's. That, to his intimate knowledge, the faithful of both churches had been orderly and quiet at their burials; that the grave yard was given for all the Catholics in the city, and further, that he, the Bishop, held the deed, duly executed and duly recorded. The Bishop invited the gentleman to come to his house and see the instrument, which he did, noted the page of records, and dropped the matter.

"The Bishop then went to the trustees, expostulated with them for having, after his express prohibition, begun the walls, which were already two or three feet out of ground; he required them to demolish the work, and, if they wished to build, to build according to any plan they might prefer, but for the objects he had sanctioned, not for the enlargement of a church already very large. He then spoke to the Very Rev. Mr. Guth, to whom the trustees had referred him as having sanctioned the work. Mr. Guth expressed himself much grieved and very sad, acknowledging that he had sanctioned the work; but declared that, if now demolished, he could never hold up his head again, and would have to withdraw to hide his shame. The trustees came, they begged pardon, but, as so much was done, they entreated that they might be permitted to finish the part begun. The Bishop, deeply touched at the grief of Mr. Guth, whom he greatly respected, hesitated. At length he said that he could not approve, but he would overlook, and not notice the act, provided no more was attempted than the part already begun. The promise was given, but not kept."

In a printed pamphlet,* Bishop Timon himself writes as follows:

"Deception and misrepresentation have their day. Truth gradually finds its way to souls that have no interest in being deceived. Thus, in 1844, August 16th, alarmed by the number that had dropped off from them, the trustees begged pardon of Bishop Hughes, and promised submission to the laws they had resisted.

"The Bishop then visited the church, and gave them a pastor. But, alas, the germ of evil still remained, and showed itself in many forms. In 1848 a plan was presented to Bishop Timon for

---

* "Documents and History of the Affairs of St. Louis Church."

enlarging St. Louis church, building two towers, etc. He not only disapproved of it, but absolutely forbade it, as a plan which would spoil what was then, in its beautiful simplicity, a truly noble church. Bishop Timon went out to visit his diocese. At his return he found the monstrous addition which he had forbidden, already far out of ground. The trustees threw the blame on their pastor, but the Bishop knew that a large share belonged to the trustees, for he had spoken at length to them; they had shown him the plan; to them, and to them alone, he had uttered the words of strong prohibition; no occasion had occurred for the same language to be used to their pastor. Yet, at the request of the pastor, the Bishop withdrew his orders for demolishing the works begun; declaring, however, that he could not sanction it, but that he would remain silent under certain conditions, which were accepted, but *which were not fulfilled.* A most useless expense for disfiguring their church, and a large debt, were the results of this disobedience.

"The Bishop brought Sisters of Charity to teach a free school for the girls of St. Louis church; the trustees declared to the pastor that they did not want them, and thus frustrated the desire of the Bishop to secure good parochial schools for that flock. But why enumerate? the very grave digger was officially advised by the trustees to resist the Bishop's orders. And secret insinuations were in continual use to cause disquietude, distrust, and trouble amidst a *good,* simple, and *well disposed* people. The correspondence, now given *verbatim,* will itself prove this. During the Bishop's absence in Europe, the pastor found his position so unpleasant that he quit it: the French, who had suffered much from the trustees, also left St. Louis church, and founded a new congregation in the church of St. Peter.[*] The Bishop, at his return, tried to remedy the evil. The trustees and their adherents rejected his propositions; but on August 30th, 1850, they themselves prepared, in rather bad English, the following document, which the Bishop accepted:

---

[*] Corner Clinton and Washington streets.

"'To the Rt. Rev. John Timon, *Bishop of Buffalo:*

"'The undersigned, trustees of the Roman Catholic church of St. Louis, in the city of Buffalo, regret that misunderstanding has arisen between them and their Bishop, regarding the rights and duties that devolve on them under the laws of the State, in the administration of the affairs of the said St. Louis church.

"'Whatever may have been the character or extent of our past differences, we regret them, and pray the Bishop to forget them. We propose to the Bishop that he and his successors in office, and we, abide and be governed by the following rules and regulations:

"'On our part we acknowledge that, according to the laws of the State, the titles of the temporalities of the church are vested in the Bishop and his successors in office, in trust for the sole use and only purposes of the congregation. That the Bishop, for the time being, according to the spiritual and Divine laws, is guardian of the church and its property. We bind ourselves to do nothing having reference to spiritual matters without the permission and consent of the Bishop, and truly and faithfully to observe and fulfill his command in that regard. We propose to administer the temporal affairs of the church under the counsel and advice of the Bishop, as becomes the children of God and of the Bishop. We acknowledge that the Bishop and pastor appointed by him for the time being are accountable to God as guardians of their flocks, and as such we acknowledge that they have the right to superintend the schools attached to the church, and we pledge our best exertions in aid of the clergy for the success of the school and the education of the youth. The trustees shall, under the direction of the Bishop, select the teacher or teachers of the school, and no teacher shall be appointed without the sanction of the Bishop or pastor. We consent and agree that the rector appointed by the Bishop for the time being, shall preside over the deliberations of the trustees, and have his vote. The undersigned trustees shall not and will not expend over one hundred dollars at any one time on any improvements, repairs, or building, or in any manner, without the knowledge and consent of the Bishop, and we ask and desire that the Bishop and the rector for the time being, will use their power, advice, and influence to prevent the election hereafter of any person as trustee who may be known as a person of immoral character or who fails to perform his duty as a christian, and we pledge ourselves never to wish for or assist in the election of any such person.

"'Finally, we wish sincerely to coöperate with the clergy in all things tending to the glory of God, the good of ourselves, the welfare of our people, and to the prosperity of our church.

"'Dated BUFFALO, August 3d, 1850.
    (Signed.)
                                "'N. OTTENOT,
                                "'J. HABERSTRO,
                                "'JNO. CHRETIEN,
                                "'JACOB WILHELM,
                                "'GEORGE ZIMMERMAN.

"'Mr. Eslinger had removed to Wisconsin.
"'Mr. Handel had resigned.'

"To induce the Bishop to waive his opposition to the useless expense of the addition to St. Louis church, and to convince him that they would be prudent in not contracting debts beyond what the church could easily pay, the trustees, over and over again, declared to the Bishop that the debts they might contract would be on their own individual responsibility. The Bishop did not wish them to suffer, but he ought, at least, to have been consulted when the trustees laid aside the check which their own declaration had placed on future imprudent enterprises; yet, before Bishop or pastor knew anything of it, the trustees transferred the burden to many generous members of the congregation. They or their abettors acted with regard to Bishop Timon as, after having demanded pardon of Bishop Hughes, they had acted with him; then they published that they had triumphed; that Bishop Hughes had been forced to cede. It was only after some good christian had translated into German, and published the trustees' apology, inserted in the *Commercial Advertiser* of 10th August, 1844, that the good Germans of the congregation were undeceived. So, also, after signing the above document, they publish in the German papers of Buffalo that they had triumphed, and of course that Bishop Timon was forced to acknowledge his error. Bishop Timon, who sought no honor of triumph, was silent until, emboldened by his silence, they had these articles translated into English for a population who, being unacquainted with the preliminaries, could not easily detect the falsehood. Then an answer was published; the document was shown to the editors of two principal gazettes, in which the false boast of victory had been published, and those editors, with generous indignation for the attempted deception, published in a few words the facts and their convictions. Various other arts were used. It is scarcely possible that the trustees would descend to some of them, it was the work of the party.

"After having taken advice from pious, learned and distinguished priests, on Easter Sunday, Bishop Timon addressed the following letter to the congregation:

"'Having long borne with patience from the trustees' acts of usurped authority which have plunged your church in debt, and others which have caused this, once the most flourishing congregation in my diocese, to gradually fall away, so that whilst St. Mary's church has six or seven hundred children in the parish schools, you have but a handful; and, under incessant insinuations that your Bishop wants to do *now this, now that*, the spirit of unholy distrust and of murmuring has entered the fold, and the piety of many has grown cold; it becomes our duty to remedy so sad a state of things. We are the more impelled to this by a step taken without our knowledge, and which we only learned a few days ago. It seems that many of the congregation were called upon to assume the payment of a debt for a needless addition to this church, began without my permission, and against all the laws of the church and the diocese. Now, under proper management, the resources of this church would suffice to pay the debt. You know, beloved brethren, that when you invited the Jesuits to come and serve this church, these fathers proposed that they would assume the debts of the church, and furnish as many German priests as might be necessary for your fullest spiritual comfort. Second, That this church should remain for ever the parish church of the German Catholics of this congregation, and that the Rev. Father would build school houses for your children. Now, if the Jesuits could offer such advantageous conditions, why did the trustees burden many of you with personal obligations for this debt?

"The promises these gentlemen made to me last August, have been broken in a most important feature. They bound themselves in a written article, that the parish priest should be president of the board; yet they have elected a lay president, contrary to the letter and the spirit of our agreement. Beloved brethren, you ought to know that even in Protestant churches of this State, the pastor is generally the only president of the board; so that those trustees wish to have your church under a far more Presbyterian government than most of the Protestant churches themselves. We know not what thus presses those gentlemen to meddle with the affairs of God's house; the priest or Bishop never thinks of meddling with the affairs of your houses, or with the affairs of houses consecrated to civic or political uses; though by his taxes the priest pays in part for those houses affected to civic uses, he willingly leaves the care of them to men of the world; but the priest, the man of God, the Bishop, as minister of God, is bound to take care of God's house. We willingly use the help of laymen in temporal affairs, but then upon the laymen whom we call to help us the power descends from above, it does not come from below; the Bishop and the priest are called by God through a superior power, which also comes from God, and the laymen we call to aid us have their power also from above, through the Bishop's nomination; then all is in peace, and God's blessing dwells in His houses. We now name five responsible men, N. N. N. N. N., as administrators of this church in temporal affairs. We also name Father C——, the priest you desired, to be pastor; he will be assisted by two other clergymen, in whose zeal and piety you and we have full confidence. We declare that, henceforward, the so called trustees have no right in this church. The property is vested in us for your use. If they wish to be trustees, let them find a church in which to exercise their functions, but they will never have a priest to minister.'

"The Bishop having understood that the most unfounded statements had been made by the adverse party, had, on the following Sunday, a letter read to the flock, as follows:

"'*Beloved Brethren:* On that holy and most solemn day, when our Blessed Lord rose from the dead, and twice wished peace to His redeemed, I sought to procure the true and holy peace of this congregation by the declaration made to you last Sunday, and from which my love for you and for your happiness and peace in time and eternity, will never permit me to recede. But, with grief, I learn that now, as heretofore, men whom the spirit of party blinds and agitates, whisper among the people insidious doubts, and false, malignant insinuations. It is for your peace that I should notice them; for me to be calumniated or to be praised is all the same, and whether I succeed or do not succeed in my efforts for your peace, God will reward my upright intentions. I seek but my God, and your salvation and happiness, for His glory. I have not long to live; I seek for nothing on earth, and it is my joy to know that when I die, all that is entrusted to me shall remain for the uses for which it was given, and I will retain nothing but my coffin and my shroud. Hence what I now say to you is not to defend myself, but to prevent the father of lies from destroying your peace.

"'First, Beloved brethren, it has been said to you that I wished to take your church. Now, from my first coming among you, to many questions and proposals I ever returned the same answer, that I abhorred the very idea of permitting this church to be ever diverted from its application to the use of the German congregation of St. Louis church. I never wanted your church except to hold it in trust for you according to my deed, and to the very declaration of your trustees. I wish your church to be administered as almost all the churches in America, and as all the churches in my diocese but this, are administered; so that your trustees may not so fetter the action of your clergy, that they can do little for your spiritual comfort, little for the education of your children. I now declare solemnly to you, as I often declared to your trustees, that I do not want your church, except (in the very words of the donor, Mr. Lecouteulx,) 'in trust to me and my successors in office of Bishop for your sole use and benefit.' I do not want the revenues of your church, do not even want to meddle with them; the revenues of your church shall be henceforth more carefully, more exactly, and most scrupulously applied to the sole use and benefit of this congregation and church. Alas, had I taken this measure three years ago, your beautiful church would now, I am sure, be finished, be well ornamented, and be out of debt.

"'Let any of those who resist the Bishop show me a text of scripture which constitutes them your pastors and guardians of your church rights. Be not deceived, beloved brethren; hear the blessed apostle saying to you, 'obey your pastors and be subject to them, for they watch, as having to give an account to God of your souls.'

"A few days after, a committee, having as their president a gentleman who seldom came to church, and who never approached the sacraments, speaking in the name of the congregation, but really representing a minority of the flock, handed to the Bishop the following document, containing self laudations, many vague words, and worse:

RESOLUTIONS.

"'The committee appointed by the incorporated Society of St. Louis, to draw resolutions concerning the contents of the pastoral, published from the pulpit instead of the sermon, on the feast of the Easter, A. D. 1851, by Rev. Mr. Raffeiner, by the orders of the Rt. Rev. J. Timon, Bishop of the Diocese of Buffalo, Erie county, State of New York, by which (pastoral) said congregation of St. Louis is to be forcibly debarred of her legal administration of the temporal affairs of the church, in virtue of the State Charter of the 2d December, 1838, and to propose the same resolutions to the meeting adjourned to the 27th of April, 1851,

(9)

for their approbation, has the honor to answer with this the wishes of the said congregation, and respectfully to propose its resolutions to their examination.

"'1st. *Resolved*, That the society of the St. Louis, before all, regrets most heartily that for several years they have been so often disturbed in their truly christian peace and indefatigable zeal in doing good, by their own clergy, the Rt. Rev. J. B. Timon, Bishop, included, and are yet disturbed, for this only reason, that they (the congregation,) refuse to give over to the Rt. Rev. Bishop Timon, as his free and absolute property, their beautiful new church of St. Louis—which they have built with their own means, and which was solemnly consecrated—so that he might, as the rumor has gone abroad, appropriate the same for the use of the Irish congregation. And, whereas, the Rt. Rev. Bishop, (since all his previous attempts to grasp at said St. Louis church have rebounded against the firmness of St. Louis congregation, which constantly fought, and always will fight for its rights,) has betaken himself to violent measures, which not only are in direct opposition to the laws of the State, but may turn very pernicious to the holy Roman Catholic religion in the Union.

"'2d. *Resolved*, Whereas, the Rt. Rev. Bishop refused personally to communicate to the committee appointed legally by the board of the trustees, composed of Messrs. J. Haberstro and Anton Diebold, the pastoral published from the pulpit in St. Louis church, on Easter Sunday, (either the original or a copy thereof,) St. Louis congregation cannot but regret that the Right Rev. Bishop should have caused to be published from the pulpit upon one of the holiest festivals of the year; and at the solemn Divine service, in place of a religious discourse, that which he feels not inclined to entrust to two citizens.

"'3d. *Resolved*, That the congregation of St. Louis will not take the least notice of the said pastoral, since said congregation was incorporated as a religious society under an act of this State, passed April 5th, 1813, with the consent of the generous donor, Louis Lecouteulx, and also with the consent of the Right Rev. Dubois, Bishop of New York; and that, although at that time, when the well known lot on which the St. Louis church stands, the society as such had no legal existence, and the land had been deeded in trust to the Bishop of New York and his successors, that trust has entirely ceased since the act of incorporation, December 2d, 1838, and was transferred to the incorporated society of St. Louis, which shall see to it, that in all circumstances their charter may be preserved in all its strength. That the society of St. Louis will always call for his advice in the administration of the temporal affairs of the church.

"'4th. *Resolved*, Whereas, neither the board of trustees, nor the society of St. Louis, had ever made to the Rt. Rev. Bishop J. B. Timon, or to the Rev. Fathers Jesuits, or to any body whatsoever, any proposition that the said fathers of the Society of Jesus might take charge of the religious (spiritual) affairs of St. Louis society. This is founded on an error, of which the Rev. Bishop must be as well convinced as the board of the trustees, for, when the trustees were invited by the Rt. Rev. V. G. F. Guth to call at the Bishop's instantly and in great hurry, they had not the slightest knowledge of the plan of giving St. Louis church into the hands of the Rev. Fathers Jesuits; they were opposed to having the Superior of the Jesuits sent for, until the Right Rev. Bishop told them personally, as they were retiring, that he had spoken over the matter with his Vicar General G., so as to appoint the Fathers Jesuits for this place, etc., etc. That some other individuals, moved by ambition and self-interest, had been working to the same purpose, is perfectly well known to St. Louis society. St. Louis society had been till now attended by secular priests, who stand under their Bishop, and never preferred against them any complaint, notwithstanding the many chances of doing it. It only wishes to have such pastors who will do honor, not only to St. Louis church, but to the whole Roman Catholic religion in the Old and New World.

"'5th. *Resolved*, That the reproach about religious schools of St. Louis church lies not at the door of the trustees or of the congregation, but rather of the clergy of said church, as no teacher was appointed to said school without the consent of the pastor, if not by his strong and formal request; but that, as soon as the teacher had the misfortune of calling on himself the displeasure of the pastor, there was no more mercy for him, and he had to leave the situation. This is a fact.'

"Several other 'resolutions' of minor importance, but each one strongly marked by misrepresentation and disregard for truth, follow. The document was duly signed, and dated April 27th, 1851.

"To this document, in which every paragraph contains misrepresentation, false insinuations, and absolute falsehoods, the Bishop addressed the following answer:

"'From a committee, styling itself your organ, and having for president a gentleman who never practices his religious duties as a Catholic, I received a paper full of falsehoods and insult. Judge for yourselves, beloved brethren. That document says that 'this congregation has been disturbed in its truly christian peace, by the clergy and the Bishop, only because they refuse to give up to Bishop Timon their church as his free and absolute property.' Now, my brethren, did I ever ask you for such a thing? Have I not, on the contrary, often and most solemnly declared that I want nothing but to maintain the trust for you, as Mr. Lecouteulx had given it; and that I wished that trust to be administered for you by some from amongst yourselves, viz: by some laymen whose power, deriving from their Bishop, might come from above. How then dare those men say, in a public document, that the only cause of disturbance is my wish to get the absolute property of your church? I understand well enough the laws of my country, to know that the trustees could not give me such absolute right, even if they would, nor even could you, beloved brethren, give such right, and far am I from wishing it. Still those men persevere in the slanderous assertion, which originated with their party, in order to sow distrust between you and your Bishop, and, in this document, they even dare to say, 'the Bishop wants to get the free and absolute property of this church in order, as rumor spreads, that he may give it to his Irish congregation!' May God have mercy on such deluded and deluding men, who dare to say that I even thought of taking St. Louis church from you to give to the Irish! But who was it that set so lying and slanderous a rumor in motion? Was it not the very party that now dares, in a public document, boldly to endorse it?

"'Beloved brethren, we need waste no more words on this subject. Any man of sense, any christian will now see that the Bishop and the priests of a God of peace and truth, can have no fitting connection with an order of things which allows the father of lies to insinuate his malicious suspicions, first in a whisper, then more boldly, and finally in a public document, openly and unblushingly, striving to deceive God's people, first by insinuation and doubt, then by bold assertion, until, as occurred with Eve, they honor and esteem their spiritual authorities as long as they live up to the rules of the Roman Catholic Church, of course, *the trustees of St. Louis church being judges!*

"'I might rely on the law, and appeal for my rights to the courts, but, beloved brethren, I am not so fond of law as to engage in lawsuits for it, unless my duty compel me; your Catholic spirit, and the mild exercise of my Episcopal right, will, I trust, suffice. I seek but for the salvation of the souls entrusted to my care; provided they find peace and holy piety, though in a shed like that in which the Redemptorists long worshiped, I would be better satisfied than to see them in a splendid church, in which the spirit of lies and rebellion would be continually gnawing away the vitals of true piety.

"'If, therefore, beloved brethren, the resolutions handed to me be really the resolutions of a majority of the congregation, (which I do not believe,) I must only withdraw the priests immediately. It is your duty to manifest your sentiments. Therefore let those who love their God in their religion, and who adhere to their Bishop, as to the visible centre of Church unity in this diocese, let them declare themselves freely and fearlessly. God will bless and protect those who stand up for His cause. May He inspire into your hearts holy zeal and courage, to confess Him before men, that He may acknowledge you before His Heavenly Father.'

"This letter produced a due effect upon what appeared to be a large majority; they remained after mass in the church; the party adverse to the Bishop retired; whilst the pastor was exhorting those within to give a calm and fearless declaration of their sentiments, the turbulent party, finding themselves a feeble minority, and that the good and peaceable had not, as usual, gone home, rushed into the church, insulted the pastor, menaced him with personal violence, and ordered him out. He retired, bearing our Lord in the most blessed sacrament out with him. For several succeeding Sundays, an unauthorized, uncatholic worship was held in the church. It became the Bishop's duty to interfere. He addressed the following letter to them:

"'BUFFALO, June 14, 1851.

"'*To the faithful of the congregation of S*t. *Louis church:*

"'After exhausting all means of patience and of kindness to induce the trustees and their abettors to permit the laws of the Church to be freely executed in your congregation; after having known that your pastor was insulted in the church, menaced there in presence of the trustees, and ordered to leave the house of God, and thus forced to withdraw; we have the grief to see that a kind of schismatic worship has been there established by the trustees; some of the sacred vestments, used in Divine worship, are placed on the children; the altars are adorned, vespers sung, the organ played, etc., whilst many neglect mass to assist at such rites. By the laws of God's Church, such acts subject those who assist at them to various spiritual penalties, and force the Bishop to declare, as we now do, St. Louis church to be under an interdict; and consequently that no child of the Church can, without grievous sin, assist there at such rites and prayers, whilst this sad state of things continues. May God save our beloved in Christ from awful punishment, such as He inflicted in times past on those who, in their worldly wisdom, rebelled against Moses and Aaron.'

"Strange how the same spirit has ever followed 'the said "corporation." Bishop Hughes never dreamed of taking their church.

Yet in 1843 the innocent Germans were deceived by the party to believe it. That same party, on the 21st June, 1851, had the following article inserted in the *Morning Express*, of Buffalo:

"'St. Louis Church.—This church, the oldest of that persuasion in our city, and the only one, perhaps, incorporated according to the laws of this State, is involved in serious difficulties with Bishop Timon, we understand in consequence of a refusal to abandon to him their church property, and the administration of their temporal affairs. A few years ago that congregation experienced the same troubles with Bishop Hughes, from a like cause, but after a rupture of two years, matters were settled to their satisfaction, they being secured in the enjoyment of their former rights. We learn that Bishop Timon has been more severe with the congregation of St. Louis than was Bishop Hughes, having, (after depriving them of their priests for the last two months,) on Sunday, the 19th inst., caused a pastoral letter to be read in all the Catholic churches of the diocese, by which he pronounces excommunication against that church and its congregation! We know nothing of the merits of this controversy, save what we hear, but it looks a little like taking us back to ages almost forgotten, when such things occur in a free country, where all religions are equally acknowledged and tolerated.'

"In the same paper of the 24th June, the following answer appeared:

"'St. Louis Church.—The upright-minded editor of the *Express* has been deceived, as was, by the same party, the editor of the Buffalo *Gazette* deceived in 1843. Bishop Timon never sought for any property in the St. Louis church other than the deed Mr. Lecouteulx gave, and the laws of the Church made it the Bishop's duty to maintain. He never even wished to administer the revenues of the church, but he was bound to see them administered in a Catholic spirit. The statements published in the *Express* of Saturday morning, are as false, with regard to Bishop Timon, as were false, with regard to Bishop Hughes, the statements in the Buffalo *Gazette*, which drew forth the following letter from that learned and distinguished prelate; the only difference is, that Bishop Timon has long and patiently borne with much more than Bishop Hughes had to bear with from the same party. . It is false that Bishop Timon has excommunicated any one of that church. When the pastor (insulted and menaced in the church by a turbulent minority who domineer there,) was, by them, ordered out of it, he did leave it. And, when many were deceived by the semblance of a public, uncatholic worship, and neglected the great act of Catholic worship, (the mass,) at which they might have assisted in different churches of the city, then the Bishop, according to the laws of the Church and the decrees of the Council of Buffalo, pronounced an interdict on the church, that is, forbade any public worship in it. If any one incurs excommunication, it will be by his own act, for refusing to obey the laws of the Church, and assisting at a schismatic worship.

"'The name of Bishop Hughes having been united in blame with the name of Bishop Timon, it is hoped that the generous editor of the *Express* will publish his letter as inserted in the Buffalo *Gazette* for April 4th, 1843.*

"'A SUBSCRIBER.'

"The following document will close the evidence now offered to the public:

"Extract from a letter written by J. A. Vandyke, Esq., a Protestant lawyer of high standing, to Bishop Le Fevre, of Detroit, on a case very similar to that of the church of St. Louis, in Buffalo:

"'Mr. and Mrs. Beaubien donated the land on which the German Catholic church is erected. I prepared the deed; it ran from the donors directly to yourself, (Bishop Le Fevre,) as acting Bishop, and to the Bishop who should succeed you in this diocese, and to his successors as such Bishop, being and holding according to the rites of the Church. It was in trust for the use of a German Catholic congregation, worshiping and to worship according to the rites and ceremonies of the Church. There

* See page 109.

existed at the time of the deed, since, and still exists, a statute in this State providing that a given number of stated hearers of a congregation may take certain proceedings, give notice, elect trustees, and fully incorporate themselves, and that, on becoming incorporated, the whole of the church property, etc., by whomsoever held in whatsoever manner or name, for the use of such congregation, should pass to and vest in the corporation. A certain portion of the German congregation went to work and incorporated themselves, and having so done, undertook to assume and exercise control over the church affairs, and, among other things, to rent pews. You, by the appointed priest, remained in possession, continued the exercise of full control, and to rent out the pews; a pew being held by one under you, was claimed by a tenant under the incorporation; his claim, and attempt to enforce it, *vi et armis*, being successfully resisted, he brought suit to gain possession of his alleged rights; it then and thus became necessary to try titles.

"'We contended that the deed, on its face, was one of special trusts, that it was a contract, etc., which prevented all interference by the statutory regulations and corporation thereunder. But we were desirous to test the principle and fix the rule in the State; a principle so important to your church, and going to the right of its existence here in its integrity and uncrippled exercise. We therefore claimed—That the *canon law* constituted part of the discipline, rules and regulations of the Catholic Church; that discipline, as well as faith, made up the Church; that it was part of that law, and hence of the Church; that the Church property could not be vested in laymen; that such was the decree of the Council of Baltimore, which itself was a mere declaration of the old canon law; that although the courts of this country would not regard the canon law of the land, yet that they would regard and enforce it as a matter of contract between church members, as part of the discipline and government of the Church, where it did not come into collision with the laws of the country. We claimed that, whenever the Church existed unfettered by the arm of temporal power, usage and custom were in accordance with the said rule of the canon law; that, in fact, no Catholic could in conscience thus join in such incorporation; that the thing was against his duty and religion; that it was fraud upon the Church and the rights of members who refused to join this faction; that said statute was only permissive in its nature; that it gave the privilege to persons and churches, who could properly avail themselves thereof, to become incorporated, but never could be construed to compel members of a church to join in an act against their religion and duty, and with a faction banded against their ministers and faith, or suffer the penalty of seeing the church property wrested from them; that if such things could be, it would be, in fact, denying the freedom of conscience and the free exercise of religion and worship of God, and would be unconstitutional, if held to apply. We proved that such was the canon law; we succeeded in obtaining judgment in the court below, sustaining us in every point; and the case going up to the Supreme Court, we recently obtained a full affirmation; thus affording to you a shield and protection of the most invaluable character.

"'As regards the information which Bishop Timon asks of you, I will briefly say: A deed is made by a donor to the church, he vests the title thereto in the Bishop, according to the law of the Church. All persons who join that church, in joining, ascribe to, and agree to be governed by, not only the faith, but also the discipline of that church. A court of law, in deciding as to the rights between litigant parties will look at that discipline as the contract. It will be seen that Catholics cannot incorporate themselves under such a law, and for such a purpose. The very attempt to do so excommunicates themselves; they are at once at war with the Church. The thing is a fraud upon the Church. The statute must be held inapplicable to a church with such a discipline and rule. And the attempt to make such an application is an attempt to prevent them from the free and unrestricted right of worshiping God according to the dictates of their own conscience.'

"If a Protestant lawyer thus speaks, and if a Protestant jury, and Protestant judges of the Supreme Court sustain him, should Catholics be less just?

(A.)

"As answer to the above plain documents, many letters full of insult and void of proof, appeared in some German papers of Buffalo, the parties even descending so low as to use the *Luegen Feind*, a scurrilous infidel gazette. The Bishop counseled his clergy not to answer such unchristian effusions. W. B. Lecouteulx, Esq., who, for long years, has not approached the sacraments, and who now, as in the time of Bishop Hughes, courts the unenviable position of leader in the war against Church discipline, published, from time to time, statements either greatly misrepresented or entirely false. Though the Bishop often and publicly explained to him how the law and practice stood in France, and offered him French books, in which that law and practice were laid down in the very words of the French legislation, still this unhappy gentleman dared to say in his letter of June 28th, 1851: 'The majority of the congregation being natives of France, *where all church property belongs to the people, who have the administration of it,* they expressed a wish that their church should be administered in the same manner.' He proceeds to state how they were incorporated, taking care to tell us that the corporation was, as indeed it is, in the most odious sense, 'a close corporation.' He tells us how soon the trustees began this sad work, the Bishop and the priests have all the blame; the trustees could do no wrong! He adds a sneer, to insinuation, which all know to be perfectly false, 'that Bishop Hughes was forced by a higher power (Rome,) to retrace his steps, through the interference of a higher power, and a few concessions on our part, (for the clergy can never be wrong,) a priest was reinstated in our church.' *See document No.* 1. Finding that the Bishop would not notice these effusions, in the Spring of 1851, after several acts of violence, and some interments against the laws of the church, the party presented to the Common Council a petition, document No. 2, to obtain exclusive control of the graveyard. The Bishop has thought it his duty to present document No. 3 to the Common Council at the same time a great number of faithful Germans presented to the Council document No. 4. But the party continued to misrepresent, and to invent. Until the Very Rev. P. Bede published document No. 5, no answer has been attempted to the plain statement he gives. May God grant that many upright and generous persons, who are deceived by a few interested and crafty men, may be undeceived by this simple narrative of facts."

No. 1.

ADDITIONAL DOCUMENTS AND NOTICES ON ST. LOUIS CHURCH.

"' BUFFALO, June 28, 1851.

"' *To the Editor of the Buffalo Morning Express:*

"'*Dear Sir:* In this letter of 'A Subscriber,' which I trace to the Reverend Francis Guth, formerly pastor of St. Louis church, and now one of the Vicars General of this diocese, our congregation is violently taxed with falsehood, which could easily be returned to its author, but which a gentleman, who respects himself, cannot do; therefore I will limit my answer to the simple relation of the causes which have brought so much spiritual severity upon our congregation.

"'Many years ago, when Buffalo was yet in its infancy, my late and much regretted father, Louis Lecouteulx, desirous to have a church in which to worship his Creator according to his persuasion, gave an extensive property on Main street, on which to erect a Catholic church and make a cemetery; he gave besides another valuable property on Delaware street, to be leased into building lots, so as to make a perpetual revenue for said church. The deed was given in trust to the Right Reverend John Dubois, then Bishop of the Diocese of New York, and to his successors in office.

"'The Catholics in Buffalo being but few at that time, and generally poor, a small church was erected on the premises given; but their number increasing rapidly by daily emigration from all parts of Europe, it became necessary to think seriously of building a larger church; but their poverty was for some time a great obstacle to its accomplishment. However, through the greatest exertions on their part, and generous donations by some of the inhabitants of this city, the present fine church of St. Louis was erected. The majority of the congregation being natives of France, *where all church property belongs to the people, who have the administration of it*, they expressed the wish that their church should be administered in the same manner, and to which, my worthy father consenting, also the Right Rev. Bishop Dubois, a Frenchman by birth, who had received the deed in trust, our church was incorporated according to the laws of this State upon religious corporation, *and under a close act of incorporation*, the 2d day of December, A. D. 1838; and from that day the trust of the property fell into the hands of the people, who had the management of its temporal affairs, and who enjoyed it *fully and peaceably* until the decease of their venerable and much regretted Bishop, the Right Rev. John Dubois.

"'The Rt. Rev. Bishop Hughes having succeeded him in office, we were left quiet but a few months, when faults began to be found with the administration of trustees; we were told that 'Church property being for the use of God, belonged to God; that laymen were improper persons to administer it; that it belonged to the clergy.' Our resistance in maintaining our rights caused our priests to be withdrawn from our church, and for two years we were deprived of all spiritual succor! At the end of that time of unspeakable misery to our families, through the interference of a higher power, and a few concessions on our part to save appearance, (for the clergy can never be wrong,) a priest was reinstated in our church, and we remained in peace until the Diocese of New York was divided into three dioceses, and Buffalo being the See of one, the Right Rev. Timon became our Bishop, who, after a short time, followed the same course as did his predecessor, and who found no way to get us to his wishes but by sending Jesuits to our church, and appointing one our pastor!' From that day mischief grew rapidly, and division appeared among us; pastoral letters were frequently read and enforced by commentaries from our Jesuit pastor, said Bishop claiming his right of trust, as given by my father. At last, no doubt as an experiment, the Bishop had one of his pastoral letters read, in which he informed the congregation *that he had dismissed our trustees and appointed others, of whom he gave the names!* This act, which nothing can justify, caused a spontaneous meeting of the congregation to take place, in which respectful but firm resolutions were adopted and transmitted to the Bishop, maintaining our trustees in office and rejecting those appointed by him. From that moment war was seriously engaged. On the Sunday following, another pastoral letter was read by our Jesuit pastor, who, in his commentaries to enforce the Bishop's rights, insulted the congregation by calling them liars and other such gentle expressions, until he exasperated the people and made them forget that they were in the house of the Lord; an act always to be deplored. Quiet being soon restored, said Jesuit pastor took occasion of it to invite those in favor of the Bishop (otherwise his wishes,) to remain in the church to be counted, and the others to go out, which again caused some disorder. The consequence of all this has been the withdrawal of the clergy from our church, and for these last two months we have been deprived of Divine service and all spiritual succor!

"'In the hope that the Right Rev. Bishop would reflect upon such a state of things, and relent upon his unjust severity toward us, we continued to frequent our church to pray in common, which, in 'A Subscriber's' letter, is called an act of 'uncatholic and schismatic worship!' What! to pray God in common in a consecrated church is uncatholic and schismatic worship? To what days are we then come to, that such things can be said in a country like this?

"'Since I am on the Rev. Francis Guth's letter, I am happy to see him affirm so positively that 'it is false that Bishop Timon has excommunicated any one from the St. Louis church;' yet I cannot make out the difference which he tries to establish between an excommunication and the interdiction which he says the Bishop has been obliged to pronounce against our church. My full belief is that it amounts to the same thing.

"'As to the Right Reverend Bishop Hughes' letter, which you have been begged to give a new insertion, I will observe that it is dated the *fourth* of April, 1843, and having answered it at the time, further comment upon it would be useless, particularly, belonging as it does to a controversy which took place so many years ago, and which has been satisfactorily settled between the parties it concerned.

"'I will conclude this already very long letter with saying, that several attempts have been made with Bishop Timon to bring him to better feelings toward our congregation, but in vain. 'Submit to your Bishop,' was the only answer that could be obtained! Myself, for one, took care to explain to him that our act of incorporation being *a close one*, it required the unanimity of the congregation to alter it or annul it, and that my firm belief was that it could never take place. His answer to me was: 'I cannot change my dispositions; a church is already in the course of erection for the dissenters from yours, and if it is not sufficient, one, or even two more shall be built, so as to leave but few persons in your church, who may then become Protestants if they please.'

"'We can now but hope to put a stop to such warfare upon incorporated religious congregations; the legislature of this State will, one day to come, and perhaps not far distant, see fit to prohibit the clergy from holding Church property, as it exists all through France and many other parts of Europe.

"'Very respectfully, yours,

"'W. B. LECOUTEULX.'"

No. 2.

ST. LOUIS CHURCH CEMETERY.

"The following petition, in relation to the Cemetery connected with St. Louis church, in this city, was presented to the Common Council, read, and ordered printed in the city papers:

"'*To the Hon. the Common Council of the city of Buffalo,*

"'GREETING: The undersigned, trustees of the St. Louis Catholic church, in this city, for themselves, and in behalf of the other members of this congregation, incorporated according to the laws of this State, on the 2d day of December, A. D. 1838, would very respectfully represent to your honorable body, that in the year 1832, when the cholera was threatening to invade this city, the Common Council rendered an ordinance prohibiting the burial of dead persons within the city limits, which said prohibition deprived your petitioners of the use of a burial ground given them by one of their fellow members, the late Louis Lecouteulx.

"'At that time, said congregation having but just finished the erection of their church, and being too poor to purchase another cemetery, their hard case was submitted to the Common Council by Alderman White; which, in consideration of their precarious situation, the damage sustained in being deprived of the use of their burial ground, and furthermore, upon that principle, that as tax-payers they would have to contribute toward the payment for any purchase made by the city, adopted a resolution granting your petitioners (the St. Louis church being the only one of that persuasion in the city,) a piece of land to be used as a cemetery, being part of a certain tract of land bought by the city of Wm. T. Miller and others, and situated out of its limits. At the time of said grant, the congregation of the St. Louis church not being yet incorporated, Dyre Tillinghast, Esq., then city clerk, inquired of the late Louis Lecouteulx in the name of whom the conveyance for said grant was to be made, who told him, 'that having himself made grants of lands to said congregation, he had conveyed the title *in trust* to Right Reverend John Dubois, Catholic

Bishop of the Diocese of New York, and that he thought that the conveyance for said grant made by the city should be executed in the same manner;' which was effectually done, but with an unfortunate omission, the words IN TRUST *not being inserted in said conveyance.*

"'The consequence of that unfortunate omission for your petitioners is, that the Right Reverend Bishop Timon, now Catholic Bishop of the new See of Buffalo, has lately claimed said cemetery as his own, turned out our grave-digger and appointed another, and otherwise having taken the whole control of said premises, permitting to be buried there only those he pleases, and mostly from congregations not in existence in the city at the time of the grant, to the exclusion of that of the church of St. Louis, for which it was intended, and creating himself a revenue out of said cemetery, *by charging a fee of two dollars for each body buried there!*

"'That Bishop Timon should buy lands (as he has already done,) to make cemeteries, and speculate upon the sale of them into small lots to those willing to buy them, your petitioners have nothing to say; but when that spirit of speculation extends to that cemetery given by the city for the use of our congregation, surely we have a right to complain, and to seek redress at the hands of the donors.

"'The congregation of the St. Louis church, since the demise of their worthy Bishop, John Dubois, have been sadly tormented by his successors in office, for their resistance to annul their act of incorporation. They are now under the displeasure of Bishop Timon for no other motive; and, as a last experiment, to bring them to obedience to his arbitrary will, he has thought fit to withdraw the clergy from their church, and by so doing to deprive them of all those consolations derived from religion.

"'Your petitioners can but hope that your honorable body will see fit, as grantors, to give them that relief which they claim, by enforcing the use of the grant as intended by the city, or by any other measures which your honorable body may think fit, so that the congregation of the St. Louis church may re-enter into the

(10)

full possession and control of their cemetery, where the remains of their friends have been deposited for the last twenty years. And your petitioners will ever pray and feel grateful for your so doing.

     "'J. HABERSTRO,
     '"JOHN KOCH,
     "'GEORGE ZIMMERMAN,
     "'HENRICH ENTRUF,
     "'MATHIAS HAUSLE,
     "'ALLOISUS ALLENBRAND,
     "'GEORGE FISHER.'"

No. 3.

"'*To the Hon. the Mayor and City Council of Buffalo:*

"'*Gentlemen:* Profound respect for your honorable body induces me now to act contrary to the resolution I had taken, never more to notice the misrepresentations of men who wish to belong to our Church, provided that Church consent to be taught and ruled by them. They inform your honorable body 'that Bishop Timon has *lately* claimed said cemetery as his own.' Now I have *lately* claimed nothing more than I, and my predecessors, claimed from the beginning.

"'On the 19th of February, 1848, W. B. Lecouteulx, Esq., stopped me in the street to inform me that he was about handing in a petition to your honorable body. After reading it, I told him that it contained many things that were not true, others misrepresented or exaggerated; and that, further, I held the deed of that cemetery. He came to my house, read the deed, and I heard no more of an attempt to appropriate to a small fraction of the Catholics of Buffalo what had been given for all. On the 2d of March, 1833, the Honorable Mayor made a deed to Bishop Dubois of the land in question. Different congregations were formed from those who, in March, 1833, worshiped in St. Louis church. Those of St. Patrick's church first migrated, but still retained their rights on the cemetery; and about five years ago the Irish Catholics made a collection for repairing the fence. The Germans of St. Mary's church erected a poor shelter, in which they could worship in peace, when the trustees forced Bishop Hughes to withdraw the priest from St. Louis church; and, though those Germans subsequently bought a graveyard, yet they never renounced their rights. St. John's church had equal claims. St. Peter's withdrew, with the *then* pastor of St. Louis church, (the Rev. Mr. Guth,) when he and they found the yoke of the trustees too heavy. St. Michael's church, too, was formed from St. Louis. The present pastor was pastor of St. Louis church, when in the peaceable discharge of his duty he was insulted in the church, ordered out, and menaced. He retired meekly, bearing with him the holy sacrament; but neither he nor his flock abandon their just rights.

"'In August, 1849, I received information from St. Louis church that the old graveyard was full; then, on the 15th of August, 1849, I consecrated as a graveyard, a piece of ground which had been purchased for another object. Publicly, and before a large concourse of people, I read aloud the rules which should govern the allocation of lots. They were: 1st, That the poor should have graves free of charge; 2d, That as the land had been bought and fenced in, *not by contributions or by public money*, but by funds advanced by *one individual*, those who had means should pay a moderate rate for graves; that the money thus obtained would go to liquidate the debt on the graveyard, and that, as soon as that debt was paid, the revenue accruing from subsequent sales should be applied solely to keeping the cemetery in order and adorning it.

"'The whole amount received, up to this time, from that new cemetery, is less than one-third of the sum advanced on it.

"'Having been warned that it was no longer decent to bury in the old cemetery, I told the pastor of St. Louis church that it should be closed, but that if Catholics, *from any parish of the city*, greatly wished, through affection for the dead there interred, to be buried near their friends, he, the pastor of St. Louis church, might give permission; requiring, however, two dollars for each grave, and retaining the money thus received to form a small fund, which should be solely employed in keeping up the fences, lest, in some years, hogs and cattle might rummage amidst the graves of the dead. But I was soon informed that I was deceived as to the state of the graveyard. I then revoked that order, and burials ever since have been going on as before, without charge. This the trustees of St. Louis church well knew. Well did they know that I never received a cent from that cemetery, that I never sought it; yet they dare tell you that Bishop Timon permits to be buried there only those he pleases, to the exclusion of the church of St. Louis, creating himself a revenue of the said cemetery. May God have mercy on men who can descend to such means!

"'With profound respect, honorable gentlemen, your most obedient, humble servant,

"'+JOHN TIMON, *Bishop of Buffalo.*'"

No. 4.

"'BUFFALO, April 5, 1852.

"'*To the Hon. Common Council of the City of Buffalo:*

"'The undersigned, who were members of St. Louis church of Buffalo, at the time the deed hereinafter referred to was given, do respectfully remonstrate against your honorable body taking any action on the petition of the trustees of said church, relative to the Catholic burying ground.

"'It is with feelings of deep regret that we are called upon to act in this matter. Many years since we emigrated to the village of Buffalo, here to make this our homes, where we could enjoy the religion of our fathers. About that time, the Hon. Louis Lecouteulx made a donation of a very large piece of land, sufficient for church and burying ground purposes for a long time yet to come, had not your predecessors prohibited the use of said ground for burial purposes. At this time there was but one

Catholic church in Buffalo, organized under the Bishopric of New York; this was then and is now called the St. Louis church, in which the French, German, Irish, Italian, and English Catholics all worshiped the same God, and kneeled at the same altar. At this time, on the 2d March, 1833, the city of Buffalo, by Ebenezer Johnson, Mayor, etc., Dyre Tillinghast, Clerk, under the corporate seal of said city, for the consideration of five dollars in the deed expressed, conveyed to John Dubois, Roman Catholic Bishop of New York, and to his successors in the holy office of Bishop, in trust forever for the sole and only uses of a Roman Catholic burial ground, eighty-eight feet front of land, running back to the road, etc., (being the land which has been used for that purpose since the day of the grant,) which deed was, on the 4th April, 1833, recorded in Erie County Clerk's office, in liber 20 of deeds, at page 455, to which we beg leave to refer. From the day of the said grant until the present time, the Catholics of Buffalo, who have now, independent of St. Louis church, seven church organizations, viz: St. Patrick's, St. Mary's, St. John's, St. Michael's, St. Peter's, St. Mary's of the Lake, and St. Joseph's, which churches have been organized by members of St. Louis church, who, for convenience and brotherly love, have aided in erecting such church edifices, and who are all Roman Catholics, and owe ecclesiastical allegiance to the Right Rev. John Timon, Bishop of Buffalo, and successor of the venerable and departed John Dubois, late Bishop of New York.

"'Our kindred and friends lie buried in said grounds; our wives, our children, there rest in peace, and where we wish that our bodies may be interred. In said ground our wives, children, kindred and friends have found a common resting place; by your grant we are entitled to rest there. Nearly twenty years since you done one of the most solemn acts you could perform; you donated to us the right to have our bodies interred by the side of our wives and children.

"'You are now called upon by the trustees of St. Louis church to act disgraceful in the sight of God and man, and say you, the city of Buffalo, have repudiated your act and deed, and have permitted a self-constituted body of priestless men, without any ecclesiastical power or authority, to assume the control of that which now belongs to, and is held in trust for, the members of seven churches, regularly organized.

"'We admit that we have reason to believe, and do believe, that the grave-digger has been dismissed. We do not know the reason, or when the same was done; but we do know that this same man left the bodies of the dead so near the surface of the ground, that your honorable body was compelled, at a large expense, to cover the same with earth during the Summer of 1849. If he was not discharged for this reason, he should have been.

"'In regard to pay for interment, all we can say is, that the deposed grave-digger has, for nearly eighteen years, charged for his services about double what is charged in other grounds, and we deny most unequivocally that any other charge has been made for interments.

"'With this information before you, we ask who is right?

"'Very respectfully, your ob't servants.'"

Here follow the names of forty-four members.

"'*Mr. Editor:* Bishop Timon adheres to his resolution of not noticing the misstatements of a gentleman who insists on remaining a Roman Catholic, but who has long neglected to practice its most sacred duties. To me it seems that the Bishop is over delicate in his views of charity. To me it seems that, as some may be deceived, misrepresentation tending to foment division and strife ought to be contradicted. Extracts from a few letters will suffice for this. The first is from P. A. Lecouteulx, Esq., received by Bishop Timon in August, 1851, with permission to make it public. Delicacy for the feelings of a gentleman in this city, induced the Bishop not to use that permission. I lately, with difficulty, obtained leave to copy it, and now give extracts to the public:

"*Right Rev. Sir:* If hitherto I have not intervened in the difficulty which exists between you and the Germans of the congregation of St. Louis, it was in hopes that, touched by your forbearance, they would yield, acknowledging your authority and the inviolable rights which you and your successors have over the church of St. Louis and its dependencies. Hence I waited till now. But now that you are forced to interdict the church of St. Louis, (having also read in the daily papers that the trustees of St. Louis church maintained that its temporal property ought to remain where my father, L. F. Lecouteulx, the founder of that church, had placed it, namely, in the trustees, intimating thereby that it was due to his memory to maintain his will,) I consider that I would be culpable if I remained silent longer, without raising my voice to refute the shameless calumnies spread about against you by a faction of the German congregation of that church. I also thought it my duty to publish the wishes of my father, and to demand a strict fulfillment. Previously to the year 1829, the Roman Catholics were not very numerous; they were French, Germans, and Irish. My father having requested of Bishop Dubois a priest for the Catholics of Buffalo, received him into his house, and placed at his disposal a room in which mass was said. This place soon became too small. My father made then a donation to Bishop Dubois and to his successors, of lots for the use of a Roman Catholic church, and for the establishment of a school, a Presbytery, etc. The Catholics, French, German, and Irish, caused immediately a small church to be built at common expense; they also built the priest's house, and some time after a school house. Besides the lots alluded to, my father gave money for these buildings. The Catholic population having rapidly increased, and the church not being able to contain them, the Irish formed a congregation apart; but as they had, in common, concurred in the erection of this church, my father, through a sense of justice which always characterized him, made donation of a lot to this congregation. St. Louis church remained with the French and Germans, but the population having rapidly increased, the old church became too small, and the congregation was obliged, in 1838–39, to build upon the same site the vast edifice which now stands there. The building was constructed under the direction of Rev. Alexander Pax, and finished by the aid of voluntary contributions, and by the joint efforts of all the Catholics, and even of strangers.

"'Every thing went on well, and the most perfect peace prevailed between the French and Germans up to the death of my father, which took place in 1840. Disorder then began. (*The date fixed by Bishop Hughes for the beginning of troubles is* 1841.) The trustees commenced to arrogate undue power to themselves, justifying their illegal usurpation on the ground of having been incorporated, and having then acquired the exclusive right over the church and its dependencies, saying that in this they fulfilled the will of my father. I can affirm that this demand of incorporation has been made without the concurrence of my father, who, as the founder, ought, at least, to have been consulted. I am even led to think that he was ignorant of it. He had, indeed, often spoken to me of his desire to have Marguillis or Counselors, such as we had in France. But I affirm, that never did he wish that trustees or administrators (especially by election,) should be appointed and be invested with a power thus repugnant to the Holy Roman Catholic Church, for which he had the greatest respect; if such an intention had been manifested to him, he would have opposed it with all his might. Further, he knew that, in the position of the congregation of St. Louis church, composed in part of French and Germans, it was necessary that the power should be in the hands of the Bishop and of the pastor of the church, in order to maintain the just rights of all, and to prevent the majority, which was already German, from trampling on the rights of his compatriots. It is evident that it was for this my father made the donation of the property to Bishop Dubois and to his successors;* the trustees knew, as well as I did, this will of my father; hence it was only after his death that they laid claim to the property and administration of the church. It

---

*"The act authorizing incorporation then existing."

is useless, sir, for me to retrace here what has been the deplorable consequences of the unhappy system adopted by the trustees. You have developed them better than I could in your historical document relative to this affair. I shall not, then, limit myself to its sad consequences for the French.

"'At the time of the nomination of trustees by election, the Germans of the congregation of St. Louis were most numerous; the French never obtained but a weak minority; finally the French, disgusted at the vexations they had to suffer, withdrew from the elections.' (*Mr. Lecouteulx here enters at large on various complaints of the French against the trustees; some of them were submitted to the Bishop for arbitration. Mr. Lecouteulx complains that the trustees violated the agreement then entered into, and continues:*) 'It would be too tedious to enumerate all the vexations which the German trustees inflicted on the French part of the congregation; they became intolerable, and forced the French to quit their church during your absence, with the pastor of St. Louis church, who could no longer risk the dignity of his ministry by suffering such usurpations. It is evident from what I write that there has been a determination since my father's death to get possession of the property of the church, and to chase away the French. To attain this, the most iniquitous arts have been resorted to, and, to justify all, they dare to say that they execute the will of my father. This assertion is an outrage on his memory, and I regret it with indignation.

(Signed,) "'P. A. LECOUTEULX.'"

"W. B. Lecouteulx several times has published, in our city papers, the assertion that in France all the Church property belongs to the people, who have the administration of it. Now, before and since his first publication of this misstatement, in presence of several respectable gentlemen and in my presence, Bishop Timon repeated to Mr. Lecouteulx the very words of the French laws upon this subject, and invited Mr. Lecouteulx to read the text in the original French, the Bishop adding that he had several works published in France, giving, *in extenso*, the

French laws on church property; but Mr. Lecouteulx did not wish to read the laws, that he might with a quiet conscience assert what suited his purpose.

"After calling the Bishop *(administrateur ne)* administrator *ex officio* of church property, the French laws provide as follows:

In parishes of more than five thousand souls there shall be nine counselors, if the population be less than five thousand there must be five counselors; when the counselors are nine, the Bishop shall name five and the Prefect four; when there are only five counselors, the Bishop shall name three and the Prefect two. The pastor shall always be, *ex officio*, the first member of the council; he may depute his vicar to fill his place. The Mayor also shall be a member and have the second place; but if he be not a Catholic, he must name a Catholic who will fill his place. The council shall meet four times a year. It cannot meet oftener but by the authorization of the Bishop or the Prefect. The council names the marguilliries, or what we would call the acting trustees. Vacancies in the council are filled by the remaining members. If the council neglect to fill a vacancy for one month after such vacancy occurs, the Bishop then names to that vacancy. Reparations of any moment cannot be made without the approbation of the Bishop. That of the Prefect is also necessary, particularly if help from the public treasury is required.'

"The statements about to be made were volunteered by the writer, as Bishop Timon had no correspondence, mediate or immediate, with Mr. Pax, nor had he the least expectation of receiving any communication from him.

"Extract of a letter from Rev. A. Pax, dated 4th September, 1851, from Dubling Depart. of Moselle, France:

"'*Right Rev. Sir:* Deign to permit a priest, who for eight years was a missionary in Buffalo, and under whom the church of St. Louis was built, to express to you his sentiments of condolence for the grief which that church causes to your paternal heart. Permit me also to compliment you upon the wise firmness and apostolic zeal with which you defend the rights of the church from the usurpation of the trustees. I learned with extreme sorrow the excesses to which arrogant impiety impelled those trustees and their adherents. And also with joy I read the letter by which you *interdicted* the profaned church of St. Louis. This measure was necessary in order to terminate usurpations and schismatic pride. I pray to God that He would deign to open the eyes of those senseless men, and call them from their wanderings to sincere repentance.

"'A sad prelude to these events was, that Bishop Dubois, of venerable memory, always believed that Mr. Lecouteulx had ceded the lot to him personally. Hence he strongly urged me to accept that mission and to build that church. 'For,' said he, 'the usurpations of trustees are not there to be feared, because the ground belongs to me.' Were it not for this conviction, I would not have built the church, of which each stone was watered with my sweat. The church was not yet finished before I was undeceived. Then began the domineering pretensions and the usurpation of the trustees, and their stubborn opposition to the kind and zealous efforts of Bishop Hughes. The vexation I had to undergo injured my health, and, more than my other labors, forced me to return to my native climate.

(Signed,) "'PAX, *Cure of Dubling.*'"

———

"P. A. Lecouteulx, Esq., residuary legatee of L. Lecouteulx's estate, declares that his father never wished such a corporation; Rev. Mr. Pax declares that Bishop Dubois never wished it. A Protestant lawyer, before the Supreme Court, quotes the universal teaching and legislation of the Roman Catholic Church, and says: 'It will be seen that Catholics cannot incorporate themselves under such a law, and for such a purpose. The very attempt to do so excommunicates them; they are at once at war with the Church.' The Supreme Court decides in favor of the Bishop according to those principles.

"'Wherever the affairs of St. Louis church, or your trustee system, was mentioned, all, both the clergy and the laity, were greatly surprised at the wondrous pretensions of congregations and Catholic individuals to the ownership of Church property. In all Europe, in modern schools, or in schools of former days, wherever common law is taught, it is an undisputed principle that the Church of Christ, Christ as embodied in the Church, is the only legitimate owner of Church property. Not some members of the Church, nor any particular association of Church members, but the Bishop, not *in his private capacity*, but as *he who is divinely* appointed to rule and govern the Church of God, is the only legitimate administrator of Church property.'

"Thus think Bishops, clergy, ninety-nine out of a hundred Catholics in America, and nine hundred and ninety-nine out of a thousand Catholics in the world. Are we to believe them, or Mr. ———? The question is not whether the Church is right or wrong in her faith and discipline; but whether, in our free country, she is free to exist, according to her faith and discipline; whether a minority may or may not have the power of forcing the majority, either to observe regulations directly adverse to the spirit and laws of the Church, or to abandon their just rights in the joint occupancy of Church property, and, for conscience sake, and for peace sake, build, at their own expense, poor shelters in which they may worship unmolested. I entreat the public to notice a fact that stares each one in the face. Bishop Timon had rights to St. Louis church: like the Bishop of Detroit, he might have maintained his position; but he wished not to have litigation, even with a small and misguided portion of his flock; he abandoned the possession of St. Louis church and its dependencies to the men who thirsted for power; he aided to build, or formed poor churches, in which the large majority of those who not long since worshiped in St. Louis church now worship in peace. Yet, lately, *for a poor grave yard already filled*, in which even the refractory members of St. Louis church were maintained by the

Bishop in equal rights with other Catholics, the trustees, after acts of violence, during which, at least, one body was lawlessly interred! after uttering, in their petition to the council, false accusations against their Bishops, have instituted suit!

"PETER BEDE."

---o---

CHAPTER IV.

THE BISHOP AND THE MENDICANT.—BISHOP TIMON VISITS BALTIMORE TO GET SISTERS FOR AN HOSPITAL AND ASYLUM.—RESOURCES.—SISTERS ARRIVE.—HOSPITAL OPENED.—ATTACKED BY REV. JOHN C. LORD, A PROTESTANT MINISTER.—DEFENDED BY REV. B. O'REILLY.—THE ORPHAN ASYLUM.

GREAT men are highly distinguishable for some prominent characteristic in their genius. Some excel for their magnanimity and piety; some for administrative and executive abilities; in some again moral courage and a zeal for the dissemination of the principles of revealed religion predominate; and so on to the end of the catalogue.

In the subject of this memoir, however, charity was the predominant characteristic. Indeed, to that extent had nature endowed him with this virtue, that sympathy for the sufferings and miseries of humanity, whether orphan or sick, indigent or abandoned, led him to make the most extravagant sacrifices, even to his personal attire, in order to wipe away the orphan's tear, or rescue from degradation or want the infirm and old. It is related by his physician, James P. White, M. D., that one day, whilst standing with Bishop Timon on the threshold of the latter's residence, engaged in conversation, a poor and wretchedly clad man approached them, and pitifully solicited alms. The Bishop, after asking some questions, noticed that the man had no shirt, and summoning the housemaid, directed her to bring down one of his shirts from his bureau drawer. The servant hesitated, but finally went up stairs on her errand. In a few minutes she returned, but without the shirt, and informed the Bishop there were none left in his bureau drawer.

"Why, how can that be?" remarked the Bishop. "It was only a short time ago that I had several new ones made, and now they are all gone! Have you not made a mistake?"

"No, Bishop. There *were* some in your room, as you say, but I gave them away to other poor folks, as you directed me to do. You have the last of them on you."

"Is it possible?" replied Bishop Timon, pausing for a few moments to think on the matter; and, as he gradually recalled the almost forgotten circumstance, an air of satisfaction overspread his features, and at the same time he took from his pocket some money, handed it to the mendicant, and bade him go and procure the necessaries of which he stood most in need.

Overflowing with the exuberance of this virtue for the miseries of his neighbor, Bishop Timon now began to look about him for a suitable site on which to erect an orphan asylum and an hospital.

For this purpose, in March, 1848, he visited Baltimore, and obtained a promise of two Communities of Sisters for the institutions just mentioned. It will seem strange to many of us, at the present day, if we pause awhile and reflect upon the resources then at the Bishop's command, with which he had to commence his plans and purposes, and contrast those poor beginnings with the magnificent progress of these institutions to-day; it will seem strange to many of us, how he has succeeded so successfully in stamping the impress of his genius upon the few plastic materials then at his command, and his success will compel candid minds to rank him among the most remarkable men of the age, irrespective of the character of his calling.

In 1848, the population of Buffalo was not then as large as now, nor were its commercial and manufacturing interests as largely developed, although the city from various causes was rapidly swelling in point of numbers, and its wealth proportionally increasing with its population. There were but three Catholic churches in this city then, but by no means the splendid edifices that adorn our streets now; the wealth of the Catholic portion of the people was limited, whilst the seeds of discord, planted in the breasts of many by the prejudices and misrepresentations of disaffected persons, in a certain measure served to dampen enthusiasm in the Catholic heart. Besides, the Bishop personally was poor; his acquaintance and influence with men of position had not as yet any availability; and hence, restricted on all sides, except so far as his confidence in the Providence of a good God, and aided by that indomitable and indefatigable energy of purpose, that had frequently converted more discouraging circumstances into harvests golden with promise and reward, he resolutely laid his plans, placed his shoulder to the wheel, and triumphed above the insinuations and mistrusts of the weak-minded.

On the 3d of June, 1848, the promised Communities of Sisters arrived in Buffalo. There were in all six Sisters of Charity, three for an orphan asylum and three for an hospital.

It was with considerable difficulty that a suitable place could be obtained in which to commence the practices of their vocation. At length, after some trouble, the house where St. Vincent's Orphan Asylum now stands, was prepared for them. But there was no house for the hospital. This, however, he soon obtained. The site where the present imposing edifice now stands was selected, as being the most suitable to purchase, and time has since demonstrated the wisdom that made the selection. Originally its dimensions were more limited, whilst prosperity and patronage have since nobly verified the prediction of that unfortunate but heroic servant of Christ, the lamented Bernard O'Reilly,* in his defence of this institution, against the "bigoted" attacks of its opponent, Rev. John C. Lord, a Protestant minister, who, under an anonymous signature, wrote an article for the press, urging that no appropriation by the State Legislature should be given to the hospital, principally because it was sectarian in its character. The prediction,

"That the time will come, (for sober reason is not long absent at a time,) when this community will pronounce a severe, but

---

* Afterwards Bishop of Hartford, Conn., consecrated Nov. 10th, 1850, and perished at sea January, 1856, in the ill-fated steamer Arctic.

merited sentence against the Rev. John C. Lord for his action in this matter, unworthy the christian, the clergyman, and the well disposed man."

The hospital, in its flourishing condition to-day, is the mute but eloquent sentence and rebuke that may be inferred in the above prediction.

On page 252, "Missions in Western New York," we read:

"On the 21st of June, 1848, the Bishop bought from the managers of the Buffalo Orphan Asylum, the house and lot which they then occupied, as they wanted to build on a large lot, which Louis Lecouteulx, a good Catholic, had given for a General Orphan Asylum to this corporation; having subsequently put two orphans under their care, and having been refused permission to send a priest to instruct them, when well, or aid them on their death bed, he withdrew the children. The Bishop was informed that most of the children in that asylum were Catholics, but that no priest could have access to them. After getting the deed, and making the first payment, he found it difficult to get possession, when it was known that he had bought it for the Sisters of Charity and for a hospital. After fixing various days for giving possession, and failing, the Bishop, on the 5th of July, went to the Director, from whom he had bought it, and said: 'This delay is a great inconvenience, as the Sisters for this house have now no place. You say that you cannot find a suitable house; I will then take all your orphans, put the girls with the Sisters of Charity, and keep the boys in my own house; and, when you find a suitable place, you can take them back; only I will request you to leave the Catholics with me, and to take back the Protestant orphans only.' The next day they began to move, and, on the 8th of July, the Sisters entered into the hospital, in which, under God's blessings, they have saved many lives, and done an immense amount of good.

"This charity hospital had scarcely been opened over one year, when Buffalo was attacked with epidemic cholera. As no cholera hospital then existed, the Sisters of Charity promptly tendered to the City Council the use of that institution for cholera patients. All who came or were sent, were very kindly received; and, though the city soon took measures to establish a cholera hospital, yet, as the Buffalo *Medical Journal* says: 'The number of patients received in this, the city institution, was two hundred and forty-three, of which one hundred and fifteen recovered. The Sisters' Hospital, however, received one hundred and thirty-four patients, of which eighty-two recovered. Considering the character of hospital cases,' continues the *Medical Journal*, 'the results of the charity hospital, as declared by the rate of mortality, certainly affords grounds for much satisfaction. * * * We are free to say that, whatever credit is due to the institution for the large proportion of recoveries, belongs to those under whose immediate charge the institution is placed. * * * Each patient admitted to the hospital was, at once, placed under the charge of one of the Sisters, and received her unceasing and assiduous care, as long as it was requisite. Scrupulous exactness in the execution of all medical directions, and fidelity in the administration of remedies, could be confidently depended upon, together with all other attentions and appliances which the circumstances of the case might suggest. The degree of patience and endurance exhibited by the Sisters of Charity, in their unwearied labors of mercy during the period of epidemic, was a matter of astonishment, not less than of admiration. Night after night, as well as on successive days, they were at their post, never manifesting weariness or diminished zeal, and during the whole period not one was debarred by illness from the exercise of her voluntarily assumed duties.'—Buffalo *Medical Journal*, Vol. V, No. 6, pp. 319 and 332."

Thus, scarcely had the hospital been opened more than one year, than Buffalo was attacked with epidemic cholera. Now was the moment, or occasion, in which to try the temper of men's souls, and to test the utility and permanency of this noble institution. Medical journals and the files of the public press of that day, will testify in ardent terms to the heroism exhibited in behalf of suffering humanity by those self-sacrificing women,

(11)

the Sisters of Charity. No privation, no labors were too severe for those noble types of tenderness and care, the hospital Sisters of Charity.

Oh! unfaithful would be the pen that could pass over lightly the sacrifices of women who have left their happy homes, their parents' comfortable firesides, their friends and relations, to enter an arena of life variegated with so many vicissitudes and trials, and under which many a noble heart has fallen. Let the pæans and eulogies written and spoken by the tongues of even those who disagree with them in faith, be heard; and how eloquent and how sublime is the pathos that tints the phrases of gratitude and admiration uttered in behalf of the Sisters of Charity. Night after night, day after day, they were at their post of danger, fearless of the contagion, whilst others, with less christian fortitude, shrank from the slightest acquaintance with the disease.

Not only are these remarks true with regard to the Sisters of Charity at the hospital, but even the Sisters at the orphan asylum showed their devotion in caring for the little orphans rapidly gathering under their charge. From the "flats" and from other places of the city where poverty prevailed to a great extent, children were gathered together into the asylums, and rescued from destitution, misery and vice, in order to become, as they have since done, industrious and respectable members of society. Many children thus provided for were the orphans of parents who had died at the hospital from cholera, and who otherwise, if left to the mercy of the world, might have perished physically as well as morally. Silently, devotedly, and faithfully did they labor in their mission, indifferent to the vanities and allurements of the world, exhibiting a moral heroism that challenges comparison. Heroism in man, by nature the sterner sex, is noble, is sublime, especially in defence of woman; but when woman sacrifices upon the altar of duty and religion the diffidence and fears of her sex, the ties that bind her to her kindred and friends, and all the advantages and pleasures the world might afford her, oh! then this exercise of christian fortitude *transcends* sublimity; it becomes angelic. Hence we may say, without reserve, that to

Sisters of **any** religious order whatsoever in the Catholic Church, and devoted to the amelioration of the human race, too much encouragement cannot **be** given, since they are centres from which **radiate,** in all **directions,** the sweetest and most heavenly rays of christian charity.

Necessarily, an institution **commenced under** disparagements and **embarrassments, had to** struggle to gain a foothold on the confidence **of the public.** In order **to extend its field of usefulness, it required help and** resources, without which it is impossible **to support any** undertaking. **For** this purpose, **through** the assistance of **kind** friends, steps were taken to obtain **an appropriation from the State** at large, on the ground that the charities **bestowed by the Sisters** of the hospital were general and public, **and not confined to** Catholics alone; and hence, being an institution **incorporated** according to law, not sectarian in its character nor its objects, and **in which persons of every** race, clime, or creed **were received and cared for, it was no** more than just, that such an institution deserved **a share of the** public moneys, appropriated by the State for charitable purposes.

No sooner, though, had the appropriation been **asked for, than** it excited the venom **and** bigotry of a particular **class. In** the estimation of these, it was not conformable with our form of government **to** bestow appropriations on "Romish institutions," and **the public,** through the daily papers, was asked whether

"**Roman** Catholics were to be the almoners **of** Protestant **charities to the** poor and destitute? whether there was no other **way of taking care of the** sick and maimed than to turn them **over to the Sisters of Charity?** Had it come **to this, that the sick were to be neglected unless the State** endowed the **institution? If they (Protestants,) were so dependent on** Romanists, **it were high time they bestirred themselves."**

These and kindred expressions, offsprings of provoked "bigotry" and suspicion, were numerous, and were contained in a public discussion in the columns of the Buffalo *Daily Express,* **between two prominent individuals* of this city, who, as**

---

* Rev. John C. Lord, and Rev. B. O'Reilly.

champions for either side, labored, the one to undermine, the other to sustain, the existence and support of the hospital. We do not desire to resurrect the rancor and heat of controversy which, to a more or less degree, were engaged on both sides, and which, as the correspondence published in full will reveal, resulted frequently in a departure from the main topic in order to launch invectives at each other, particularly on the part of the Rev. John C. Lord, who first introduced the side and, in our opinion, irrelevant issues of "Romish superstition," "despotism," "Bloody Mary," etc., etc. No doubt time has somewhat softened the vehemence of opinion on the part of the Reverend gentleman as to the usefulness of the hospital, and served to undeceive him in regard to its "sectarian" character.

In the controversy we find it assumed that because the hospital stood on a lot deeded in the name of Bishop Timon, and because Rev. B. O'Reilly and a few Catholic laymen were a corporate body to govern and protect the institution, according to law, that therefore the hospital was sectarian in its character, and hence the appropriation asked for was an indirect application of the Romish Church for funds from the public at large. How shallow the argument. But it is not our province to go deep into detail and sift the matter; it is self-evident. Was it not plain that a religious body of women, irrespective of the church to which they belonged, who devoted their lives to caring for and nursing the sick, the poor, the lame and wounded, were worthy of encouragement, especially when it is considered that there are few who have the moral courage to sacrifice the comforts of life for this calling? What difference did it make in whose name the title of such an institution might be, provided it were incorporated according to law, and bestowed its charity upon all, irrespective of creed or clime? But time and experience have dissipated the falsity of its "sectarian character." Even this the Rev. John C. Lord will honorably admit, having been called at least twice to the hospital, if not oftener, to attend sick calls of those adhering to his church.

And when we unhesitatingly assert that the hospitals instituted under Protestant management stand no comparison with hospitals under the good Sisters of Charity, (meaning no disparagement to Protestant institutions for the good they do,) we re-echo the testimony of those who have investigated the subject; we repeat the opinion of physicians whose vocation in life bring them in direct acquaintance with the workings of such institutions. But with regard to the Buffalo hospital, the appropriation asked for was entirely proper and just, nay, even *humane*, for further reasons.

If, as it was further assumed, the appropriation was intended for the spread of Romish institutions, etc., etc., if a fear of this kind prevailed, could not an investigating committee have been appointed by the citizens to examine the account books and papers of the hospital, and find there, to the satisfaction and silence of the "great spirit of enquiry," the sources to which every cent of the money so appropriated had been applied? This mode of procedure would have been more consistent, and more in accordance with true nobility of character, than in expressing in print the *speculative* reasonings of a bigoted and prejudiced mind, thereby unjustly trying to throw a firebrand into an institution of charity filled, or nearly so, with helpless human beings, who, through their "ministering angels," the Sisters of Charity, called upon the generosity and benevolence of the American people for support and for aid. This is why it was *humane* to ask for the appropriation.

At the time the petition was in circulation for further appropriations, there were debts upon the building, in consequence of additions, repairs, enlargements and the improvements necessary in order properly to meet the increasing wants and maladies of the public generally. The beds were nothing more than pallets of straw, without sheets, until Bishop Timon, on the strength of his own credit, obtained several pieces of muslin, out of which the good Sisters managed to do the best they could.

Again it was assumed that the hospital was "a kind of nunnery;" the affidavit of a young man, once an inmate of the hospital, was produced to show that " Protestant patients in the hospital had been assailed with arguments and motives to induce them to renounce their faith." There was a shudder at the idea that the Sisters of Charity were to be the "almoners" of public charity; and it was declared that appropriations for such institutions, in which the public had no ascertained or ascertainable rights, "was not only an outrage upon the Protestant community," but even "unconstitutional."

But the result of to-day puts to shame the advocates of such nonsense. After struggles and privations, too numerous to rehearse, including such opposition as the pen of bigotry could raise, the hospital has, in the Providence of a good God, nobly triumphed above the mean insinuations and shallow sophistry of those whose casuistry was parallel with their bigotry.

The character given to the hospital, that it was "a kind of nunnery," and that it was not certain when the Sisters might be called away to another sphere of duty, was simply absurd. To have said this much, was to have betrayed an ignorance, not only in what monastic institutions consist, but even in what manner "Catholic Sisters of Charity" are associated together. John C. Lord even admitted his ignorance on this point, when he said in the discussion:

"I do not know the precise tenor of the vows of a Sister of Charity. I have *understood* they are not those of perpetual celibacy, though, I believe, it is deemed a reproach to look back; the cloister is the natural terminus of the novitiate." Then he merely *understood*, and admitted he did not know anything about what he was trying to discuss, although he undertook to call the hospital a "kind of nunnery." The affidavit alluded to, made by a young man named Charles Heinz, however much supported by the affidavits of one or two other men, may pass for what it was worth. It was only one affidavit against thousands, not of Catholics alone, but of Protestants, who could testify to the contrary. Nay, when the affidavit was made, the young man had but shortly before left the hospital, not entirely recovered from the sickness with which he had been so sick, and not entirely in his mind. He knew nothing of the English language, having been but a short time in this country, and if he did consent to make an affidavit, it seems that he acted more as an irresponsible party. But we leave the matter to the reader to infer, especially after he shall have made a careful and just estimate of testimonials of hundreds of others, who have been loud in their praises of the worthiness of the hospital in every respect, if it is a Roman Catholic institution.

The numbers who have been helped and cared for by the "Buffalo Hospital of Sisters of Charity," and whose names and places of residence may be found in the "book of record," are the most eloquent testimonials that could be referred to in vindication of the hospital against the unjust aspersions cast upon it by Rev. John C. Lord. They will prove how their false fears of "Black Ghosts," "Romish Superstition," "Nunnery," were soon dissipated after they had entered the institution. One,* who has since gone to his grave, and who, when well, as the editor of a German newspaper, was most abusive towards the hospital and the Sisters, because his reasonings were based upon false premises, could testify how, with tears in his eyes, when he himself experienced the humane treatment of the Sisters, (having subsequently been forced to ask charity of the hospital on account of sickness,) he repented of the unfavorable and unjust manner in which he had criticized them. The colored people sent from the jails and poorhouses, people of every "creed, color or country," during raging epidemics, such as cholera, persons wounded from accidents on railroads or steamboats, all can testify in more eloquent terms than our feeble pen in behalf of the interested charity, mercy and goodness of the Sisters at the hospital. Hence, how puerile and imbecile were the reflections of John C. Lord, who, (judging him by his controversy,) evidently under the cover or shield of the propositions he advanced against giving an appropriation, coveted the discussion of another issue, that of "Roman Catholicism." Any one wishing to take the labor to peruse that famous discussion, as revised and enlarged by him in a printed pamphlet afterwards, in which he challenged Rev.

---
* John Marley.

Bernard O'Reilly to a public discussion on "auricular confession," and in which he made a dying appeal to the Catholic laity, particularly urging them not to be misled by their priests, but to think for themselves, will discover the "cloven foot" of the gentleman, and infer the notoriety he sought to obtain, and will wonder that we should have paid so much notice to the matter at all. But we felt a little constrained to do so, in justice to history, particularly of an institution of which Bishop Timon was the sole originator and founder.

Rev. Bernard O'Reilly did not escape censure for his conduct in this matter. Bishop Timon, on his return from Europe, severely reprimanded him for having had any thing to do with the discussion in his absence, and remarked at the time, that the best defence that could have been made for the hospital, would have been to allow it to speak for itself, as it has since nobly done. But, thanks to the liberality of men of more enlarged views and less prejudices, the hospital received the appropriations, with which it has done immense good for the city of Buffalo and vicinity.

In the meantime, whilst the hospital was exerting and taxing its utmost energies towards caring for "cholera cases," the good Sisters at the orphan asylum also contributed towards a large share of public good. Not only (as has been already intimated,) were children provided for who had been taken from the "flats" and other places, but even children whose parents had died in the hospital from cholera and other diseases, were received into the orphan asylum, and rescued from conditions of life with which they necessarily must have become assimilated, to the detriment of their morals as well as their mental and physical being, if it had not been otherwise ordained.

Thus the first two works of charity originated in Buffalo by Bishop Timon, had gained a foothold on the soil, and despite the rude and unwelcome breezes that shook their feeble beginning, they gradually gained growth, to culminate finally into two of the finest institutions in the city.

CHAPTER V.

BISHOP TIMON AND THE ACT OF INCORPORATION.—ST. JOSEPH'S ORPHAN ASYLUM.—CORRESPONDENCE.—BISHOP TIMON TRAVELS THROUGH MEXICO, ETC.—LEARNS SPANISH.—RETURNS HOME.—LECTURES ON MEXICO.—NUNCIO BEDINI ARRIVES.—HIS DEALINGS WITH ST. LOUIS CHURCH.

Bishop Timon was an indefatigable worker. We mean to say by this that he spared neither time nor his own personal comfort to carry out his plans. This will appear so much more remarkable when, advanced in years, we find him still vigorous and indifferent to ease, and the care that old age requires.

An interesting circumstance, as an illustration of this trait in his character, will aid to corroborate our opinion.

Towards the close of the session of the Legislature, in 1851, Bishop Timon was in Albany, anxious to secure the incorporation of an institution since known as "St. Joseph's Boys' Orphan Asylum."

It was late in the session, and there seemed scarcely time to introduce and pass a bill. But the Bishop, however, after soliciting the kindness of a member to assist him, proposed to obviate the difficulty in his own way, provided the latter would give his support to the measure. The reply was of course affable and affirmative. They parted. During the long hours of the night sleep never closed the vigilant and waking eyelids of the Bishop, but poring over manuscripts and books, he could be seen silently and rapidly drawing up the required papers, until, with the dawn of morning, he finally laid his pen aside with an evident air of wearied satisfaction.

As early as possible after breakfast, with the papers in his pocket, the Bishop sought his friend, to whom he presented them, with the observation, "the papers are all ready." The latter, after examining them, introduced the requested act of incorporation, of which these papers were the original, and much to his astonishment it passed, as though the best legal talent had been employed on them.

Although not incorporated as a charitable institution until 1851, still the feeble beginning of "St. Joseph's Boys' Orphan Asylum" dates back to the year 1849.

It was during this year, in the month of August, when the cholera raged fearfully, that the first efforts were made in Buffalo for a boys' orphan asylum. Bishop Timon and his clergy were compelled to take this step, as the orphans of very poor parents, who had been swept away by the pestilence, were principally supported by them in Buffalo, until they were removed to Lancaster, in April, 1850. As has already been stated, this institution was incorporated on the 2d of August, 1851, under the title of "St. Joseph's Boys' Orphan Asylum." It continued in Lancaster until the 19th of April, 1854. At this time, the zealous Bishop most earnestly desired, (in addition to the usual branches of education,) that these orphans should learn a trade, to adapt them afterwards in life to habits of industry. The resources of a location outside of the city limits rendered this impracticable. Therefore, on the 19th of April, 1854, the orphans were removed from Lancaster to Buffalo, to a building located on Best street, but scarcely adequate to their wants and number. Here they remained, however, until August 27th, 1856, when, at the earnest solicitation of the managers of the asylum, Bishop Timon donated sixty acres of ground, contiguous to the Holy Cross Cemetery on Limestone Hill.

A few letters here given, will give the reader an idea of the zeal of the good Bishop:

"To ———.

"BUFFALO, August 26th, 1854.

"*Dear Sister:* I just returned from a visit to a part of my diocese, and about to start to visit another portion of it, when I received your letter. It is a pleasure to hear from one whom I esteem so much as a good and faithful servant of God in works of charity. I hope that you still continue to pray for me, for, alas! *I have too little time* to pray for myself.

"Your Sisters are well, the orphan asylum is full, and we have one now for boys at Lancaster.

"Recommending myself to the kind prayers of your good Sisters, I remain, in haste,

"Most respectfully,

"Your obedient and humble servant,

"✝ JOHN, *Bishop of Buffalo.*"

"To ———.

"BALTIMORE, November 15th, 1855.

"*Dear Sister*: I have received your kind letter on my return from Emmetsburgh. I was much pleased with all I saw, and you may be sure that I was much pleased to see ——— apparently in excellent health. I will try to stop at Wilmington* for a few hours, in eight or ten days, as I return to Buffalo.

"Pray for most respectfully,

"Your humble and obedient servant in Christ,

"✝ JOHN, *Bishop of Buffalo.*"

"To ———.

"BUFFALO, October 22d, 1853.

"*Dear Sister:* Many thanks for your kind letter, kind remembrance and pious prayers. Continue to pray for your old father in Christ, who will not forget you in his prayers.

"Father Burlando wrote to me from Paris, saying that the Superior General is pleased with the prospect of a foundling asylum, etc., here, but that he wishes me to wait till Spring. Hence I have not written, as I intended to request the Mother Superior to send the community she promised for that institution, of which, *no doubt, you* and ——— will form a part. Tell this, if you please, to Mother ———, and present her my respects and best wishes for time and eternity.

"Dear and respected Sister,

"Your humble and obedient servant,

"✝ JOHN, *Bishop of Buffalo.*"

*The Bishop did not stop at Wilmington, where he arrived at midnight. At daylight he came to say mass, and spent a few hours, when he left for Philadelphia, practicing such condescension to oblige a poor Sister of Charity.

"BUFFALO, February 6th, 1854.

"*Dear Sister:* It gives me great pleasure to hear from you and from *Emmetsburgh*, although I am often vexed that *Emmetsburgh* is at *Emmetsburgh*. Business calls me to Baltimore and Washington. I have just time to go, or perhaps one day more. I started as a last time to give that one day more to a trip to Emmetsburgh, but the cars were detained, and I had to hurry home again to labor. God's blessed will be done. He ordains some to labor, others to sweeter rest in Him.

"Present my respects and best wishes, that God restore health to your excellent Mother Superior. Tell her that I would vote for her canonization, not now but fifty years hence, if she would send a good book-keeper and a Sister for the pharmacy at our hospital.

"Most respectfully,
"Your humble and obedient servant in Christ,
"✠ JOHN, *Bishop of Buffalo.*"

The necessities of the diocese, as well as the new projects set on foot or about to be commenced, particularly a Cathedral, of which more will be said in the succeeding pages, induced Bishop Timon, in 1853, to pay a visit to Spain, Mexico, and other countries, in search for pecuniary aid. Although familiar with several languages, still the Bishop was not so thoroughly conversant with Spanish as to feel confident in the use of that tongue upon his travels, particularly through Spain. Accordingly, when he reached New Orleans, he took up his abode there for a time, in order to acquire a little more proficiency in the Spanish tongue. For this purpose he placed himself under the instruction of a Spanish priest. Intuitively the Bishop was an apt and ready scholar; his acquisition of knowledge upon any subject whatever was quick and decisive. This characteristic likewise predominated in him under other circumstances. In moments of emergency or necessity, when it was dangerous or even disadvantageous to procrastinate, he almost invariably adopted the safest plans, and expressed the most wise views, if he took any action in the matter at all.

Punctually every morning at six o'clock, both pupil and tutor met together for the morning's exercise. So rapid was his acquisition of this language that in a few weeks he resumed his journey, able and *confident* to satisfy all demands upon his Spanish education. Bishop Timon profited vastly on this journey, both pecuniarily and mentally.

On his return from Mexico, he gave an interesting discourse in St. Patrick's church, for the benefit of St. Vincent de Paul's Society, on his journey through that country, and as he found it. He treated the subject in a very graphic manner, and as it was considered at the time a very remarkable address, no doubt the reproduction of it in the pages of this book will not be altogether superfluous.

LECTURE ON MEXICO,

DELIVERED IN ST. PATRICK'S CHURCH,

ON SUNDAY, SEPTEMBER 15TH, 1853.

"*Fellow Christians, and Fellow Citizens:*

* * * * * * * * * *

"Not in the mere human order do I wish to consider Mexico. I am no politician. During all my life as a clergyman I have kept aloof from politics. Should any party wrong my religion, I would fly to the defence of the truth committed to my charge. In doing this, should I say a word or do a thing that might offend any party, it would only be because that word or that act was necessary to defend a sacred right, a Divine truth, from unprovoked attack. I leave the mere human order to men of this world; but much in the human order has connection with the superhuman order. The history of Mexico, as regards faith and morals, regards also eternity; regards the end where virtue is rewarded, and faith changed into the blessed vision of God. In that order alone I wish to treat my subject. I have indeed required that the blessed Sacrament be, for greater reverence, removed to the lower chapel; yet I do trust that, though not in our usual mood, neither word nor action here will be unworthy of the sacred place, or the presence of Him whom we adore.

"My stay and my position in Mexico gave me extraordinary opportunities of examining the religious state of that country. The judgment I have made upon it, with all simplicity and sincerity, I will now communicate; and, lest it might be thought that I make hasty assertions on points that have been viewed in a quite different light by some, I have taken notes, which, as far as may be needed, I beg permission to read as we proceed.

"In the vast and fertile territory of Mexico, blest with every variety of climate, and with nearly all the productions of the vegetable and mineral kingdom, exists a population most interesting indeed, but in number wholly inadequate to reap the exuberant harvest which nature is ready to offer. Where thirty millions would scarcely suffice, between seven millions and eight millions are found. Nearly four millions of these are of Indian race, *pure* and *unmixed*, about two millions are of Indian mixed with other races, and about one million three hundred thousand are Creoles, descendants in unmixed blood from Europeans, chiefly Spaniards. All these are Catholics. According to statistical returns to government in 1850, there were only five thousand four hundred and twelve foreigners in the whole republic. Of this small number, three thousand and forty-seven were Spaniards. To allow for deficient returns, we may double the number, and still find there very few of foreign birth. It is important to remember these elements of the Mexican population, when we judge the nation in a civil or religious aspect. A great proportion of the inhabitants are Indians or of Indian race, pure or mixed, and they are christians. Trace back this people to their painful, wild, migratory and slavish life in the thirteenth century; see them, up to the fifteenth century, wretched and struggling with extreme poverty in their reed habitations, amidst the marshes of the Mexican lakes, and from their fishes and wild fowl snatching a precarious subsistence.

See them in continual, bloody wars, the slaves of a despot, and the slaves of a horrid idolatry, which consumed yearly about fifty thousand human victims, and called them to horrid cannibalism. See them now, all christians, living in profound peace, the convulsions around scarcely affecting the pure Indian race; murderous wars of tribe against tribe no longer exist; famine is almost unknown. Occasional labor and the rich, teeming fruit of a prolific soil amply supplying their simple wants, see them, with touching devotion, offering the adorable victim of our altars to the true God alone, to thank Him for the blessings they enjoy, and to beg Him to guide them safe to the better land, where holier blessings await them. See all this, and then look at what they were but a few centuries ago, and you will find a progress, not great as with us, nor in the same direction, but, under circumstances the most disadvantageous, great for them.

"In substance the same remarks have been made by a most interesting Protestant writer, who, alas! too often utters words of sarcasm against Catholic faith. The parallel in the extract proves that in Mexico, as elsewhere, the religious instincts of our nature and vague remembrance of primitive revelation established practices more or less like the time-honored practices of the Catholic Church.

"'The Aztec worship,' says Prescott, 'prepared its votaries for the pomp and splendor of the Roman ritual. It was not difficult to pass from the fasts and festivals of the one religion to the fasts and festivals of the other; to transfer their homage from the fantastic idols of their own creation to the beautiful forms in sculpture and painting which decorated the christian cathedral. But, if the philosopher may smile at the reflection, that conversion, under these circumstances, was one of form rather than of substance, the philanthropist will console himself by considering how much the cause of humanity and good morals must have gained by the substitution of those unsullied rites for the brutal abominations of the Aztecs.'

"As to Prescott's assertion that 'the form is changed, not the substance,' I would remark, that all religions contain some good;

as there is no pure poison on earth, so is there also no pure error. Some truths mingled even with the folly of idolatry. The substance of those truths the Indian retained, and added the substance of other truths as yet unknown. The secrets of eternity will tell how blessed an effect this change operated in the order of sanctity, and even of time. I do not say that all are good, or that no evil mingles with the good; alas, such is the condition of our fallen nature, that in every nation we find '*Bona mixta malis, et mala mixta bonis,*' good mixed with evil, and evil mixed with good. Why should the Indian or Creole of Mexico be an exception?

"The Mexican has indeed his vices, but he has also his virtues; parental and filial love, hospitality, humility, unbounded charity, meekness, patience, resignation, and other touching virtues, are general in Mexico; but it is also true that some vices are probably more common in Mexico than elsewhere. Gambling is for many a passion; lying is not held in due horror; and among the lower classes thieving is too common. Those vices, however, are far from being general; they are vices common to the Indian race, and, alas! but too frequent in our own favored country. In Mexico, however, as here, those who practice our holy religion either never had, or soon cease to have, such practices. Now when we consider that, for the last forty-three years, Mexico has been in continual agitation, convulsed by civil wars and revolutions, those deadly enemies of faith and morals, we must gratefully adore that special Providence which has not only preserved a distracted country from more horrid crimes, and from wider spread corruption, but which has also kept even the late Indian pagans in the practice of many touching virtues, in general piety, and in the blessed unity of christian faith.

"To judge correctly of a painting, much depends on the point whence we view it. So it is also in judging a community or a nation. If we view solely in the light of time, solely as regards earthly pilgrimage, we will form judgments of what is good and what is bad, widely different from the estimate we would form, should the light of eternity mingle strongly with that of time.

and if, under the decided conviction that the practices, rites, and
belief of the Roman Catholic Church are absurd or idolatrous,
we estimate a nation's religious character through its exterior
demonstrations, we will pity or despise what a Catholic would
admire. If our estimate for the good, the sublime, and the beautiful be exclusively found in a narrow circle of the cold North; in
the warmer climates we will judge practices superstitious and
unnatural, which appear natural and holy to minds and imaginations that glow in the sunny South. Thus a fine writer, viewing
with a Protestant eye the Catholic ceremonial, and its powerful
effect on the Mexican idolater, says:

"'The Roman Catholic communion has, it must be admitted,
some decided advantages over the Protestant. The dazzling
pomp of its service, and its touching appeal to the sensibilities,
affect the imaginations of the rude child of nature, much more
powerfully than the cold abstractions of Protestantism. The Protestant missionary seeks to enlighten the understanding of his
convert, by the pale light of reason. But the bolder Catholic,
kindling the spirit by the grandeur of the spectacle, and by the
glowing portrait of an agonized Redeemer, sweeps his hearers
along in a tempest of passion, that drowns everything like reflections. He has, however, secured his convert by the hold on his
affections.'

"Without stopping to inquire how far God has willed that the
sensibilities,' the imagination, and all *our* nature, (and, indeed,
all nature should serve in the great work of confession and salvation,) we see to this day the ceremonies which once swept the
pagan Indian along in a tempest of *holy* passion, now, like the
letters in our Bibles, recalling to the minds of his christian
children truths which first awakened the father's heart to deep
emotions of christian piety. And those who attend the sacred
rites during the Holy Week, see the powerful effect which the
living lessons of our christian ceremonies have, not only on the
meek and humble Indian, but also upon the most instructed
Mexican Creole or Spaniard.

(12)

"It is true that most of the Indians, and many of the Mexicans, are employed in low offices. It is true that, (as in the days of Cortes, a friendly monarch could send almost an army of *temanes*, or men of burden, to do the work of horses or oxen,) so even now are there many *temanes* who carry burdens which astonish us. Yet, generally the hopes of religion sweeten this toil; often, too, do they give to the Indian countenance, an expression of calm and of cheerful content, which the rich might envy.

"Speaking of the Mexicans in the sixteenth century, Prescott says:

"'The whole nation, from the peasant to the prince, bowed their necks to the worst kind of tyranny, that of a blind fanaticism.'

"He then speaks of their human victims, and their feeding on human flesh, and says:

"'Cannibalism suggests ideas so loathsome, so degrading to man, to his spiritual and immortal nature, that it is impossible the people who practice it should make any great progress in moral or intellectual culture. The Mexican furnishes no exception to this remark.' Prescott continues in these words: 'In this state of things it was beneficently ordered by Providence, that the land should be delivered over to another race, who would redeem it from the brutish superstitions that daily extended wider and wider, with extent of empire.'

"We know how slowly, how reluctantly a nation changes the wild, unfettered, savage life, for the life of restraint, which high civilization imposes. It required ages to bring the Greeks and the Romans, the Gauls and the Britons, to anything like our form of civilization. Hence, apart from the result on our faith, we need not wonder at this assertion of another Protestant writer on Mexico:

"'The Indians of Mexico,' says he, 'are divided into numerous tribes, speaking upwards of twenty languages, wholly distinct from each other. Their character remains much the same as it is alleged to have been at the time of the Conquest. Indolence, blind submission to superiors, and gross superstition, are as much their characteristics now as formerly. The form of their religion is changed, and that is all; they take the same childish delight in the idle ceremonies and processions of the Catholic Church, as they once took in the fantastic mummeries of their aboriginal idolatry.'

"Excusing the words of insult, the writer expresses what was always true of every barbarous nation, during ages of slow progress from Indian life. In Mexico conquest, forms of government, climate, nature itself account for deficiencies. What there is of progress is due to religion alone; and for the whole nation, in all classes, it is indeed religion alone that has preserved something of nationality, and some bond of union, to prevent the dissolving, destroying effect of civil wars for more than a generation. The mild climate of Mexico, its perpetual Spring, exempts the native from the necessity of protection from winter cold; plants of giant vegetation, yielding fruit at all seasons, render famine almost impossible. The stern law of necessity, which in northern climates says 'work or die,' is not known in Mexico. Hence, many cabins of the poor, still like those described by the Conquerors, are small huts of lava, of rough stone without mortar, or of reeds, poles, brambles, or rushes, the thatch which covers the hut being often the only part impervious to the winds or to the driving rain. That hut gives shelter to a family, some times so large that all can scarcely stand erect in the narrow space. Yet, there the domestic ties are so strong and tender as often to diffuse around sweet and cheerful content; some picture or image of the crucified Saviour and of His blessed yet sorrowful mother, teach lessons of resignation and patience. The Holy Week, and occasional pilgrimage give, in the religious order, a touching variety to life. In the fairs that frequently occur, the Indian and his family think they enjoy as much as the greatest believe that they enjoyed at the 'World's Fair' in the Crystal Palace. Along a sweet valley, embosomed in the giant Andes accompanied by the truly learned, pious and estimable Bishop Mungiua, I once rode to visit Indians who reside in the romantic island of a lake in the mountain plain. I shall not easily forget their looks of mingled cheerfulness and piety. Ambition and the cursed thirst of gold never tormented them. The scene reminded me as much of the first christians as any thing I ever noticed out of the holiest cloisters.

"Near Lagos, late on Sunday, accompanied by the pastor, I visited an Indian village; a beautiful square lay in front of the church, in which the Indians had passed the morning and most of the evening in religious duties. The sun was setting, diffusing its mellow rays over a scene of fairy beauty. The fragrance of a thousand plants, unknown to our clime, seemed the incense of nature to the God whose blessings were spread so luxuriantly around. All the men of the village were gathered in the square; the men of age sat, in Indian fashion, on the ground, conversing together, telling of the past, or commenting on the sermon; and the smile and the frequent laugh told how happy they were. Near them the young men danced their ancient Indian dances, to their old Indian music. The worthy pastor and I enjoyed the simple, innocent gaiety which sweetly terminated a day, the greater part of which had been given to God's worship.

"The author lately quoted charges the Mexican Indians with gross superstition; others have charged them with a tendency to idolatry. The latter charge is unfounded; a close examination of acts supposed to have been idolatrous, would prove them to have been merely superstitions; and superstition is found in all nations, and in every religion and sect. Read Robert Burns for a graphic description of superstition in Scotland. Superstition is defined by Webster to be, 'excessive exactness or rigor in religious opinions or practice,' and 'excess or extravagance in religion.' Superstition, then, when it does not imply fanaticism, is better than infidelity or cold indifference to religion. Neither are good, but of two evils, I prefer that which is foolish excess or extravagance of good, in the order of eternity, to that which is its total negation.

"The Indian, late an idolater, and still, alas! too ignorant, is no doubt inclined to superstition; but the clergy make great efforts to correct this inclination. Unhappily, there are not enough of priests to instruct them; though the Bishops have seminaries in which the Indian languages are taught to the young clergy, still the supply is not sufficient; many priests cannot yet speak the language of the tribe to which they minister; and the Spanish, though understood, generally, by the Indians, in all that relates to visible things, is a very imperfect medium for conveying to them spiritual ideas of the invisible world. As to this, the separation from Old Spain was also a loss to the aboriginal race; many of their kindest instructors and Rev. fathers were forced, under the law which expelled all Spaniards, to leave their Indian missions. Spain, too, in granting lands, has considered the Indians as minors; they had the free and full use of their lands, but could not sell them; when independent, they were free to sell. To speculators then, for a trifle, they did sell, and soon were forced from the sweet home of happy days, to wild and almost inaccessible mountain tracts. Notwithstanding all this, I found the Mexican Indians, generally, far better, and far more happy, than I had been led to expect; far above our Indians, and still farther elevated above their idolatrous forefathers. Thus the blessed influence of the Catholic religion, triumphing in Mexico and in the South over conquest, continued civil wars, and some individual acts of cruelty, has preserved the Indian race. At this day, in the America which was settled by Catholics, about eighteen millions of Indians in unmixed blood, are found; they are christians, and take part in government, whilst on our part of the continent the Indian race is almost extinct.

"In the mixed race and among the Creoles, instruction is widely diffused; many are truly learned. It would take too long to give the names of gentlemen of the highest standing and of great wealth amongst the Mexicans, the Creoles, or pure Spaniards, whose extensive learning is only surpassed by a munificent charity, by a deep spirit of religion, and by devout attention to religious duties. A fervent and touching piety is indeed very common, in the highest ranks as well as among the poor. Few nations, in proportion to population, have more numerous or better filled libraries. Thus the cathedral library contains thirty thousand volumes, that of the College of St. John Lateran twelve thousand. A great proportion of the population approach to the holy sacraments; among them, consequently, great faults must be rare. Among those who do not approach the sacraments, certain faults must be common. Some of these are inherent in the Indian nature; some others that characterize men of a warm clime, who do not serve God, may be found more frequent in Mexico than in lands where the same natural causes do not exist; whilst faults and sins that are common with us, are almost unknown in Mexico. I traveled there some thousands of miles, over roads nearly impassable, yet, even in the rainy season, when the drivers and servants were working knee-deep in water, the most vexatious accidents often occurring, I never heard either driver or servant utter an oath or a blasphemy. I might enumerate other sins of a horrid type, alas, too common amidst the pride, wants and passions of overstrained refinement, and which are very rare in Mexico. I visited many prisons in the republic, spoke to the culprits, administered confirmation to them, aided to prepare some for execution, yet not on a single visage did I trace that deep and dark impress of crime, which I have noticed searing the countenance of many a culprit in prisons of other lands.

"Again I repeat it, I do not say that all are good, or that the good have not their faults. Why should we expect there perfection, which we might seek in vain here or in any spot on earth? But I do record my deep conviction that, before Him who reads the heart, the balance of virtue and vice probably stands as fair in Mexico as in any other land; and that I would sooner cast my lot for a blessed eternity with many a meek, humble Mexican Indian, than with the proud Pharisee, who thanks his God, 'that he is not like other men.'

"The most erroneous ideas exist as to the clergy of Mexico. They are represented as excessively numerous, immensely rich, ignorant and vicious, ruling the country and thwarting the onward march of government. So often and in so many ways have those charges been made or insinuated, that I went to Mexico prepared to mourn over evils, most of which, I soon found, existed but in the imagination of enemies of our religion, or in the facility of weak minds to readily believe and echo what enemies have said.

"The Archbishop of Mexico, Don Lazaro de Garcia, is a profound canonist, a learned and truly pious man. His revenues amount, it is said, to twenty-four thousand dollars per annum. He spends almost all in works of mercy and zeal, and in encouraging learning. He needs but little for himself, since his mode of life is simple, retiring and austere. In his Archepiscopal palace, his own rooms are very plain and poorly furnished. The poor cot in which he sleeps is the same which he used at college, when yet a student; he rises before day, visits but little, and labors till late at night. His meals are very plain and frugal. The president of St. Anna's Council, Bishop Mungina, possesses extensive learning, great talents, and unblemished reputation, and, like his predecessor, Bishop Portugal, is revered by his flock, and by the poor beloved as a father. The many valuable works he has published would do honor to a prelate in any country. The Bishop elect of Guadalajara has written some works which prove his learning and talents; in the sacred ministry he displays virtues which make him dear to his people. The Bishop elect of Monterey has talents of the first order, and those talents are well cultivated. He speaks several languages; but his humility and his many christian virtues grace him still more than his acquirements. I might speak truly in the same strain of many eminent clergymen, with whom I had the honor of becoming acquainted. I might declare that generally among the canons and the higher clergy, I met with men who would be worthy of their post in any country. Yet, I do not say that there are no unworthy men in the sacred ministry. Alas, there was a Judas among the twelve! and one bad priest will attract more notice than twenty good. The good are unobtrusive, they are often hid from the public eye in their holy labor for the poor sick, and for God; the bad are ever abroad, and seem to have an ubiquity which magnifies their numbers. There are evils in the clergy, but a merciful protection of God has prevented still greater, which political events must otherwise have caused. On the clergy, in some measure, as on the laity, the convulsions and revolutions of forty-three years have had a deleterious effect; but also, in consequence of these convulsions, for several years not a single Bishop was to be found in the whole republic; young clergymen had then to be sent to various dioceses of the United States for ordination. I need not say how discipline would naturally relax, and studies languish under the total privation of the chief pastors.

"Another evil now, as formerly, exists in Mexico, and might account for much relaxation of discipline. Bishops are too few; it is morally and physically impossible for them to fulfill the duties of their office. France has seventy-seven Bishops and fourteen Archbishops; Ireland, with seven millions of Catholics, and a territory not more extensive than a single diocese of Mexico, has four Archbishops and twenty-four Bishops; and Mexico, with seven or eight millions of Catholics, and a territory so vast, has only one Archbishop, and nine Bishoprics, with actually only six Bishops, the former incumbents being dead. Of the four last Bishops of Guadalajara, but one, during a very long administration, was able once, and only once, to visit all his diocese; the other three visited but a small part; the whole four died on the visit, one as he completed it, the others as they labored along it. Were there, in an army, but one captain for a thousand men, one colonel for ten thousand, and one general for a million, what would become of military discipline? The Church of God is an army 'in battle array.' In Mexico there are rank and file enough, but officers are wanting. Thanks to God, the Bishops, the clergy and the people are awakening to a sense of this truth, and two new Bishoprics are already erected. God grant that many others be soon created!

"It has been stated here that the Church controls the government. On the contrary, in Catholic Mexico, the government has but too often oppressed the Church. Unequal and ruinous burdens were imposed on the clergy; much of the parish lands was seized; monasteries and religious houses were and are occupied by force as barracks, leaving but a part of their own house to the religions. Bishops were often thwarted and checked in their efforts to correct abuses. Still, the very legislature which refused to recognize Sr. Clementini, the learned and estimable Nuncio of the Pope, expressed their general and high esteem of the secular clergy. And strange to say, whilst censuring the lives of the monks, they refuse to permit the Pope's delegate to correct the very abuses of which they complain. Oh, that the Church in Mexico were perfectly free! Oh, that the successor of St. Peter had full permission 'to confirm his brethren;' then whatever relaxation may affect the clergy would soon disappear.

"Much has been said about the riches of the Mexican Church and clergy. As to the mere edifice, some twenty or thirty churches may be called rich; several others, decent and well furnished; but a very great many are poor, and some are very poor. As to the clergy, those who know the use to which they have generally applied any surplus revenues, would wish that they were richer. Many, not only of the churches, convents, hospitals, asylums and colleges, but also of the bridges, aqueducts, public roads, and public squares or walks, are due to the clergy, who projected them and paid for them. The learned and pious Bishop elect of Guadalajara, furnished me with an account of the works of public utility which, in his own days, the Bishops of Guadalajara had began and perfected at their own expense. The mere enumeration forms a small volume. In every part of the republic I found works of this kind, constructed wholly or in great part at the expense of Bishops, canons, or other clergymen. Alas! few would now be able to do so much! Long since a law was passed which virtually abolished tithes; the glebe lands have been sequestered, the churches despoiled. The liberals have endeavored to swell the revenues of the Church, by taking into the count hospitals, asylums, colleges, convents of nuns, and even the amount paid them for tuition. Let us apply the same rule to our own country. One who appeared to know, declared some time ago that the corporation of Holy Trinity church, in New York, was worth eighty millions of dollars, and was richer than the whole Church of Mexico. I can scarcely believe it, but I well believe that if, to the riches of that one corporation we add the possessions and revenues of all the other Protestant churches in the city of New York, and the property and revenues of all their hospitals, asylums, colleges, Bible societies, tract societies, charities, etc., we would find a total exceeding all the riches possessed by all the churches and church establishments of seven millions of Catholics in Mexico.

"By statistical tables published in Mexico in 1852, the number of secular priests in the republic was estimated at three thousand two hundred and twenty-three. The Bishops have since been making great efforts to obtain a number more adequate to the wants of the country. Some of the seminaries count upward of five hundred seminarians; then we may now estimate the secular clergy at about four thousand five hundred; the regular clergy may be estimated at about three thousand; making an aggregate of between seven and eight thousand, or an average of one priest for every thousand souls. How different from idolatrous times, three hundred years ago, when, in the city of Mexico alone, five thousand priests were attached to the service of the temples. It is true that the clergy in Mexico are not fairly distributed; some places abounding and others very deficient. Still the number, compared to duties, is not great; and when we know that many are employed in colleges in teaching, and in other functions, apart from the sacred ministry, we feel that the clergy must often be unable to meet the demands on their time and labor.

"The writer I have just quoted fixes the entire revenue of the Mexican clergy, derived from every source, even from offerings at baptisms and marriages, burials, devout practices, etc., at eight or ten millions, and, in a note, he says he thinks he has exceeded the true amount. But then, even according to his account, the average of the Mexican clergy's revenue, from the Archbishop of Mexico to a poor curate or vicar, would be about one thousand dollars per annum, or about two hundred pounds sterling yearly for each minister of the altar. Contrast this with the revenue of clergymen in England, or indeed with the revenues of many clergymen in our own country. I found many priests in Mexico who were poor, yet who still were generous benefactors of those who were poorer than themselves; I found some who were rich, and who made most noble use of their riches. I found some monks who did not appear edifying; but I also found many of exemplary life. Among the Carmelites and the Reformed Franciscans, among those of St. Ferdinand in Mexico, or near Guadalajara, at Zoppapan, I could not but see worthy successors of the holy men of whom a Protestant writer, Prescott, thus speaks:

"'Twelve Franciscan friars embarked for New Spain, which they reached early in 1524. They were men of unblemished purity of life, nourished with the learning of the cloister, and like many others whom the Romish Church has sent forth on such apostolic missions, counted all personal sacrifices as little in the sacred cause to which they were devoted. The missionaries lost no time in the good work of conversion. They began their preaching through interpreters, until they themselves had acquired a competent knowledge of the language. They opened schools and founded colleges, in which the native youth were instructed in profane as well as christian learning. In a few years, every vestige of the primitive *teocallis*, or pagan temples, was effaced from the land. The uncouth idols of the country shared the same fate. In about twenty years from the first advent of the missionaries, one of their body could make the pious vaunt, that nine millions of converts had been admitted within the christian fold.'—*Prescott*, C. of M.

"Mr. Prescott, generally, when he speaks of what he knows or has closely studied, speaks in praise of the Catholic Church. It is only when he speaks from second hand knowledge, that he utters a word of insult. Thus, his notice of the Dominican friars is as favorable as that which I have quoted of the Franciscans. I could add to his list an enumeration of most regular and edifying convents of Carmelites, Augustinians, and Franciscans, in which I lodged, and in which I marked evidences of holy life. I could speak of the few Jesuits fathers in the same style of praise in which a most amiable, learned and distinguished Protestant spoke some few years past. It is true, Madame Calderon de la Barca is now a Catholic, but when she wrote her 'Life in Mexico,' she was not a Catholic. But I fear to trespass too much on your time, and I sum up by declaring that during my stay in Mexico I found the evil much less than I expected, and the good immeasurably greater than I could have expected.

"More than forty years ago, our General Pike, ascending Red River, and unknowingly trespassing on the Mexican territory, was taken prisoner, and brought to the City of Mexico. In his work, (though a Protestant,) he gives a flattering description of the Mexican people and clergy. Were he again permitted to visit that land, he probably could not now, after long years of civil wars, give equal praise. Yet he would see enough to join with me in the judgment I have pronounced, and also to join with me in adoring and blessing that special Providence of God, which has prevented forty-three years of revolutions from working the full sadly deteriorating effects so usually and so fatally produced."

In the Spring of the year 1853, Monsignore Bedini, Archbishop of Thebes, was sent by the Papal government at Rome, as Apostolic Nuncio to the court of Brazil, and, in the course of his journey, was authorized to hand a complimentary autograph letter from the Pope to the President of the United States. In addition to this, he was charged to look after the interests of the Church in America, and report to the Holy Father the wants, condition and the prospects of religion in this country. Power was delegated to him to adjust local differences between congregations and their spiritual heads, and among many other things, he was empowered to settle the long and uninterrupted spirit of rebellion in St. Louis church, in Buffalo. On the preceding pages we have given a very detailed explanation of the trouble with this congregation, from originally printed documents, found among the posthumous writings of Bishop Timon. It will be necessary here only to sketch briefly the visit of the Nuncio, and allude to his importance, in any further consideration of this memorable trouble.

The efforts of Bishop Timon to settle the difficulty of Church discipline, affecting his authority as Bishop, had been in vain. As has already been seen, the condition of the church had been in a very unsettled state. Correspondence, containing resolutions for better behavior, or defiant resistance; communications to the public papers of the day unfriendly to the Bishop; a petition to the Common Council of the city, and also to the Legislature of the State, to notice and adjust their claims; all these and other forms of insubordination, gave the Bishop much trouble. The arrival of the Nuncio, therefore, seemed an auspicious event.

As soon as was practicable, a time was appointed for an interview between the trustees of St. Louis church, and His Eminence the Nuncio. The following correspondence will sufficiently explain the result:

AFFAIRS OF ST. LOUIS CHURCH.

DECISION OF THE APOSTOLIC NUNCIO.

"The trustees of St. Louis church visited the Apostolic Nuncio on the 22d inst., and presented a memorial containing the details of their alleged grievances.

"The Nuncio delivered the following answer in the course of Tuesday, the 25th instant:

"'*To the Trustees of St. Louis Church, Buffalo,*

"'*Gentlemen:* I have read, with great attention, the memorial which you handed to me, relative to the unhappy difficulties existing, or which did exist, between some members of St. Louis congregation and their Bishop. Deplorable, indeed, is the condition of that congregation. Instead of enjoying in peace the comforts of religion—practicing it, and honoring it in love and charity—discord and bitterness are found; and even in the temple a sad desolation reigns. A truly christian heart cannot remain longer in such a state. Indeed, the Catholic who would not seek to be delivered from it, by a reasonable submission to authority, would excite just doubts of his faith, and of his sincere will to follow the Divine teaching of that faith. But the appeal which you have made to the Holy Father, and which you again make to me as his representative, proves, I hope, that you wish to terminate those unhappy dissensions, and that you, as is just, expect that result from his authority and counsels.

"'I see no necessity for passing in review all the details or all the assertions of your memorial. The root of the evil and its remedies are very evident. My whole attention shall be directed to point them out.

"'I thought it my duty, first of all, to examine carefully the original deed of the church lot. I find that in the year 1829, it was given by Mr. L. Lecouteulx '*for the sole and only use of a Roman Catholic Church and Cemetery;*' consequently its whole administration, whether in the measures taken to provide for its wants, or to remedy any abuses that may arise, should be founded on the principles and laws which regulate the discipline of the Catholic Church.

"'Furthermore, I find that the original deed was made by Mr. Lecouteulx to Bishop Dubois, with the condition that the property should remain in his hands, and in those of his successors, for the purpose above mentioned. Now, such a donation having been accepted by Bishop Dubois, and the church having been built on a lot thus acquired, the principles which regulate its administration admit of no doubt.

"'In your statement you speak of a 'Charter' obtained afterwards, and of your duty to observe the laws of your country. I will ever be among the first in exhorting you to observe the laws of your country, and to be invariably faithful to your duties as citizens of this vast and illustrious Republic. You know well, as Catholics, that not only nothing prevents your fulfilling such duties, but that for you, as such, they become even more sacred. I must remark, however, that to observe the laws of your country *is one thing;* to avail yourselves of your privileges for the purpose of arraying yourselves in opposition to your Church, and to the authority of your Bishop and clergy, in the free discharge of their duty, *is another and a quite different thing.* I sought in vain for some proof of Bishop Dubois' consent to the Act of Incorporation, procured on the 2d of December, 1838, nearly ten years after the original grant. But even supposing that he gave it, certain it is that he neither could nor ought to have consented to any thing incompatible with the basis of that grant. No one could, by subsequent rights, no matter how obtained, justly destroy rights enjoyed previously by the ministers of the Church, according to the rules and discipline thereof.

" 'The question, then, always remains the same: What were the essential rights of the Bishop in the church of St. Louis, according to the original deed, and the laws of the church which should govern it? Evidently rights obtained later should aim at preserving the *original ones*, not at destroying them.

" ' But in this question it is not necessary to advance beyond its strict limits. If there were questions of revenues accruing from property or capital given or acquired for the use of the church, which was in itself productive, the rights and the obligations of those who administered them, or who claimed a share in the administration, would depend on the conditions stipulated by the donor and accepted by the church, according to her own rules of discipline; and the decision of difficulties that might arise could only be based on her laws, and on the above named conditions. But I find nothing of this in the case before me. Here there are no possessions or capital to be administered which can, properly speaking, be said to be productive. Only the offerings of the faithful are to be received and distributed, whether these offerings are given during the public worship, or are previously agreed upon for the use of pews during Divine service. Can there be any thing more exclusively subject to the ecclesiastical ministry than this kind of revenue? The pews are not, of themselves, productive; you yourselves, whilst your church was closed, could see this. The oblations and the contributions for pews take place only in view of the Divine service, and that it may be carried on, and they must be appropriated to meet the expenses incurred in performing it, or to support the ministers appointed by the Bishop to celebrate the Divine mysteries. Those contributions, then, are but the direct result of the sacred ministry, and consequently must be subject to the free administration of ecclesiastical authority. The Bishop who sends thither the ministers has the right to prescribe the mode of collecting such contributions, and of distributing them, so as fully to accomplish the sacred intentions for which they are given.

"'He has, also, the right of making such changes or modifications in the rules governing such matters as may become necessary from time to time. The canonical prescriptions which guide the Bishop in his actions are, on the other hand, well known; they prevent the possibility of abuse, or provide an efficacious remedy for it. These very prescriptions not only give the Bishop *power*, but they impose on him the *obligation* of remedying abuses which might occur in the administration, however legally acquired, of property and revenues of any kind which belong to the Church. But, as in your case there is question solely of pious oblations or contributions, which, after all, are but voluntary, there can be no doubt that the Bishop has full right to determine the manner of regulating them, and he, more than any one else, will take a deep interest in applying them to their holy destination. When, therefore, your Bishop informed you that he would name, out of your own congregation, a certain number of persons to receive and distribute, for the use and benefit of the same, the aforesaid oblations, whether offered during the holy sacrifice, or given for the use of pews by those who occupy them during the Divine service, it was manifestly your duty to submit, as he had an undoubted right to make such arrangements.

"'Your very memorial shows abundantly that the system of administration heretofore existing was very defective, since you have only disorders to deplore; and your very assertions prove clearly that to cure them fully and radically, your Bishop could not have acted otherwise than he did.

"'Mention is often made in said memorial of an intention to change the nationality of the church of St. Louis, and, by giving it to others, to take it away from those to whom it was first given. But the existence of such an intention is denied by the Bishop, (I have no proof of it,) I cannot even believe it possible; and if ever it were attempted the Holy See is ready to make the execution of such an attempt impossible.

"'You say also that, since your charter of incorporation gives to the trustees elected by the congregation the administration of oblations, and the above mentioned contributions, you cannot cede it, without failing in your duty. Here I call to your mind what has been already stated. When, in such an affair, you use the rights which the civil law gives you, you are bound to make your action harmonize with your duty as Catholics. The privilege which the civil law here grants is *permissive;* you *may* use it or *not.* It is your duty to consult the principles of your faith, to ascertain when and how you ought to use it.

"'Without examining the legal rights which accrue to you as trustees under your charter of incorporation, and without determining by whom and in what way the thing should be done, it suffices for me to state what the Bishop may lawfully decide and require, and to this the congregation, either by mere consent or by direct and immediate action, should conform. Consequently, I declare that those who refuse fail in their duty, and by thus hindering the Bishop in the free exercise of his holy ministry, they become responsible for all the sad consequences that may result. Furthermore, I cannot believe that any law of the State will prevent your conforming to the discipline of your church; on the contrary, I know that the spirit of justice, which so strongly characterizes the legislation of this country, will never make the accomplishment of its duties impossible to a religious congregation, nor compel them to adopt a course that would necessarily produce disorder and confusion. But if by chance it were otherwise, I am convinced that you need only make the case known to the legislative body, and they would grant such modification of the law as would place your legal position in harmony with the laws of the Church to which you belong. I know that such acts of justice, in favor of other corporations, have already emanated from the Legislature of this State, and I cannot believe that a like concession, so evidently just, would be refused to the Catholics of this Republic, when once they make their wants known, and sincerely seek a remedy. In the meantime, if you but do your duty, nothing need prevent the administrators named by the Bishop from discharging their duties, even legally, in the church of St. Louis; and I counsel you to take the necessary steps to effect this object as soon as possible. The Bishop does not ask for himself the administration; he is ready to place it in the hands of members of your own congregation, but appointed by him. All that these may receive in the church, shall be used for the congregation itself; and at fixed periods shall give an account of their administration to the Bishop as well as to the faithful that frequent the church. Thus peace and order have been restored to other congregations; and the same will doubtless happen here, as soon as you have the sincere desire of restoring order, and of enjoying the precious advantages of a holy and lasting peace.

"'I request you to reflect most seriously and conscientiously on what you will do after this answer. You undoubtedly are free to submit or not to my declaration, and to follow my counsels; but the Catholic Church is also free to recognize those that are truly her children, and those that are not. After so many dissensions, disorders, and painful agitations, it is time to return to peace, and to make the vineyard of the Lord flourish in union, in charity, and in humility, without which it is impossible to please God. The congregation of St. Louis church, by adopting the course indicated, which alone is just and indispensable, will give a noble proof of faith and charity, and a sincere desire for order and peace; will crown all my efforts with the most happy success; and they will have a very large portion in the benedictions which the Catholic Church and its visible head bestow on her zealous and obedient children. But if they refuse, I can only see in them persons faithless to their duties, who make use of their privileges, not to edify in the Church of God, but to destroy;

who, by placing obstacles to the free exercise of Episcopal authority, can never be received as obedient sons of the Church of God, who has confined solely to Bishops the power and the right to govern it. '*Posuit episcopos regere Ecclesiam Dei.*'—Acts xx: 28.

"'The Holy See will ever perpetuate the succession of worthy and holy pastors, and the common father of the faithful is always ready to provide for the spiritual wants of the flock in every part of the world, by providing such pastors, and by the prescriptions, the rules, and the holy discipline of the Church. You now know his decision, his counsel, and even his earnest recommendation in regard to the question at issue; you have only to comply with this earnest recommendation to merit still more fully his paternal care and holy benedictions. Your submission to the laws of the Church will ever be a pledge of your submission to every other law to which you are subject, as it is impossible to be a good Catholic, and not be at the same time a good citizen of your country.

"'C. BEDINI,
"'*Archbishop of Thebes, Apostolic Nuncio.*'"

THE TRUSTEES' REPLY.

"'OCTOBER 25th, 1853.

"'*Excellency:* We have read the esteemed answer given by you at our last interview, (this morning,) with a great deal of attention, and we see therein, with great astonishment, that you say '*among a few members of the congregation,*' (although we are very numerous.)

"'It appears to us that you have been misinstructed in that regard, and we would propose to your Excellency the contrary, if his Excellency think it necessary, by calling a general meeting of the congregation in St. Louis church, at any time your Excellency may appoint, within forty-eight hours. We know *positively* that the *congregation of St. Louis church is yet three hundred family fathers strong.*

"'Furthermore, we see nothing in your Excellency's answer, but a repetition of the demand made by the Right Rev. Bishop Timon, that is, *entire submission, and that our act of incorporation should be annulled, and that the appointment of a committee instead of a board of trustees, should be made by him, which has been the cause of our difficulties.* Up to the time of the beginning of these difficulties, we never meddled with the spiritual, leaving it entirely to the pastor and Bishop, but as to the temporalities we had always the control, subject nevertheless to the yearly inspection of the Right Reverend Bishop and pastor, (and at any time within the fiscal year,) over the amount expended and received, and which the pastor always found correct. As to the annulling of our act of incorporation, there is not the least shadow of thought, as we believe that *temporalities* have nothing to do with *spiritualities.*

"'If your Excellency thinks that, by having another interview, (the Right Reverend Bishop in person present,) a reconciliation can be effected, we leave it to your Excellency's own discretion, praying you to inform us of the appointed time to such an interview, if one is to be had.

"'In hopes that a reconsideration of the past transactions will be made, and that a more favorable discussion in our favor will take place,

"'I have the honor to be, with high respect, your Excellency's most sincere and obedient servant,

"'N. OTTENOT,

"'*Secretary of the Board of Trustees of St. Louis Church.*

"'To his Excellency, C. BEDINI,
  "'*Apostolic Nuncio, at St. Mary's Church.*'"

FINAL ANSWER.

"'*To the Trustees of St. Louis Church:*

"'I informed you that I was ready to hear you again, as I was told that you had something to add to the letter of your secretary, in answer to mine of the 25th inst. I also wished to know for certain if that letter was the expression of the sentiment of the board of trustees. In our last interview you told me that you had nothing more to say, and that the aforesaid letter was the expression of your sentiments. I made known to you at the same time that I had not authorized any one to say a word to you regarding the question at issue, as it was fully treated in my letter, and I was decidedly unwilling to communicate any part whatever of my decision by word of mouth, or by any one's intervention, so as to avoid effectually all misunderstanding.

"'Now, then, it becomes my duty to say that your answer is truly painful, especially to an envoy of the Holy Father, to whom you referred your case. The sad conviction forces itself on me that you disregard altogether Catholic principles, consequently that if you persist, it only remains for me to deplore the sad position in which you place yourselves in the face of the Church; but the responsibility of this rests entirely on yourselves.

"'Buffalo, October 26th, 1853.

"'C. BEDINI,

"'*Archbishop of Thebes, Apostolic Nuncio.*'"

CHAPTER VI.

The Church Property Bill.—Hon. Mr. Putnam and Hon. Mr. Babcock.—Bishop Timon's Reply.—The Foundling Asylum.—Ground devoted by Louis S. Lecouteulx.—Cottages secured.—Cholera.—Bishop Timon carries Infants in his Arms to Places of Safety.—Buys a Farm for a Cemetery and other Uses.—Sentence of Excommunication against the Trustees of St. Louis Church.—Father Weniger mediates and restores Order.

In the year 1853, during the great Know Nothing excitement, a bill was introduced by the Hon. James O. Putnam, in the Legislature of the State of New York, at the instigation of the trustees of St. Louis church, of Buffalo, which, in substance, was done to necessitate the transfer of all ecclesiastical property to the trustees. As the custom generally of other denominations, (non-Catholics,) was to vest their Church property in corporate bodies, of course this affected *Catholics* only.

Much debate was elicited upon that famous bill, particularly from Hon. Erastus Brooks, Senator from New York, and one of the editors of the New York *Express*.*

Among the champions of that famous Church Property bill was the Hon. Mr. Babcock, who, in his speeches, uttered so many remarks at variance with known facts,† that Bishop Timon felt compelled, under the signature of *Veritas*, to publish a reply by way of correcting the erroneous statements of the gentleman.

REPLY TO MR. BABCOCK'S SPEECH.

"Absence for some months, will account for so late a notice of the Hon. Mr. Babcock's speech on the 'Roman Catholic Church Property Bill.' Love for my country, which each absence increases, and regret that in an American Senate, an American Senator should, in malicious insinuations and sweeping denunciations, utter the oft refuted calumnies of by-gone years against the faith of many of his own constituents and against individuals, press me to offer some remarks to a generous public.

"The Hon. Senator has indeed 'read history badly,' or he has only read such history as forced the Count de Maistre to declare that, for nearly three hundred years, it had been 'a vast conspiracy against the truth.' Innocent the III, Gregory VII, Boniface VIII, were not bold, ambitious, unscrupulous men. Hutter, then a Protestant, in his 'Life and Pontificate of Innocent III,' and Vought, a Protestant and a German, in 'The Life and Pontificate of Gregory VII,' vindicate the character of those much calumniated Pontiffs. Voit, the eminent Protestant historian, shows Hildebrand, Gregory VII, to have been a truly meek and humble follower of the Redeemer, and calls him 'the savior of the liberties of Europe.' The character of Boniface VIII has been

---

* As the reader will get a very comprehensive idea of the details, etc., of this bill, from the controversies and writings of Archbishop Hughes, which are already published, we will avoid giving a lengthened analysis of the same. So far as Bishop Timon took part, however, will appear in this work.—THE AUTHOR.

† We mean no offence to the Hon. Senator. But as many things said by him were subsequently corrected by Bishop Timon, we are left to presume, that the sources from which he got his information must have been poisoned.

often and ably vindicated. Mr. Babcock assumes, as an undisputed fact, 'the encroachments of the ecclesiastical power upon civil rights,' yet he ought to know that the majority of christians consider their by-gone 'encroachments' to have been the *encroachments of the civil, or rather of secular despotic power on Church rights*. By the words 'Papal See,' Mr. Babcock evidently understands the Pope, the Papacy. Now, he must know that the vast majority of the christian world hold the Papacy *not* to be a human organization, 'nor its agencies to have been for evil;' he should also know that 'the Papal Dominion' held no possessions in England; then, indeed, the Church property was eminently English and popular, as proved, not long since, at the bar of the House of Lords; the canon law required the incumbents of Church property to divide the revenues thus: One-fourth for the clergy, one-fourth for the poor, one-fourth for hospitality, one-fourth for the public buildings.

"Thus, also, 'the Papal Domination' holds no possessions in the United States; Roman Catholics indeed hold property, Church property, according to the rules and discipline which, they know, will best secure the safety of that property and the peace of congregations. The Hon. Senator may say, 'I quote from such and such an historian,' but certainly, the Hon. Senator knows that the vast majority of christians tell a very different story. Who is to decide upon this question of truth, and upon other questions in which his assertion is contradicted by three-fourths of the christian world? Will the Senate summon distinguished clergymen on each side, hear them on oath, pass some years in reviewing their authorities, and then decide who is right and who is wrong? If this can be done, why not leave controversy, either in strong unproved assertion, or in inferences and broad allusions, to scenes less dignified than an American Senate?

"How coolly the Hon. Senator informs the Legislature that 'under Henry VIII, the English exchanged one despot in Italy for another in Britain!' With what dogmatic assurance he makes the very erroneous assertion 'that the canon law was promulgated after the twelfth and fifteenth centuries, that it is utterly repugnant to civil liberty;' adding insult to his error when he says, 'I have not found it necessary to war against their faith, however erroneous I may deem it; if their practices tend to the subversion of our republican institutions and the destruction of true liberty, theirs is the offence, not mine.' The Hon. Senator has indeed read history in vain, if he knows not that the faith which he attacks by such insinuations, molded the former despotic governments of the Old World to that high degree of freedom which they enjoyed before the Reformation. The Senator should know that when Luther began his sad work, there was not a despotic government, nor a standing army in Europe. He should know that then all the governments in Christendom were either republics or limited monarchies, 'with parliament or courts as powerful,' says Macaulay, 'as any that ever sat in Westminster.' The Senator should *know* history before delivering lectures upon it in an American Senate. The Hon. Senator has also had the politeness to call names. Catholics are not Romanists. The Church of Rome is not in America, it is in Italy. There is no 'Roman Bishop' here. The Hon. Senator shows his learning in theology by informing the Senate that 'the canon laws are no part of the *faith* of the Roman Church at the present day.' But the Hon. Senator has forgotten to inform us when the faith of the *Roman* Church, 'at the present day,' changed from what it was in other days, or when laws regarding discipline, which *may* change, ever formed part of faith, which *cannot* change.

"When uttering most erroneous statements, Mr. Babcock says: 'I am credibly informed, from the most respectable sources.' Yet the Hon. Senator has been publicly assured that his statements were not true, and has been called upon to prove them, or to name persons and places, that his statements may be disproved; but he is *silent;* the poisoned dart is cast, he cannot give proof; he must by this time know that he was cheated, but he skulks from manful assertion, or manful retraction.

"In no church of Buffalo were the outer doors closed, and the people coaxed or coerced into signing the remonstrance against the bill; the remonstrances were *not* 'manufactured in New York under the direction of Archbishop Hughes;' those from this city, for instance, were printed in Buffalo, at the *Republic* office. The Catholic body in this State would, in far greater number, come forward at any time to sign a remonstrance against such a bill. The Senator tells the Senate that 'Bishop Timon was consecrated in St. Louis church' and talks of a breach of faith on the Bishop's part, against the rights of a church in which he was *consecrated*. Alas! for the Hon. Senator. Bishop Timon *was consecrated in New York!* He never received any sacred rite in St. Louis church! He has, indeed, celebrated the holy mass there; he has often administered the sacrament of confirmation there; he has preached for them; he has labored hard to direct or prepare himself for all that was necessary to consecrate that church; for two years he sought to save a worthy and large majority of that congregation from the withering influence of a small minority, or rather of a few men who wish to be Catholics in faith, and Presbyterians in practice and discipline; but all this would not render the Bishop worthy of 'impeachment' for not totally abandoning the discipline of his Church to the mercy of such men.

"When Bishop Timon was invited by the trustees of St. Louis church to consecrate it, he asked them 'if the deed was in the Bishop's name?' remarking that the decree of the Council of Baltimore prohibited him from consecrating any church the title of which was not in the Bishop. The trustees assured him that the title was in the Bishop, and to convince him, brought him an attested copy of the deed, which the Bishop still holds. A few dates will now suffice to show Mr. Babcock how he has been deceived by an unhappy man, whose talent for misstatement is perhaps unrivaled:

"Bishop Timon reached St. Louis church late at night, on the 22d of October, 1847. Whilst there, he was employed in giving directions, and preparing himself for the consecration of the church, and just stayed long enough to consecrate it, and to confirm two hundred and twenty-seven persons. The church was consecrated on the 21st of November, 1847. The Bishop moved to St. Patrick's church on the 23d of November, having stayed at St. Louis church about one month.

"He who will compare these facts and dates with the statement of Mr. Babcock to the Senate and people of New York, cannot but deeply regret that the Hon. Senator should have lent the influence of his name and high station to calumny.

"The worthy priest, who, in the new church of St. Michael, is still the honored pastor of a majority of the former congregation of St. Louis, left that church, bearing with him the blessed sacrament, when he was publicly insulted in it, menaced, and ordered by the daring minority to quit it. Can the Bishop be blamed for not sending there another priest, when all who lived under the domination of the trustees either fled from it, declaring the post untenable, or importuned their Bishop to deliver them from such tyranny? Can the Bishop be blamed for refusing to go to law even with a misguided portion of his flock, or for not urging his claims, valid or invalid, but donating lots and money to aid in building sheds in which the faithful portion of his flock may worship in peace? Can the Bishop be blamed for refusing his services to men who refuse to accept his terms? Is the Bishop bound by any law to guide men who refuse to be guided by him; but who call that right which he calls wrong, and that wrong which he calls right? Would not a Bishop of the Protestant Episcopal Church refuse to sanction sacred rites in a church in which a minority, after insulting their pastor, and chasing him away, repudiated the discipline of the Church to which they belong?

"I need scarcely say that the touching jeremiad of the Senator 'is all a farce.' Those Germans who really wish to be Catholics and hear mass, have now, as formerly, all the sacraments administered to them. Those who wish to be Catholics according to their own rule, still go to St. Louis church, and make the prayers that suit them.

"Mr. Babcock is equally unfortunate in all his operations; it is not true that 'through the intervention of Cardinal Fornasi, the

Pope's Nuncio at Paris, Mr. Lecouteulx succeeded in his mission.' But it is true that the trustees begged pardon of Bishop Hughes, promised amendment, and obtained forgiveness for their reckless and insulting conduct!

"The Senator says: 'In France, for instance, the Church property is held by the municipal council, composed exclusively of laymen.' Alas, here again the same evil genius was at the Senator's elbow, to tell him what is not true. In France, no parish church or its property is held under the name of a municipal council, or of a corporation, or of a layman! Permit me to cite a little of French law; the French text will be at the Senator's service at any time:

"In 1801 a concordat was made between France and the Holy See; the twelfth article reads thus: 'All metropolitan, cathedral, and parochial churches, and all other churches necessary for worship, shall be delivered up to the care of the Bishop.' This law remains in force to this day, in that part of Catholic Europe which was affected by the French revolution.

"On the 18th June, 1827, a concordat was made between the King of Belgium and the Holy See. The first article is: 'Art. 1. The concordat of 1801, between the Sovereign Pontiff and the French government, being now in force in the southern provinces of Belgium, shall henceforward apply also to the northern provinces.'

"In the French decree concerning *Les Fabriques*, passed 30th December, 1809, we find: 'Of Sales,' 'Article 1. The alienation of Church property cannot be valid, unless authorized by the Emperor, (King, etc., as rulers changed,) *and by the Bishop*, the administrator *ex officio* of Church property.'

"'Sec. 2. Art. 1. The council of administration of a church shall watch over the preservation and repairs of the church, and administer the revenues. In parishes of more than five thousand population, there shall be nine councilors; the Bishop will name five and the Prefect four; in parishes of less than five thousand souls, there will be only five councilors; the Bishop will appoint three, the Prefect two. The pastor of the church shall always, *ex officio*, be the first member of the council; he may depute his vicar to fill his place. The council shall name the 'marguilliers,' (acting trustees.) Vacancies that occur will be filled by a majority of the council; if they neglect this for one month, the Bishop must then name to the vacancy.'

"Americans would perhaps only pity the Hon. Senator for his gullibility in believing the statement of 'his respectable informant' in French law. But deeply mortified will the candid American be, when he finds the same Senator mistaking the laws of our own country, in order to satisfy those bigoted feelings to which he well alludes when he says: 'As a private citizen and a Protestant, I may have *a duty* to perform in regard to the growth of Romanism, very wide of that incumbent upon a legislator.' What sort of a *duty* he may have to perform, Mr. Babcock says not. It may not be to burn our convents, as in Philadelphia; still he may have a duty to perform in regard to the rapid growth of Romanism!

"If Mr. Babcock had studied the law which he read in the Senate, he must have seen that the clause first enacted forms a Church government merely human, (the pastor having of right no more to do with the trustees than the man in the moon.) Other societies were not satisfied. The Protestant Episcopal Church obtained a special enactment, declaring that the pastor of the church is, *ex officio*, member and president of the board of trustees. Other Churches, too, claimed exemption from that ultra-human form.

"The Reformed Dutch Church obtained this concession: 'Be it enacted, that the minister or ministers, and elders and deacons, of every Reformed Dutch church or congregation, now or hereafter to be established in this State, shall be the trustees for every such church or congregation.' Even the Presbyterians found themselves aggrieved by the earlier act; hence, in 1822, they obtained this exemption: 'Be it enacted, that the minister or ministers, and elders and deacons, of every Reformed Presbyterian church, now or hereafter to be established within this

State, shall be the trustees of every such church and congregation.' In 1825, the 'True Reformed Dutch Church' obtained the same favor.

"Roman Catholics can only incorporate by a clause so ultra-Presbyterian, that even Presbyterians have asked and obtained laws to exempt them from its rigor. To the honor of the legislators who passed it, we may say that it was never intended for Catholics, (Catholics were then but a handful; the law seems to ignore their very existence,) no officer of their Church is once designated. The Hon. Senator says: 'Full ninety-nine hundredths of all the religious societies in the State are organized under the provisions of this law.' Is this an evasion, or special pleading? Under the clause against which the Catholics protest, it will be fair to say that only a small minority of the religious societies are incorporated. Take away the Protestant Episcopal Church, the Reformed Presbyterian Church, the Reformed Dutch Church, the True Reformed Dutch Church, and see if 'ninety-nine hundredths of the religious societies of the State are organized' under the form which aggrieves the Catholics.

"The Hon. Senator says that 'the Senator from the 11th, and others in and out of the Senate, claim that the Reformed Dutch Church has similar powers, and is a close corporation.' He is wholly mistaken; the constitution of that Church provides for the election of the elders and deacons by the body of the church, and for certain periods. But as regards the point at issue, either the Hon. Senator does not know what law is, or, in his high office of Senator, he descended to special pleading to mislead the Senate.

"Men who would vote for an individual to be trustee, would not afterwards refuse a vote to the same person were he a candidate for a spiritual office. Through an error, repugnant to the legislation of the Holy Scriptures and to the experience of man, many unthinking persons consider the church edifice and the revenues of the church as entirely distinct from the church in its spiritual character. In vain do we tell them that they might as well consider the body, its nourishment, its functions, and its actions, as entirely distinct from the soul. In vain do we show them how, by God's eternal law, the soul acts on the body, and the body and the functions of the body have their powerful influence on the soul. In vain do we show them that to legislate for the human body, because it is flesh, as you would legislate for the animal body, which is also flesh, would be enslaving the immortal spirit: still they affect to consider the church, not as the house of God, but as the house of Mr. Somebody, whom they represent, and the church revenues, not as something consecrated to God, and belonging to Him, but as something belonging to them and their's. Such persons will vote for Mr. B. as a trustee, because he is a very clever fellow; for Mr. C., because he is a great financier; for Mr. D., because he is a good Democrat, etc. Ask their vote to elect the same person into some known spiritual office, and they will shrink from the proposal.

"The Hon. Senator gives us extracts from the canon law which go most strongly to prove that the Bishops, and at least ninety-nine hundredths of the Catholics in the United States, know and act according to the principles of their Church, and that Mr. Lecouteulx and a very small minority, who care little for sacraments or discipline, neither know nor act according to the religion they profess. I do not here seek to prove that the Catholics are right, and that Mr. Babcock's religion is wrong. I merely say that Mr. Babcock's extracts, proving that the Bishops and the priests are right in their construction of the laws and discipline of their churches, prove also that they are worthy of praise, and not of blame, when they peacefully withdraw from men who do not believe as they do, and abandon the church edifice and its prospects, rather than go to law or act against their conscience.

"How different from Mr. Babcock's were the sentiments of the honored men who legislated for New York near the time of the heroes and sages of our Revolution! The very act passed 6th of April, 1784, which enacts the clause against which alone Catholics protest, says: 'It is ordained and declared that the free exercise and enjoyment of religious profession and worship, without discrimination or preference, be enjoyed by all religious denominations.' On the 7th of March, 1788, the New York

Legislature passed the law which now figures as one of the clauses of the present law. The preamble is as follows: 'Whereas, by the usage of the religious societies commonly known by the appellation of the Reformed Dutch Churches, the minister or ministers, and elders and deacons for the time being, have the management of the temporalities of the respective congregations, and the said congregations cannot therefore avail themselves of the benefit intended by the 'act to enable all the religious denominations in the State to appoint trustees, etc.,' without departing from such usage which has been long established, therefore, be it enacted, etc.' Then follows the law which constitutes the offices in the spiritual order, and their successors in that order, trustees to manage the temporalities. On the 17th of March, 1795, a law passed exempting the Protestant Episcopal Church from the rigor of the law of 1784. But let us hear the very words of the Protestant Church and of the Legislature: 'Whereas, the Protestant Episcopal Church in this State hath represented that the 'act to enable all the religious denominations in this State to appoint trustees,' passed 6th April, 1784, directs a mode of incorporation which subjects it to a variety of difficulties, leaving the congregations not incorporated to the alternative of foregoing the benefit of incorporation, *or of submitting to an entire alteration and subversion of the usual and peculiar government of the respective congregations of said Church;* for remedy whereof, Be it enacted, etc.' Then follows that which now stands as a clause of the law of our present Digest or Revisions.

"In that of 1784, against which Catholics, like the respectable Protestants above cited, protest, for the very same reason, because they cannot use it 'without an entire alteration and subversion of the usual and peculiar government of the respective congregations of said Church.' That law of 1784 which ignores the existence of the Roman Catholic Church and of its ministers, terminates with the noble and generous proviso, which, if it have not the power of law in the book, will, I am sure, in every generous heart, be a law to give to Catholics that relief which

Protestants claimed and obtained. 'Be it further enacted, etc., that nothing herein contained will be construed, adjudged, or taken to abridge or affect the *rights of conscience*, or private judgment, or *in the least* to alter or change the religious constitution or government of either of the said churches, congregations or societies, so far as respects, *or in any wise concerns, the doctrines, discipline, or worship thereof.*'

"VERITAS."

It was always the intention of Bishop Timon to establish, in connection with the hospital, a "Foundling Asylum" and "Lying-in House;" as many infants, whose parents had died in the hospital, had no friends to whom they might be given, and consequently, in the very beginning, these children were at first cared for in a wing of the hospital; but, the number of children increasing, and the attention necessary to be paid to them, resulting in serious damage to the interests of the sick in the hospital, Bishop Timon was constrained, though with much difficulty, to seek other lodgings in which to commence a new institution in his diocese.

Mr. Louis Stephen Lecouteulx, who had donated other valuable pieces of property for religious and charitable purposes, had intended to give a certain piece of ground, (at present occupied by a magnificent building called "St. Vincent's Infant Asylum," situated on Edward street,) to the Bishop, for any charitable purpose he might see fit to promote. Upon the death of Mr. Lecouteulx, senior, his son, P. A. Lecouteulx, kindly donated, according to the terms of his father's will, this piece of property for such an asylum; but, owing to a want of funds, Bishop Timon hesitated for a long time to build upon, and thereby take possession of the land. Legally, after a certain number of years, the property would have reverted to the lawful heirs of Mr. Lecouteulx, senior, and indeed, the time fixed by law for such issues had nearly expired, when, by mere accident, Bishop Timon discovered the oversight. No doubt, the necessities of the case, too, very materially aided in awakening him to the critical situation of affairs. He immediately had the ground properly fenced in, and two or three small cottages moved on to it, and in these humble dwellings he began "St. Vincent's Infant Asylum." This was in the year 1853. Just at this juncture the cholera broke out in the United States, and the hospitals were literally choked with patients, many of whom died. Mothers with infants died almost every day, and these latter helpless beings, thus deprived of their natural protectors, immediately found a home and careful nursing in the new asylum. Bishop Timon himself frequently assisted in carrying over in his own arms* to the asylum, little infants from the hospital whose parents had just died. But, in a very short time, even these cottages were found to be too small and inconvenient to answer the purpose required. The present handsome edifice was projected, for which a subscription was at first started, with which to commence building. In the meantime, Bishop Timon, in 1853, succeeded in getting this asylum incorporated, according to law. The work already begun on the new building was now pushed on with renewed energy, so that, on the 24th day of June, 1854, it was ready to receive its first entrances. Since then improvements have been made, aided by kind donations from the State.

How imperceptibly the decrees of Divine Providence manifest themselves through the zeal of devoted and pious men. Thus, in a few years, from rude beginnings, noble institutions of charity have sprung up on every side, to the advancement of the interests of the community in whose midst they have been built. Where, a short time ago, were uncultivated acres of land, over whose wastes have swept the howl of the wind, there now stand monuments of mercy, whose splendid piles rear in grandeur to the skies, as if in thanksgiving for the inscrutable designs of God. In the meantime, Bishop Timon, in the year 1853, purchased for the sum of twelve thousand dollars, *which he actually had to borrow*, a small farm for a cemetery, and consecrated forty acres

---

* The Bishop had early joined the order of St. Vincent de Paul, and in this act of charity, imitated the example of the illustrious founder of the Sisterhood of infant charity.

(14)

of it. This cemetery is located on Limestone Hill, near Buffalo.

The difficulty with the St. Louis church rebels became daily more complicated and defiant, so that Bishop Timon, who, in the exercise of charity and forbearance, had overlooked many and oft repeated violations of Church discipline, at length felt himself impelled to adopt a more stringent and decisive course. As has been seen from the correspondence between Monsignore Bedini, the Pope's legate, and the trustees, the Nuncio used the following remarkable words:

"The congregation of St. Louis, by adopting the course indicated, which alone is just and indispensable, will give a noble proof of faith and charity. But if they refuse, I can only see in them persons faithless to their duties, who can never be received as obedient sons of the Church of God."

The trustees "could not see" this kind of advice, and hence compelled the Nuncio to wind up the correspondence in the following painful language:

"Now, then, it becomes my duty to say that your answer is truly painful, especially to an envoy of the Holy Father, to whom you referred your case. The sad conviction forced itself upon me, that you disregard altogether Catholic principles, consequently, that if you persist, it only remains for me to deplore the sad position in which you place yourselves in the face of the Church; but the responsibility of this rests on yourselves."

The authority and kindness of the Nuncio failing to adjust the difficulty between the trustees and *their duty*, the matter, of course, was left entirely in the Bishop's hands. He readily availed himself of the authority thus left him by the Nuncio, in writing, which was as follows:

"I consider them as not being Catholics at heart, and, Right Reverend Sir, should your Episcopal ministry inspire you to declare so, in order that good Catholics may know *who* are their brethren and who are not, and that those who now are led astray may no longer be deceived as to right or participation in the benedictions and benefits of the Catholic Church, I leave it to your discretion and to your holy inspirations."

This judgment was approved of by the Holy See. The trustees, however, in the public papers, published, amidst many untruths, their determination never to comply with the decision of the Holy Father, and this, finally, determined the Bishop's course of action, and rendered his duty more imperative and decisive.

Therefore, on the feast of the Octave of Corpus Christi, June 21st, 1854, Bishop Timon issued his major or greater excommunication against the trustees,* (seven in number,) declaring further, "that all who may accept the office of trustee of St. Louis church, *to continue the present unholy opposition to Church discipline*, will, *ipso facto*, incur the same major excommunication."

For nearly two years after the excommunication of the trustees, Bishop Timon allowed no priest to officiate in St. Louis church. A black flag was flung to the breezes above the church, by some misguided people, and, although obliged to act as he had done towards the leaders and promoters of strife in the congregation, Bishop Timon often wept tears of sorrow for the condition of the congregation itself, thus deprived of spiritual help. But he did not altogether despair for their future.

On the feast of Pentecost, May 27th, 1855, at the earnest solicitation of the distinguished missionary, Rev. Father Weniger, S. J., the interdict was solemnly removed, and the church reopened. The following is the permission given for the removal of the interdict:

"BUFFALO, May 18th, 1855.

"The pious, learned, and zealous missionary, Father Weniger, (wishing to labor for the salvation of souls in the only German church of this diocese which has not yet heard his noble and truly christian eloquence,) requests me to withdraw the interdict from the church of St. Louis, and the excommunication from the trustees. I can refuse nothing to this worthy priest of God; consenting, therefore, to his request, I hereby declare, that the excommunication will cease as soon as the holy *Triduan* in St. Louis church will begin.

"✝ JOHN, *Bishop of Buffalo.*"

---

* Names are here omitted for charity's sake, as the excommunication over them has since been removed.

Father Weniger succeeded in obtaining some concessions to ecclesiastical laws and discipline on the part of the trustees, though the good father has himself since acknowledged that it was not without reciprocal concessions on his part. At first, Bishop Timon was not fully satisfied with the manner in which Father Weniger was dealing with the affair, and went frequently to the St. Louis church parsonage to see him about it. At length, the matter went so far that Father Weniger respectfully suggested to the Bishop, "One of us has to leave Buffalo, until the settlement is effected." Bishop Timon consented to go to Pittsburgh.

In the statutes of the Diocese of Buffalo, (page 26, Art. XIX.,) may be found the Bishop's conduct towards this church, and there will also be found the affirmation of the entire clergy, that the Bishop acted wisely, and even was not strict enough with this congregation.

The *erring men* at last yielded, and once more the holy sacrifice was offered in their church. Thus ended, seemingly, this long and stubborn difficulty of St. Louis church. We say seemingly, because since then frequent misunderstandings have taken place, threatening the life of their pastor, and casting under the table in the waste basket any official communication to the board of trustees from the Bishop. In fact, this trouble may be compared to the eruptions of a volcano like Vesuvius. Frequent small eruptions from the mouth of the crater, indicate that the fires of matter, once so destructive and dangerous, are not wholly extinct, and are likely, at any moment, to assert their former ascendency irrespective of the dire consequences that may ensue.

So with St. Louis church. The great eruption has been calmed down. But the frequent insults to Episcopal authority since, and the insolence and ill-bred behavior to its priests, are indications enough to show that the fires of rebellion are still aglow, although under subdued discipline. God spare the church of the future in this city from the further scandal of insubordination of the laity against due Church authority. Amen.

CHAPTER VII.

EDUCATION.—CONVENT OF THE SACRED HEART.—ST. JOSEPH'S COLLEGE.—OBLATE FATHERS ARRIVE.—ST. JOSEPH'S COLLEGE.—DISCOURAGING CIRCUMSTANCES.—IT FAILS.—CHRISTIAN BROTHERS.—MISS NARDIN'S ACADEMY.—INCIDENTS.—SISTERS OF THE GOOD SHEPHERD.—A DETAILED REPORT.—OTHER RELIGIOUS ORDERS.—PROVINCIAL SYNOD.—ITS RESULTS AND IMPORTANCE.—BISHOP GOES TO ROME.—DOGMA OF IMMACULATE CONCEPTION.

THE next want in this diocese that manifested itself very plainly to the Bishop, was that of education. As early as 1848, Rev. Julian Delaune, late President of St. Mary's College, in Kentucky, under the auspices of the Bishop, opened the College of the Sacred Heart, at Rochester; but it met with difficulties, and closed in 1852. The exertions of the Bishop, however, in the cause of education, were not confined to this college; he sought to endow his diocese with a house of religious women, devoted to the highest order of teaching, and therefore rejoiced to find that the ladies of the Sacred Heart were able and willing to aid him. Accordingly, a colony came from Manhattanville, New York, in 1849, and founded a convent of their order in Buffalo, which, however, was, in 1855, transferred to Rochester, as a more central point for their academy.

The subject of education seemed to impose special claims upon the Bishop's attention, and, as a matter of urgent necessity as well as of vital importance, he did not forget the youth of both sexes.

In 1849, he opened another institution in Buffalo, known as St. Joseph's College. He placed it under the tutelage of the clergy, and gave it the above name, out of a special veneration he held for St. Joseph. The early career of this college was a varied one, transferred from one portion of the city to the other, it was temporarily located in the Episcopal residence attached to the cathedral.

Bishop Timon was particularly anxious for its success, and the encouragements he held out to the laity, and the degree of talent he employed, were such as to reveal the interest he evinced for the mental as well as moral culture of his flock.

But, unfortunately, the many complicated labors that engrossed his mind, the numerous missions he had personally to attend to, the pecuniary embarrassments in which he struggled, and the insufficient interest and enthusiasm manifested on the part of the laity in general, all these combined were so many agencies at work that undermined the foundations upon which he had to build for the education and culture of Catholic youth, and caused the trembling superstructure to totter, with a prospect of finally passing out of existence entirely. In this emergency, however, that ever watchful interest and energy of purpose of the man came to the rescue, and for a time prolonged the doom that threatened the hopes of the college. Bishop Timon then invited to his diocese the Oblate Fathers, and transferring the future of the institution to their fostering care, removed the college to York street, on Prospect Hill, near to the church of the Holy Angels. But in spite, as it were, of the zeal and determination of the good Bishop, the institution did not seem to "grow." It lingered along spasmodically, as we have seen, and although the good Oblate Fathers brought the best of talent to bear, (particularly during the administration of Father Chevalier,) it did not prosper. There seemed to be a general apathy among the Catholics at large; education, although a necessity and an advantage in their estimation, did not awaken a corresponding enthusiasm in their callous bosoms. Like a ship leaking at every pore, gradually sinks as she fills with water, although her crew labor incessantly at the pumps, and finally engulfs beneath the closing waters of the ocean, thus St. Joseph's College, gradually sinking for want of sufficient support and encouragement, finally engulfed in the darkness of obscurity, and was blotted out of existence for the time being.

It was a source of great grief to the feelings of Bishop Timon, to witness this result of his labors thus far in the cause of education in the diocese, and although the prospects were dubious and the future uncertain, he relied firmly in the Providence of God, "who doeth all things for the best." Nothing daunted, therefore, by the adversities and ill-success of his efforts in this particular, he, subsequently, by dint of renewed energy, succeeded in re-establishing the college, though on another basis. Grown wise by experience, and having witnessed in his travels, both on this continent and in Europe, the grand results that were acquired by the children of the Venerable Father De Salle, or, as they are more generally known, the "Christian Brothers," Bishop Timon opened negotiations for introducing a community of these religious persons into his diocese.

In these efforts he was successful. Six brothers, from New York and Montreal, under the charge of Brother Crispian, arrived in August, 1861. The fine buildings in the rear of St. Joseph's Cathedral, are mute but eloquent testimonials of the success that has attended their efforts in a diocese hitherto apparently indifferent, or apathetic to the requirements of good education. The introduction of Christian Brothers into different dioceses, and the encouragement given them by several Bishops in the United States, was similarly imitated by Bishop Timon. He encouraged an establishment at Rochester, in St. Patrick's parish, from which, as a central house, each morning the brothers went to the different parish schools to teach.

The same was done at first in Buffalo, when, in the Fall of 1861, the erection of an academy was commenced, dedicated to St. Joseph.

But the solicitude of Bishop Timon for the establishment of schools, was not local. He endeavored to infuse his zeal for learning into other parts of his diocese; perhaps not upon so extensive a scale, but at least as interestedly. Nor were his efforts exerted mainly for the boys. He provided for the girls in the various institutions that still survive, some of which subserve other objects, such as caring for the deaf and the dumb, the infirm, the poor, and the abandoned. Among several worthy institutions that he introduced into his diocese, the first one that suggests itself is that known as Miss Nardin's Academy. It is a religious community of educated ladies, bound together in the same way as any other religious order, by rules, with this exception, that the ladies wear no habit and are secular. Their duties are to instruct the young particularly.

Bishop Timon knew the community originally in France, but secured the present number of ladies in 1855, from their established mother house at Cleveland. It will be amusing, as well as interesting, to review the labors and the zeal that the Bishop exerted in establishing this community in his diocese. After having invited the ladies to come to Buffalo, with the promise that a house would be prepared to receive them, he was considerably astonished to discover, on their arrival, that the instructions he had given to another person to provide the house and furnish the same, at least sufficiently to receive the ladies, had been almost entirely neglected.

On their arrival they proceeded to the Hydraulics, near the junction of Swan and Seneca streets, where they found the house provided for them, but nothing in it with which to commence housekeeping, not even an ordinary article of furniture. Nothing but the bare walls greeted them. The poor Bishop was in despair, and felt sad that his instructions had not been fulfilled. But the indomitable energy of purpose that had so often triumphed over sterner embarrassments, immediately asserted itself. Going across the street, to a house opposite, he obtained a tallow candle, in order to throw light upon the situation, and see what was to be done. He also ordered some hot water to be sent over, with which the travel-worn ladies might be refreshed with a cup of tea at least. Without stopping in his work, he next sent down mattresses and some other articles, and from his own personal furniture he added sheets and bed clothing. With these the good ladies made a faint beginning, and not long after, true to their mission, began to take young ladies to instruct them. In this first place of residence the community remained for some time, although it was soon discovered that the location of their institution was not a good one. Consequently, they removed to premises on Pearl street, south of Seneca street, and subsequently again removed their home from thence to the corner of Ellicott and South Division streets, at present the residence of Dr. Miner. Here they remained a few years, with varying success, until their present permanent location was procured on the corner of Church and Franklin streets, where a very fine and commodious building is in process of erection.

It was always the special desire of the Bishop that this religious community should prosper, and on many and repeated occasions he has extended towards these talented ladies marked and favorable expressions of his sympathy and interest.

One morning, during the winter of 1859, when Buffalo had been visited with very severe weather, the surface of the streets and sidewalks of the city were like one vast sheet of ice. It had been raining very severely the day before, and during the night following it froze so hard that it was dangerous to venture abroad. It being a pious practice to be present at holy mass early every morning during the week, the community, in consequence of the state of the streets, and the danger of going out on this morning, had very prudently remained at home. The watchful Bishop missed them, accustomed as he was to see them together in the church at that early hour, (six o'clock,) and immediately after mass, in his solicitude, went, at great personal risk, to call and inquire whether any thing had happened. Advanced in years, and tottering under the infirmities and cares of age, he could not rest until he had done this duty, and at the same time ascertain whether the community had provisions and necessaries of life in the house sufficient for the day. This duty performed, he returned again to his residence.

Nor was his interest in this community abated when, on Ash Wednesday of 1867, the year of his saintly death, he, in person, called at the academy to give his permission to the ladies not to fast; and this he chose to do himself, if he could thereby only spare the trouble to the community of calling on him to ask the permission. A few weeks afterwards and he, whose zeal and charity were ever warm and attached to his institutions, was a cold and inanimate corpse. But it was Bishop Timon's nature to be continually busy. He seemed to scorn fatigue, and his whole heart and soul were enlisted in the cause of the Church and charity. Besides the many beautiful religious edifices erected in the diocese, directly by the main efforts of clergymen and religious orders, but indirectly sanctioned and encouraged by the good Bishop himself, there are many institutions that may be considered, directly speaking, as the *result* of his own pious labors and encouragement. For instance, he introduced the religious order of the Sisters of St. Joseph for the Deaf and Dumb. To begin this institution upon a proper basis, he visited the various asylums for the deaf and dumb in this country and in Europe, in order to bring his experience and knowledge of the workings of these similar institutions to bear directly on his own. Frequently, when suffering under embarrassments arising from the want of the necessaries of life, he has taken from his pocket, or sent from his residence, means amounting to a hundred dollars at a time. He took a decided interest in the condition of the poor orphans gathered there, who could neither hear nor speak, and very frequently his sympathy for their unfortunate situation was such that he was scarcely able to repress his emotions and tears.

The following circular will best explain the history of this noble institution, from its beginning:

"*To the Honorable, The Senate and House of Representatives of the State of New York:*

"Mr. A. P. Lecouteulx, a distinguished benefactor, generously presented Rt. Rev. Bishop Timon an acre lot on the south-west corner of Morgan and Edward streets, Buffalo, for the purpose of establishing, in Western New York, an Asylum for the instruction of the Deaf and Dumb. Having no building on the lot, nor sufficient means to erect a suitable edifice, the Bishop found it was necessary to purchase three small frame houses which were in the neighborhood, and caused them to be moved on the lot in the Spring of 1856. Three Sisters of St. Joseph took charge of the new Asylum, and immediately opened a day school for the support of the house, to enable them to prepare it for the reception of mutes. In October, 1857, the instruction of the deaf and dumb commenced, with four females who lived in the house, and a few males who lived in the vicinity, and attended as day pupils; but were it not for the benevolence of the Rt. Rev. Bishop Timon, whose charity for those afflicted children was unbounded, every idea of its continuing to exist would have been abandoned. However, it was thought well to suspend the instruction of the deaf and dumb for the space of one year, during which time efforts would be made to erect a suitable building for this noble object. Those in charge received their knowledge of the sign language from a graduate of the Deaf and Dumb Asylum of Caen, France. In the meantime one of the community was sent to the well known and excellent institution of Philadelphia, to become acquainted with the mode which the institutions of the United States have adopted. We have now the pleasure of announcing that the building has been some time completed. The building is four stories, twenty-eight by thirty-four, affording a spacious dormitory, refectory, kitchen, etc., capable of accommodating thirty children, and has cost eight thousand dollars. The frame houses we have converted into class rooms. So far the progress of the children has been encouraging and gratifying. They are daily exercised in all useful branches of education, besides reading and writing; the females are taught needle work and other fancy work, and are exercised in household and culinary duties. The males, ('who can only be admitted as externs, the building not affording, as yet, space to divide sufficiently the sleeping apartments of both sexes,') are also exercised in habits of industry. All the pupils are preparing for the duties and practical business of life. The hours of the day are apportioned to study, work, exercise and amusement, which latter takes place in the open air when the weather permits. For the male department, little has yet been done. Many applications which we receive we are obliged to reject for want of suitable apartments, and also sufficient means for their support. The generality of the applicants, being in indigent circumstances, are in no way able to assist us. The pupils who have attended since the establishment of the Asylum are poor, and unable to defray their own expenses.

"We received no appropriation, collection or donation, excepting from the same charitable source before mentioned. Having briefly stated our circumstances, we now appeal to your right honorable body in behalf of the poor deaf and dumb children who are and will be benefitted by the continuance of this institution; having been encouraged by the approbation and signature of the most prominent citizens of the city of Buffalo, to appeal to you for an appropriation of five thousand dollars to erect an addition to this building, for the accommodation of the male portion who wish to be boarded in the institution, and who are anxiously seeking for admittance. It would be also greatly for the good of society if your honorable body would allow a small annual appropriation for the clothing and maintenance of poor deaf and dumb children.

"The lots on which the institution is built are valued at	$10,000 00
"The buildings are worth about	10,000 00
"Furniture, books, etc.,	2,000 00
	"$22,000 00

"Thirteen poor deaf and dumb children have been received, and about sixty other poor children have been instructed gratuitously by the institution.

"SISTER M. MAGDALEN, *Superintendent*,
"SISTER M. ALOYSIUS, *Secretary*.

"BUFFALO, Feb. 4th, 1865."

In the dedication sermon of St. Joseph's Cathedral, delivered by His Grace Archbishop Hughes, (since deceased,) the latter took occasion to observe that he considered Bishop Timon the most humble man he ever met. He evinced no ostentation or outward ceremony, but was always plain, simple and unassuming in his manner and habits. In addition to this compliment, the good Archbishop might have added another, not less deserved, and equally as true. He might have said that Bishop Timon was the most charitable man he ever met, for he was continually planning what new charitable feature he might introduce into his diocese for the good of humanity. He had provided for the sick, the orphan, the foundling and the youth. But these did not suffice for his view of charity. He must provide as well for the abandoned and the fallen of unfortunate females. For the establishment of such an institution of charity Bishop Timon made ample preparation. He spared no leisure hour in contriving plans by which to make a beginning, even to drawing upon his own slender resources for aid.

In the institution known as "House of the Good Shepherd," what an admirable example of his zeal and charity. As early as 1854 and 1855, he saw the actual necessity of a house devoted to rescuing abandoned women from vice, and by dint of due teaching and the exercise of christian morals and piety, to stem at least in part this torrent of destruction and sensuality with which, alas, our large cities in particular are afflicted. This convent was the first of the order sent as a filiation from the convent at Rennes. Hence a detailed report of their beginnings in this country will be very interesting:

"On the 1st of June, 1855, four Sisters of Charity of 'Our Lady of Refuge,' arrived in Buffalo for the holy functions of their institute. They had been selected by the Right Rev. Bishop from their noble house near Rennes, in France. The Superioress, Mother Mary of Jerome Tournais, stands high in her order for talents and piety, and for having had much experience in founding new houses. On the 8th July, 1855, the good Sisters opened their institution of mercy in a rented house on Ellicott street. God blessed the efforts of ladies who had left their native country, relations and friends of distinguished rank, and, *not last*, their language, to come amongst strangers, to endure poverty and want, and learn again, like children, to lisp the first elements of 'an unknown tongue,' in order to lead to the Good Shepherd lost sheep that had wandered through muddy, foul, and thorny paths. Whilst learning, in English, their A, B, C, the Sisters took in a number of houseless, unprotected females, and some lost outcasts; and, to earn their daily bread, labored for and with them, in sewing and in doing such work as the charitable might send to them.

"The Right Rev. Bishop paid their passage from France, their house rent, etc., procured them their first scanty furniture, and what the Sisters valued most of all, had an altar erected and furnished, and gave them permission to keep the adorable sacrament in their poor but neat chapel. Often has the Bishop been heard to speak in admiration of their cheerful, uncomplaining resignation to privations which they were even studious to conceal, because they were most willing to suffer, from the effects of poverty, with Him 'who became poor that, by His poverty, we might be made rich.' From first to last, the outlay of the Bishop for this institution has been nearly three thousand dollars. It would have been greater if the Sisters had not hidden their wants from him, and to his frequent enquiry if they needed help, answered so as to persuade him that they were getting on well enough; often, however, he had almost to force them to accept help, when he suspected, and subsequently knew, that they had not means to pay for their bread.

"The house on Ellicott street being too small to lodge the increased numbers that flocked to their *refuge*, the Sisters rented two houses on Washington street, whither they removed on the 1st May, 1856, the adjoining French church of St. Peter having been, through the kindness of its pastor, so arranged as to afford them nearly as much facility for worship as if it was their own private chapel.

"Most dear to humanity, to religion, to the Good Shepherd, whose sacred mission it especially embraces, must be institutions like this! In Europe they have done immense good. On this continent, in Louisville, St. Louis, Montreal, etc., the piety, zeal, devotedness, and spirit of self-sacrifice of the Ladies of the Good Shepherd are well known. In all those places they have saved many poor young women from danger and from ruin, and reclaimed many from vice. We have already evidences that the results of their labors in Buffalo will be equally consoling. Up to the 1st of March, 1857, the Sisters of our Lady of Refuge have received in their house of the Good Shepherd, sixteen penitents. All have been reclaimed, six have been given back to their parents or friends, two have been placed out, eight remain.

"In the class of preservation, which is strictly separated from the class of penitents, twenty-five have been received, four have returned to their friends, twenty-one remain.

"Thirty poor houseless women or girls have also been received, nourished and lodged, for a longer or shorter period, until situations were found for them; often, indeed, they had also to be clothed.

"If even in its poor beginning, under many disadvantages, the institution has already achieved so much, what may we not, through God's blessings, expect in the future? With reason may its benefactors thank God, who has deigned to make them His instruments for His own work of 'The Good Shepherd!' 'He who causeth a sinner to be converted from the error of his ways, shall save his soul from death, and cover a multitude of his sins.' —*St. James*, vi.

"An invariable rule forbids the Sisters ever to admit into their order any woman who has once fallen, though years of penitence and most exemplary life may have intervened. Yet, reclaimed 'Magdalenes,' who feel themselves called to a religious life, may, under the inspection of the Sisters, and in a separate house, form what is called 'the Magdalene Society;' their dress is black, whilst that of the Sisters is white. Nothing of the kind has yet been done in Buffalo; indeed, most of the reclaimed 'Magdalenes' prefer, when their good habits are sufficiently assured, to return to the world and embrace decent employments, for which the instruction they receive in the institution well qualifies them.

"The Sisters rejoice at becoming the instruments of God in making known, for His glory, the generous, zealous and charitable spirit of the venerable clergy, of different nations, in this city, who deigned to associate themselves together to aid and encourage the Sisters in their holy work of the Good Shepherd. In several meetings, those ministers of a pardoning God devised a plan of a 'Society of the Good Shepherd,' composed solely of ladies of exemplary life, who have a holy wish to aid the Good Shepherd in saving souls.

"Twelve respectable ladies in each congregation form an apostolic band of charity, which meets once a month in each parish, whilst general meetings are only required twice a year. The ladies use their influence to procure work for the inmates of the House of the Good Shepherd; direct to it females who are exposed to danger, or lost ones who wish again to find their God. The ladies also receive and hand over such alms as the charitable choose to offer for this holy work. This beneficent and most respectable society has already greatly aided the institute. May God bless these young ladies and their families for their sake!

"Twice, in the church of St. Peter, has the Bishop officiated in the most solemn rite of receiving postulants into the novitiate of the order; the crowded audience at each time, seemed deeply affected, as those ladies, renouncing the world, put off the dress and ornaments of worldly pomp, to clothe themselves with the poor and simple habit of the order, as if visibly dying to the world and its vain hopes, and putting on the plain attire of the penitent's God, who says, 'I am the Good Shepherd.' Four novices are now in the novitiate; one postulant pleads for admission.

"The subjoined account of receipts and expenses will prove how the Holy Providence of God has protected the institution. A new institution was to be founded; few understood its object or its aim; all had to be begun, much had to be purchased in haste and at a disadvantage. Yet, when we look at the outlay and see the blessed results, we are forced to cry out, 'the finger of God is here.'

TREASURER'S REPORT,

From July 1st, 1855, to January 1st, 1857.

EXPENSES:

"For passage from France,	$520 00
"For rent on Ellicott street,	320 00
"For rent on Washington street,	525 00
"For furniture, beds, bedding, etc.,	375 00
"For bill of S. Bettinger, Esq.,	81 00
"For fence,	70 00
"For charges on box from Paris,	13 97
"For fuel,	219 41
"For bread,	475 81
"For other provisions,	537 98
"Alms to poor women on leaving,	62 11
"Clothing,	170 77
"Total,	$3,371 05

RECEIPTS:

"Donation from Right Rev. Bishop,	$2,500 00
"Donation from Ladies' Society,	94 51
"Collection in churches,	59 00
"Alms,	209 50
"Work,	477 17
"Total,	$3,340 18 "

To this accession of labor in the vineyard of religion and charity, were added other pious communities. The Brothers of the Holy Infancy of Jesus were introduced into the diocese to direct the Orphan Boys' Asylum, whilst Sisters of St. Bridget, an order founded in the middle of the last century, in Ireland, by the Right Rev. Dr. Lanigan, in honor of the Virgin Patroness of the island, devoted themselves to the instruction of poor girls at Buffalo and Rochester. This impulse, given by Bishop Timon, penetrated other parts of his diocese. On the 8th of December, 1854, the very day when all the christian world exulted by its representative Bishops at Rome at the definition of the dogma of the "Immaculate Conception," by His Holiness Pope Pius IX, a colony of Sisters of St. Joseph arrived at Canandaigua from St.

Louis. Here these Sisters opened an academy. Besides teaching the youth, they undertook other works of mercy, such as providing a house for poor girls of good character, whose only alternative, previously, was the poor-house or shame.

In the meantime, a council of suffragan Bishops was convened in New York, by Archbishop Hughes. It was the first Ecclesiastical Council ever held in New York. To the Bishops of Albany, Buffalo and Brooklyn, were referred the subjects of Catholic education, and the Catholic press. The council sat for a week, during which period there were two solemn sessions. The ceremonials attending the council were grand and imposing. The decrees of the council, afterwards promulgated in the name of all the prelates of the province by Archbishop Hughes, were six in number:

"*First*, Profession of obedience and devotion to the Holy Father.

"*Second*, Promulgated a new decree of the seven Provincial Councils of Baltimore.

"*Third*, Forbade priests to mortgage Church property without permission of the Bishop.

"*Fourth*, Repeated the injunctions of the National Council of Baltimore, respecting Catholic education, and exhorted clergymen to labor zealously for the establishment of schools.

"*Fifth*, Admonished priests that it was unlawful for them to exercise functions of the ministry requiring 'faculties,' except within their own diocese or with the permission of the Bishop in whose diocese they might be sojourning.

"*Sixth*, Enjoined on all parish priests the duty of providing, as soon as possible, a pastoral residence adjacent to the church, the title of which, as well as of all other Church property, was to be in the name of the Bishop."

The pastoral, among other things, continues:

"Two other subjects have engaged the attention of the fathers in the council which has just been brought to a close. One is, the indiscriminate reception in your families of journals not at all calculated to impart either to you or those committed to your care, those solid maxims of public instruction which would tend to edification. We do not here intend to speak of merely secular papers; but we do speak rather of those which, taking advantage of certain feelings supposed to be alive in your breasts, whether in reference to kindred, country, or religion, involve you in political relations which it would be expedient for you to avoid; except, indeed, in the sense in which it is the right of every free man to give his vote freely, conscientiously, individually, as often as the laws of the country call upon and authorize him to do so. There appears to be abroad an ignorance or prejudice on this subject, which it would be our desire and your interest to have removed. It is to the effect that every paper which advocates, or professes to advocate, the Catholic religion, or which advocates some imaginary foreign interest in this country, is, as a matter of course, under the direction of priests and Bishops in the locality where it is published, and consequently authorized to speak for and in the name of the Catholic Church. Hence, when the editors of such papers publish their own sentiments by virtue of their indisputable right to exercise the liberty of the press, it is assumed by persons outside of our communion that they speak in the name of the Church, and under direction of her pastors. Nothing could be more false than this inference, and we exhort you, venerable and beloved brethren, to leave nothing unsaid or undone to remove every shadow of foundation for this inference, so absurd in itself, but yet so injurious to us."

The other subject related to the "association which is known in Europe as the 'Propagation of the Faith;'" but as Bishop Timon had no direct expression of views on this subject, we avoid details. It will be enough to observe that this society has spread all over Christendom. During the Winter of 1854, an Informal Council was to be held at Rome, at which it was expected that the doctrine of the "Immaculate Conception of the Blessed Virgin" would be defined as an article of faith. Pope Pius IX invited all the Bishops of the world, who could conveniently make the journey, to assemble at Rome on that solemn occasion.

Accordingly, on the 18th of October, 1854, Bishop Timon, in company with Archbishop Hughes, of New York, set sail for Rome.

Before leaving he named the jubilee for his diocese, for which he appointed three months time, from November 12th, 1854, up to February 12th, 1855. Among many solicitations for the different institutions of his diocese, he observed:

"The interests of religion and of this diocese compel your Bishop to undertake a voyage, painful to the aged and not without peril. We beg your kind prayers, dearly beloved in Christ, that God's holy angel *may be our keeper, both going hence and abiding there, and returning from thence hither.*"

---o---

CHAPTER VIII.

FRANCISCAN FATHERS.—THE "IMMACULATE CONCEPTION" AT ROME.—BISHOP TIMON'S RETURN.—PASTORAL ON DOGMA OF THE IMMACULATE CONCEPTION.—CHURCH PROPERTY BILL AGAIN.—BISHOP TIMON ON SENATOR PUTNAM'S POETRY.—FAVORS FROM THE POPE TO THE DIOCESE OF BUFFALO.

WHILST the pious Sisters of St. Joseph were diffusing the odor of sanctity around Canandaigua, the cause of faith was advancing multifold in every direction throughout the large diocese. The following reminiscence will be found interesting:

* "Nicholas Devereux, Esq., of Utica, owned a large tract in Alleghany and Cattaraugus counties, to which he had endeavored to draw Catholic settlers, facilitating in every way the erection of churches and the establishing of missions. But the progress of Catholicity did not correspond to his zealous wishes, and having visited Rome in 1854, he applied to the Irish College of St. Isidore for Fathers of the Order of St. Francis, to found a mission in New York, offering five thousand dollars and two hundred acres of land for the new convent. He wished seven Fathers in order to begin the mission, but as there were not so many able to speak

---

* Catholic Church in the United States, by De Courcy.

English who could be sent, it was resolved to defer the intended colony for two years. The Rt. Rev. Bishop of Buffalo, however, was in Rome, *and from his zeal* objected to any such delay. On this, some of the Fathers so earnestly besought the General of the Order for permission to go and restore the Franciscan Order in that part of the world, where their own brothers had been the first apostles,* that he consented, and the Fathers received all due faculties.

"Of this new colony of Recollets, Father Pamphilus de Magliano is the Warden or Superior, having under him Father Sixtus de Gagliano, Father Samuel de Prezza and the Lay Brother Salvador de Manarola. They are all Recollets, or Reformed Franciscans, of the same family as the early missionaries of Canada, and the Chaplains whom we have had occasion to mention.†

"Two of the Fathers were professors of Theology at or near Rome; the Superior at the Irish College, and Father Sixtus at the Convent of St. Bernadine, at Urbino. Father Samuel was at the College of San Pietro Montorio, in Rome, having just completed his studies. Father Pamphilus and Father Sixtus had long nourished a desire of devoting themselves to the foreign missions, and had selected the United States as their chosen field of labor; so much so, that a few days before Mr. Devereux's application, they had declined an invitation to proceed to Buenos Ayres.

"With the blessing of the Holy Father, and the authority to establish a province of their order, they left Rome on the 9th of May, 1855, and reaching New York on the 19th of June, proceeded to Ellicottville, where they began their labors."

During the absence of the Bishop in Rome, the beautiful churches of St. Mary's, Dunkirk, and St. Patrick's, Rochester,

---

* The Recollets, or Reformed Franciscans, had already, as early as 1723, particularly under Father Emanuel Crespel, been in this section of the country.

† The Franciscans, or Friars Minor, comprise, 1st, the Observantines, the Recollets, and the Alcantarines, who number about ninety thousand, and are subject to the Minister-General of the Order of Minors. The present General is Father Venantius de Celano, a Recollet; 2d, the Capuchins; 3d, the Conventicals; 4th, the Tertiaries; the three last having each a General of their own. The Capuchins number about forty thousand, the Conventicals about seven thousand, and the Tertiaries a number almost incalculable.

were dedicated with appropriate ceremonies. Whilst the vineyard of religion was thus carefully nurtured, and gave promise of an abundant harvest, afar, in the city of Rome, in solemn council, was transpiring an event that filled Christendom with joy. It was the defining of the dogma of the Immaculate Conception. Bishop Timon assisted in this grand event, and in the Spring of 1855 started on his journey to return early to his diocese. He arrived in New York on Friday, April 6th, 1855. On Saturday he reached Rochester, where he celebrated high mass in St. Patrick's. On Sunday, the 8th, he said mass and officiated at vespers in several of the churches of Buffalo.

In a pastoral issued on his return, he gave a very interesting and learned explanation of the article of faith of the Immaculate Conception:

"The Holy Church has now defined as of faith the consoling truth, which we always piously and fervently believed, that Mary, mother of the Holy of Holies, was conceived without sin. All praise and glory to the Divine Son, who thus elevates the pious sentiment which glorifies Him in His holy mother to the merit of faith, to the sublime rank of the highest honor which our created intelligence can render to the God of truth. Divine wisdom has, for some ages, been preparing the christian world for this declaration, by the aspirations and petitions of learned men; by miracles, some in our own country, through prayers addressed to God, under the invocation of Mary the immaculate, or through the miraculous medal; and by prophecies, like that of the venerable Mary Magdalen of the Cross, who, in 1640, predicted that in times of great trouble the dogma of the Immaculate Conception would be defined, and that soon, in China, in Japan, and in Turkey, God would triumph; or like that of the blessed Leonard of Port Mauritio, who, before his death in 1751, most clearly predicted the solemn declaration of the Immaculate Conception, with the grace of God and the blessings which heaven would then bestow.

"About one hundred years after this prediction, the Sovereign Pontiff, in days of trial and sorrow from his exile at Gaeta, looked up to the 'Comfort of the afflicted,' to the 'Help of christians.' As he shared more fully in the persecutions of the Divine Son, so also did he in the spirit and sentiment of that adorable model. Jesus loved and honored His mother, and oh, how He loved her as she clung to the cross on which He hung; His servant and chief minister, too, loved Mary, and in exile, amidst persecutions *from his cross*, he felt more strongly within him 'the mind that was in Christ Jesus.' For Jesus' sake, as minister of Jesus, drinking of his bitter chalice, loving and honoring what Jesus loved and honored, the Vicar of Christ, then loving and honoring Mary with deeper reverence and tenderer love, felt himself pressed to yield to the wishes and prayers of the holy and learned throughout the christian world. But though the inspiration came from above, he used all means of human, and even of superhuman prudence; he wrote to every Bishop to inquire what were the traditions of each church, what the sentiments, the faith and the devotion of their flocks regarding the Immaculate Conception. Five hundred and sixty-four Bishops answered, declaring that their people firmly believed in the glorious mystery. Only four out of the vast number desired, through fear of human inconveniences, that the dogma should not be defined. The Holy Father next formed a congregation of most learned theologians to examine the questions.

"During nearly six years, in labor, in prayer, and in fasting, the great work progressed. 'Certainly,' says our saintly Pope, in his bull on the Immaculate Conception, 'we were filled with no slight consolation when the replies of our venerable brethren came to us. For, with an incredible joyfulness, gladness and zeal, they not only declared their own singular piety, and that of their clergy and faithful people, towards the Immaculate Conception of the most Blessed Virgin, but they even entreated us with a common voice to define, by our supreme judgment and authority, the Immaculate Conception of the Blessed Virgin. Nor, indeed, were we filled with less joy when the venerable cardinals of the special congregation aforesaid, and the consulting theologians chosen by *US*, after a diligent examination, demanded from *US*, with equal alacrity and zeal, the definition of the Immaculate Conception of the Mother of God.' Pius IX has defined the sacred dogma, and the Catholic world has rejoiced, and Triduans, that is, three days of special joy and holy exercises, have been celebrated throughout the wide world, and continue to be celebrated in honor of the glad event. Having been appointed by the Bishop of the Provincial Council deputy to the Holy Father, it was my duty and my good fortune to be present on the glorious day of the declaration; and never can I forget the scene. Sublime in moral grandeur were even the preceding days, when all the Bishops in private congress debated on a human form of a definition, to which, in answering the Pope's encyclical letter, they had already given their warmest assent. These Bishops, of different nations, language and race, but all using the one language of the Church, spoke, as in the presence of God, with humility, cordial deference, and charity. The perfect unanimity of faith, the deep devotion to the centre of Catholic unity, were shown in forms so touching, that on the last day of our meeting the Cardinals who presided and the Bishops were moved to tears; it seemed as if the sacred dogma of unity, one faith, one life, one sympathy and one love, in all the members (however scattered,) of the mystic body of Christ, was there rather an object seen and felt, than an article of faith. On the solemn feast of the 8th of December, in the noble cathedral of the christian world, (which, architects say, will contain eighty thousand persons, and which was full of christians from every land,) one hundred and forty-three Bishops in mitre and cope, fifty-three Cardinals in mitre, and in the peculiar vestments of their order, the Pope, with his attendants, and more than one thousand priests, moved slowly down the long nave of the vast edifice, singing in different choirs the Litany of the Saints, in order to beg the Church Triumphant to unite with the Church Militant, the Church in heaven with the Church on earth, in placing so fair a garland on the brow of Mary. As always, when the Pope celebrates the Pontifical high mass, the epistle and gospel were sung in Latin and in Greek; then the Dean of the

Sacred College, supported by Archbishops of different rites, entreated the Holy Father to affix the seal of Church infallibility to a doctrine which all believed. The Pope assented, knelt and intoned the sacred invocation of the Holy Ghost, '*Veni Creator Spiritus,*' Come, Spirit Creator! The promise of Jesus Christ seemed then verified. He, with His Divine Spirit, seemed in the midst 'gathered together in His name,' animating to holy enthusiasm the mighty crowd. Spontaneously, as with one voice, they joined in singing the noble invocation. It was heard above! The response from on high seemed to move every soul. I felt, others, too, no doubt felt, that had not the Almighty Spirit then willed the solemn declaration, He, by some of the thousand events which we call accidents, would have sealed the lips of the Pontiff. But no, the time decreed by the Divine Son for the triumph on earth of His pure and humble mother, had come.

"The Pope began to read the bull; sobs of deep emotion soon mingled with each articulation; his tears, too, fell copiously; all around laymen, and priests, and Bishops wept with the Vicar of Christ, their sobs attesting their communion in the deep emotion that filled his soul. An unusually deep silence reigned, each one holding in his breath, that a word might not be lost; hence the noble voice of the Pope was heard afar off. As he advanced, his tone of emotion changed, first into holy exultation, at being thus chosen as the hand by which the Divine Son crowned His own mother; then to confidence in the power of the Son, and in the protection of the mother. Around the scene, and on the successor of St. Peter, over whose tomb he officiated, seemed to shine some reflection from the Church Triumphant in the world of glory. I thought, and many thought, that the sufferings and dangers of a long journey were amply repaid by that hour of almost blessed vision, as a christian world crowned a mother, whilst on the first christian altar the adorable victim was offered to the Almighty for the graces bestowed on Mary. Those most touching emotions still moving each soul, the high mass continued; and never, perhaps, did such a crowd assist at the holy sacrifice with feelings of religion so general, so deep and so holy.

God grant that the prayer I then offered up for my beloved flock be heard, as I fervently invoked blessings on you all, most dearly beloved in Christ; not forgetting a few misguided men, for whom I implored pardon, light of truth and peace; placing you all, each and every one, under the special protection of the Immaculate Virgin Mother.

"God, by His Church, does not now reveal a new article of faith. He only inspires her to declare that the belief in a privilege so honorable to the Divine Son and to the Blessed Mother, which was always held in the Church, forms, now as ever, part of the sacred deposit of Revelation. As youth advances to age, some truths, always believed, become still more clear and definite, as growing light shows their importance and their relations to other truths; so, also, in man's pilgrimage to the eternal home, where the light of faith shall be eclipsed by the brightness of blessed vision, doctrines, revealed and believed from the first, often become clearer and brighter, and sometimes this accession of light comes from the very contrast of error.

"The Divinity of our Lord; His two natures in one Divine Person; the procession of the Divine Spirit from the Father and the Son; Divine grace, as the free gift of God; the holiness of the married state; the beautiful vision after the death of the Holy Virgin, were truths revealed at first, and ever believed in the Church; yet, in different ages, when error attacked now one, now another, of these sacred dogmas, the Church uttered the voice of the Teacher, who 'is with her all days, even to the consummation of the world,' and defined each dogma as God's truth, 'believed always, every where, and by all true christians.' When the faithful, believing in the Catholic simplicity of faith, and in the heroism of Divine love, died martyrs for that faith, then, when none contradicted, some few articles of faith were defined in the Apostles' Creed. As a fitting place for the highest and holiest of mere creatures, immediately after the mention of the three Adorable Persons of the Blessed Trinity, we find the 'Virgin Mary.' In that venerable document, immediately after professing our faith in the Holy God, three in one, we declare our belief that the second person of the Sacred Trinity had a mother; *He was a man;* and that His mother was a virgin; thus insinuating that He, also, was God, and that, as befitted a God-man, He prepared for so holy an office the woman who was to be His mother. He was the Holy of Holies, and He was the Son of Mary; He was from eternity before her, and He loved her with an 'eternal love.'

"Then, for His own glory and for her honor, He not only created her, the second and holier Eve, in that innocence in which He created the first, but also elevated her innocence to the highest order. The word virgin was taken by the first christians in the widest sense, perpetual virginity, entire purity. As to perpetual virginity, why, indeed, put the word virgin in the creed, if it meant no more than what takes place daily in good women on earth? Yet this belief, though universal, was not an article of faith, till the year 390, when, in the Council of Rome, the errors of Jovinian were condemned, and the perpetual virginity of the mother of the Holy of Holies defined. So also was it with the Divine maternity. By the holy instinct of faith, deep in the christian heart sank the consequences of this apostolic teaching. Jesus, who is God blessed for ever, 'was born of the Virgin Mary;' then *He* was *her* son, and *she* was *His* mother, and *He* was God, and *she, His* mother, was the *mother* of *God.* Yet, only ages after, when some proud men, attempting to measure God and His love by their standard and by their cold hearts, denied to Mary the title of Mother of God, thus destroying both the mystery of the incarnation, and that of redemption, only then, in the year 431, did the Universal Church utter, in the Council of Ephesus, the voice of every christian heart, that she, the mother of *Him* who died on the cross, was truly the mother of God; and that thus, indeed, did 'God purchase us with His own blood,' and that thus truly was accomplished the sacred promise, 'that God Himself would come to save us.' In the earliest liturgies the Blessed Virgin is styled immaculate, unspotted, incorrupt, and the Greek and Latin fathers not only use these negative terms of immaculate, unspotted, uncorrupted, 'but also,' says our Holy Father in the solemn decree:

"'To vindicate the original innocence and justice of the mother of God, they not only compared her to Eve, as yet virgin, as yet innocent, as yet incorrupt, and not yet deceived by the most deadly snares of the treacherous serpent; but they have preferred her with wonderful variety of thought and expression. For Eve, miserably obeying the serpent, fell from original innocence and became his slave; but the most Blessed Virgin, ever increasing her original gift, not only never lent an ear to the serpent, but by a virtue Divinely received, utterly broke his power.

"'Wherefore they have never ceased to call the mother of God the lily amongst thorns, earth entirely untouched, virgin undefiled, immaculate, ever blessed, and free from all contagion of sin, from whom was formed the new Adam; a reproachless, most sweet paradise of innocence, immortality, and delights planted by God Himself, and fenced from all the snares of the malignant serpent; incorruptible branch, that the world of sin had never injured; fountain ever clear, and sealed by the virtue of the Holy Ghost; a most Divine temple or treasure of immortality, or the sole and only daughter, not of death but of life; the seed, not of enmity, but of grace, which, by the singular Providence of God, has always flourished, reviving from a corrupt and imperfect root, contrary to the settled and common laws.'

"But as if these encomiums, though most splendid, were not sufficient, they proclaimed in proper and defined opinions, that when sin would be treated of, no question of sin should be entertained concerning the Holy Virgin Mary, to whom an abundance of grace was given to conquer sin completely. They also declared that most Glorious Virgin the reparation of her parents, the vivifier of posterity chosen from the ages, prepared for Himself by the Most High; predicted by God when He said to the serpent, 'I will place enmity between thee and the woman;' who undoubtedly has crushed the poisonous head of the same serpent; and therefore they affirm that the same Blessed Virgin was, through grace, perfectly free from every stain of sin, and from all contagion of body, and soul, and mind, and always conversant with God, and, united with Him in an eternal covenant, never was in darkness, but always in light, and, therefore, was plainly a fit habitation for Christ, not on account of her bodily state, but on account of her original grace. To these things are added the noble words in which, speaking of the conception of the Virgin, they have testified that nature yielded to grace and stood trembling, not being able to proceed further; for it was to be that the Virgin mother of God should not be conceived of Anna before grace should bear fruit. For she ought thus to be conceived as a first born, from whom was to be conceived the first born of every creature. They have testified that the flesh of the Virgin, taken from Adam, did not admit the stain of Adam, and on this account, that the most Blessed Virgin was the tabernacle created by God Himself, formed by the Holy Spirit, truly enriched with purple, which that new Bezaleel made, adorned and woven with gold, and that the same Virgin is, and deservedly is, celebrated as she who was the first and peculiar work of God, escaped from the fiery weapon of evil, and fair by nature, and entirely free from all stain of sin, came into the world all shining like the moon in her immaculate conception; nor, truly, was it right that this vessel of election should be assailed by common injuries, since differing very much from others, she shared their nature not their fault; far more, it was right that, as the Only Begotten had a Father in heaven, whom the Seraphim extol thrice holy, so He should have a mother on earth, who never should want the splendor of His holiness. And this doctrine, indeed, so filled the minds and souls of our forefathers, that marvelous and singular forms of speech prevailed with them, in which they very frequently called the mother of God immaculate, and entirely immaculate, innocent, and most innocent, spotless, holy, and most distant from every stain of sin; all pure, all perfect, the type and model of purity and innocence by nature, fairer, more beautiful, and more holy than the Cherubim and the Seraphim; she, whom all the tongues of heaven and earth do not suffice to extol. No one is ignorant that these forms of speech have passed, as it were spontaneously, into the monuments of the most Holy Liturgy, and the offices of the Church, 'and that they occur often in them and abound amply; and since the mother of God is invoked and named in them as a spotless dove of beauty, as a rose ever blooming and perfectly pure, and ever spotless and ever blessed, and is celebrated as innocence which was never wounded, and the second Eve, who brought forth Immanuel.'

"Through liturgies, through fathers of the Church, through decrees of many Popes, establishing the Feast of the Immaculate Conception, and attaching indulgences to it, we traced the constant belief of God's Church, and we hear the fathers of the Council of Trent, when defining the communication of original sin to all the posterity of Adam, protest that it was not their intention to include in that declaration the Blessed and Immaculate Virgin. At length, in this last epoch of time, the adorable Son inspires His Vicar on earth to define the dogma. From the right hand of this Eternal Father, the devout son may well conceive that best of Sons, thus addressing His own loved mother: 'My love, undefiled one, in the beginning of My Church I inspired the apostles, though none contradicted, to define some few articles of faith and all implicitly in the clause; 'I believe in the Holy Catholic Church.' Then, after professing faith in My Eternal Father, in Me, His only Begotten Son, and in the Holy Spirit, I taught them to record thy name and My birth from thee as a Virgin. Now, as time draws to its close, though no one that claims to be a child of My Church, doubts this privilege, yet, I now urge the organs of the mystic body to weave into the fair garland that crowns thy sacred brow, the spotless lily of thy Immaculate Conception. Then, as in Divine light My love for thee shines in brighter, holier radiance, so through thee shall My graces flow more abundantly on My redeemed, to aid them in better sanctifying what yet remains of time.'

"It may perhaps be said, 'If Mary was sinless, how is Christ her Saviour?' In the noblest manner is He her Saviour. Mary is immaculate only through His merits. From Calvary back through all preceding ages, back even to Adam, flowed the efficacy of His sacred blood; back, too, from Calvary, even to the dwelling of Holy Anna, did the merits of the same blood reach to save Mary in a perfect manner, not from sin incurred, but from incurring the least stain of sin. A physician would better save his friend by preserving him from a dreadful disease, (which, without such preservation, must certainly have been incurred,) than by curing him of the same disease after it had been incurred. It is not, indeed, a little ornament to the redemption which is in Christ Jesus, that it redeemed one of the race in a manner so perfect. Mary's preservation from original sin is solely through the merits of Jesus, all her glory is His; 'tis He that so wonderfully lavished His grace upon her; 'tis He that so gloriously now crowns her merits, and who, in crowning her merits, does but crown His own gifts."

The bill introduced into the Legislature by the Hon. James O. Putnam, (reference to which has already been made, and which was the famous Church Property bill,) became a law upon the statute books.

Bishop Timon published a letter, addressed to the public papers, in which he set forth his views on the question, which substantially are the same as embodied in his reply to Senator Babcock. Some of his statements in this letter being solemnly emphatic, we reproduce a few quotations, particularly that portion in which he very humorously grinds up the "poetry" of Mr. Putnam's speech on the bill:

THE CHURCH QUESTION.

"*Mr. Editor:* To use the common phrase, 'in this enlightened age, and in this free country,' a law has passed, conflicting most probably with the constitution of our State, and certainly at variance with the maxims of our forefathers. Mr. Putnam, the father of that bill, showed its necessity by 'presenting a petition, which, in view of its great importance, he said should be printed; his motion to that effect was adopted by the Senate.' Seventeen men, who determine, right or wrong, to call themselves Catholics, signed that petition, which Archbishop Hughes calls a 'fiction in all its material parts, with a small sprinkling of truth in parts which are not material;' and ably has he proved his assertion. My name having also been introduced by the petitioners, it becomes a duty to satisfy the public that Archbishop Hughes uttered the truth in his letter, when he said, 'I am persuaded that the trustees of St. Louis church have as little reason to complain of their present Bishop as they had to complain of me.'

"First, then, Mr. Editor, I *solemnly* declare that I neither asked the trustees, nor thought of asking them, or of compelling them to surrender to me the title of said church; on the contrary, when the trustees' party spread false reports to that effect in public documents, I not only denied the charge, but also declared that no inducements, no salary, could ever tempt me to administer their revenues."

In July, 1854, a correspondent of the Buffalo *Commercial Advertiser*, answering by authority of the Bishop the same misstatement, says:

"Your correspondent of last evening infers that the offence of the trustees is their 'sturdy and meritorious refusal to convey the property of the society to the Bishop.' Strange! the documents have been published that prove that the Bishop never asked the trustees to convey said property to him, for the same reason that the Bishop already, as always, holds the deed for that property, and he believes that the laws of our free and happy country would sustain him in his right. The difficulty has never been about the property, but about the violation of Church discipline. The Bishop has over and over declared to the trustees and to others, that he never would go to law to vindicate his right to such a property; he preferred to build poor churches, even shanties, in which faithful Germans might worship in peace, and suffer the trustees to keep the material edifice and property. The Bishop has kept his word; greatly through his aid and contributions two new German churches have been erected, and are now crowded with faithful Germans. The trustees have been suffered to keep St. Louis church and its property, and the Bishop has not troubled them in their possession. If they want his services, or those of *his assistants, he* has a right to define his terms; *they* cannot force him to serve *them* on *their* terms.

"I never was opposed to a fair trustee system; I would even bear with a bad one, were it administered by Catholics in a Catholic spirit, who, as Archbishop Bedini said, 'would make their action harmonious with their duty as Catholics.' Hence, when Rev. Mr. Guth,* with the French portion of the congregation, had been forced, by the oppression of the trustees, to abandon St. Louis church, I was satisfied with the pledge and the written document which the trustees gave, that none but practical Catholics should be elected trustees, that the Pastor should be president of the board, and have a vote, and that the discipline of the Church should be observed. Each of these promises have been violated. For many years, and in several of our councils, I have advocated the expediency of a trustee system which Catholics could safely and conscientiously use; but I have always felt as a great number of the most respectable Protestant churches of this State, and their Protestant members have felt, with regard to the clause under which alone Catholics can be incorporated. I know not why men, after being informed of their error, persist in saying that the law 'for religious incorporation' passed in 1813.†

"The trustees say that the incorporation was effected with the hearty concurrence of the Bishop. Yet, the Rev. Mr. Pax, then pastor, denies it, and the Very Rev. Raffeiner, Vicar General for the Germans in the Diocese of New York, has declared on oath that Bishop Dubois *did not consent* to incorporation, and that he was much displeased when he heard that it had been effected. But why follow these 'petitions' through their wild fiction? Was I not in Europe when the oppressions and usurpations

---

* Rev. Guth was obliged to leave St. Louis church, bearing with him the Sacred Host, owing to the threats and violence used against him.

† Here the Bishop quotes and explains the laws passed in 1784, 1789, 1795, 1822, and 1825, but which are omitted here, as they are substantially contained in his reply to Senator Babcock's speech.

of the trustees forced the Rev. Mr. Guth, with the French portion of the congregation, to abandon St. Louis church, and their rights in and to it?

"My efforts from first to last were to see its revenues administered by truly Catholic laymen of the same congregation, in accordance with the laws of the Church; and also to enable the clergy to secure the decency of Divine worship, and freely administer the introductions and spiritual helps that might best sanctify the flock. How much longer I might have remained striving to obtain this end, by protestations, by kindness, or by menace, I know not. The trustee party settled that question, and hurried on their work. After publicly insulting and menacing their pastor in the very church, they ordered him out of it; he then, and then only, left it, bearing with him the Blessed Sacrament, and neither the Lord nor His minister has entered the desecrated house since; nor would any worthy priest consent, even at the request of the Bishop, to be pastor of that church, until the wound, that has been festering for so many years, be radically cured.

"Since writing the above, I have seen the speech of Hon. Mr. Putnam. Alas! alas! In the Senate of a great State, the honorable gentleman quotes Shakspeare, Milton, Wordsworth, and 'the *muse* of history;' but certainly, he deals but little in 'the unvarnished tale of truth,' in 'calm reason's holy law,' or in the sober *prose* of history. Had the Hon. Senator examined the records of Erie County, he would have found that the Bishop after purchasing, (not with the people's money, but with his own,) property for an hospital, for orphan asylums, for a college, etc., conveyed that property to incorporations or societies, who will use them for these charitable and beneficent objects. Had the Hon. Senator not lived in a world of fiction and prejudice, he would have known that Mr. Brownson neither wrote nor published the passage with which the honorable gentleman treated the Senate. Did the Hon. Senator speak prose or poetry in the wildest fiction, when he said: 'It took Anglo-Saxon Protestantism but about one century to work out its illiberality and intolerance,' or when he gave the touching picture about 'the darkest hour of the middle ages, when the English throne scarce had a being save at the pleasure of the Roman Pontiff; nearly one-half of the real estate of the kingdom was absorbed in the Catholic Church.'

"What *poetry* in the passage which represents the priest as 'armed with the terrible enginery of the Vatican, closing the door of the sanctuary, putting out the fires upon its altar, and scourging every communicant who dares *to think a thought* independent of his spiritual master!' etc. But does not the Hon. Senator know that the trustees keep the keys of the church? hence if the sanctuary is closed it is they alone that close it? Does the Hon. Senator use the word *communicant* in irony, because he knows the 'Eminent Catholic,' whose letter he read in the Senate, has not thought fit, for many, many long years, to be a communicant, or to practice other essential Catholic duties? But *poetry* itself can scarcely excuse, not the fiction, but the worse than fiction, of his passage: 'Here, sir, in the bosom of this free State, we find a hierarchy having no sympathy with our institutions, admitting no supreme fealty to the civil power, but acting under the impulsive energy of its Italian centre and head.'

"*O tempora, O mores!* The French lawyers must go to school to Mr. Putnam to learn what he teaches, which is contrary to the express letter of their code, and to the practice of France, of Belgium, etc., that 'the temporal administration of the Church is in the Council of Fabique, who are chosen by the Municipal Council, the latter being *chosen by the people* in several communes!' Had the Senator said they were elected by the Bishops, he would have been more near the truth. The people of France have nothing to do in their elections. Alas! again alas! that such hearsay statements, such narrow, bigoted views, founded on superficial reading, should be uttered in so dictatorial a tone, in the noblest Senate of our happy country.

"✝ JOHN TIMON, *Bishop of Buffalo.*'

Besides assisting in council at Rome for the Church in general, Bishop Timon did not forget his own flock and diocese in particular. He obtained a special favor from the Holy Father, of which the following is the translation:

"ROME, November 19, 1854.

"The Bishop of Buffalo humbly entreats His Holiness to grant a plenary indulgence, on the conditions usually attached to such a grace, once a year, and also a plenary indulgence at the article of death, to the present or future benefactors of the fine Orphan Asylums in the Diocese of Buffalo."

"ROME, November 19, 1854.

"The petition is granted.

"PIUS, P. P., IX."

CHAPTER IX.

ST. PATRICK'S AND OTHER CHURCHES.—ST. JOSEPH'S CATHEDRAL.—CORRESPONDENCE.—BISHOP TIMON TRAVELS THE WORLD FOR HELP FOR HIS CATHEDRAL.—DIFFICULTIES. —CORNER STONE AND DEDICATION.—FIRST DIOCESAN SYNOD.—A CARILLON OF FORTY-THREE BELLS.—EPISCOPAL VISITATIONS.—BISHOP TIMON VISITS ST. LOUIS, MO.—THE ALLEGHANY COLLEGE.—ELECTION DAY.—JUVENILE ASYLUM.

THE holy Providence that blessed the material labors of the Church Militant in the Diocese of Buffalo, was indeed mysterious; and although the necessities of religion in council at Rome, as well as the multifarious duties throughout the diocese, taxed heavily upon the age and health of Bishop Timon, still, amid all of these incessant occupations, he found time to make provision for other purposes of a more gigantic nature.

After he left St. Louis church, in 1848, he originated St. Patrick's parish, and built on the corner of Ellicott and Batavia streets, contiguous to the "Vincent Orphan Asylum," a neat brick church, in which that portion of his flock who were willing to obey Church discipline might worship in peace. Many pious German and French Catholics of St. Louis church, likewise dissatisfied with the conduct of the men who had secured themselves the position of trustees, began to form other parishes. Hence was started St. Mary's church, under the Redemptorist Fathers, in a long, narrow, brick building, in which were no pews, but where, indiscriminately, without reference to rank or sex, pious people gathered to worship, also unencumbered with trouble to their Bishop. During the Bishop's absence in Europe, in 1853, Rev. Mr. Guth was compelled to leave St. Louis church, as already stated, and with him went a great many good French people, who formed the congregation of St. Peter's.

Shortly afterwards St. Michael's church was begun. Then followed other churches, as if by magic, all over the city, so that, at the present time, Buffalo has seven churches of Catholic faith. Many of these are magnificent edifices, to say nothing of the cathedral, a masterpiece of Gothic architecture.

The wants of a rapidly increasing flock gave Bishop Timon no time for inaction. On the contrary, though continually busy, he conceived the project of building a place of Divine worship that should be the crowning act of his Episcopal labors. It was to build St. Joseph's Cathedral. As early as 1850, he made preparations for this purpose, and consulted with his architect, P. C. Keely, Esq., into whose able hands he committed its erection.

"TO SISTER ———.

"BUFFALO, April 29, 1854.

"*Dear Sister:* I returned last night from seeing the Mother Superior in Albany; unhappily, her sufferings did not permit her to go further. Your esteemed letter and the pious gift were handed to me; accept my thanks. The prayer for the chaplet of the Immaculate Conception was indeed very beautiful. I hope that you and other good Sisters will offer up the chaplet and the prayer to obtain God's protection upon the poor Bishop of Buffalo.

"If I can, I will pass by Emmetsburgh as I return from Pittsburgh, though, alas, I know not what sudden call may prevent me. Pray that I may be enabled *to finish my cathedral, for now it makes me a perfect slave.* May God, in mercy, accept the sacrifices which I must daily make.

"With great respect and esteem,

"Your obedient and humble servant,

"✠ JOHN, *Bishop of Buffalo.*"

"TO SISTER ———.

"NEW YORK, May 13, 1854.

"*Dear Sister:* It gave me great pleasure to receive your letter, and that of Sister ———. Thanks to both for kind remembrances. Your remarks about our poor beginnings touched me much. Yes, dear Sister,*_then, when I hardly knew where to find what would meet the expenses of the next day, God gave such peace and joy_ that we were all happy; blessed be His holy name. And let me try to serve Him well now, when prospects seem more smiling. The Orphan Asylum goes on well, as does the Hospital. The Protestants have lately appealed to the public for their Orphan Asylum, and they say, 'See how the Roman Catholics keep up their benevolent works; it is a shame we do not imitate them.' Though trying all I can to get up a cathedral, still we do not neglect your children. I even hope this season to make an addition to their house. Pray for us, and pray in an especial manner for

"Your devoted father in Christ,

"✠ JOHN, *Bishop of Buffalo.*"

In order to meet the expenses of this costly undertaking, Bishop Timon visited Mexico, Spain, some parts of Europe, and the greater part of the United States, soliciting aid for his cathedral. His zeal and his name, already well known for energy, piety and charity, opened almost immediate entrance to the generosity and liberality of christians every where. The King of Bavaria, especially pleased with the zeal and charity of Bishop Timon, remitted

---

* The emphasis is the author's.

ST. JOSEPH'S CATHEDRAL,

BUFFALO, N. Y.

him a handsome donation, subsequently, for his charitable institutions. As has been seen from his "Lecture on Mexico," he profited well from his travels in that country particularly, and the fund of knowledge he gathered in his travels abroad, he made judicious disposition of in improving the affairs of his diocese.

Still his efforts met with obstacles of an unexpected nature. It is to be regretted that these pages should record them, but justice to the Bishop, as well as a desire to give the reader a fair estimate of the difficulties that had to be overcome in the origin of the cathedral, renders reference to them important.

It seems that after the Bishop had bought the property on which stands the cathedral, and the fact had become known that a Catholic church was to be erected on it, a murmur of dissent was expressed by some of the property holders of the immediate neighborhood. A proposition was advanced to "buy off" the property at a higher figure than the Bishop had paid for it. But, of course, to this he would not consent. Subsequently, after the building had been erected, and the roof was about to be put on, there was one individual, at least, who would subscribe eight thousand dollars to help to tear down the entire structure.

In the Fall of the year 1852, the corner-stone had been laid, and now, in June, 1855, the cathedral was ready for dedication. The Buffalo *Sentinel** contained an interesting account of the ceremonies, a part of which we quote:

"It was a consoling sight to behold, in this splendid edifice, some fourteen prelates and about a hundred priests, all bound by the laws of charity in the same faith, bowing down together in adoration of the Blessed Sacrament, of that God for whom that house was just built. It was pleasant to find about three thousand of our fellow citizens assembled under one vast roof, of all nations and tongues, hearing the eloquent and gigantic Archbishop

---

* A Catholic journal and the Bishop's organ, started in June, 1853, under Mr. Michael Hagan, and ending in 1864. This paper was ably conducted by its editor for nearly ten years of arduous labor. In 1864, it ceased to be the Bishop's organ, and a new paper, call d the "*Western New York Catholic*," was commenced, under the auspices of Mr. D. M. Enright. Mr. Hagan felt justified in pursuing a certain course and policy in the control of his paper, not altogether in accordance with the Bishop's views, and, as no terms of agreement could be settled upon, the Bishop withdrew his name and influence from the paper.

of this province battling against modern paganism, as an Ambrose, or an Augustine, when they stood with holy pride over the scattered ruins of ancient paganism, and launched the thunderbolts of their oratory on a wondering populace. The most attentive silence, joined to noiseless awe, that follow the Catholic priesthood through all their ceremonies, was observed by all; nor did any thing occur (excepting the heavy rain sent by God for man's benefit,) to mar the happy observance of them by priesthood or people. All hearts were gladdened, and praised the Lord for His goodness in blessing the city by so grand a tabernacle of His covenant with men, where they may pray and He may hear."

The dedication of the cathedral and church was performed by the *Bishops of Albany and Brooklyn, assisted by numerous priests, deacons, and acolytes.

The sermon was preached by the †Archbishop of New York, who took for his text Paul's Epistle to the Ephesians, ii, 13:

"13. But now in Christ Jesus, you, who sometime were afar off, are made near by the blood of Christ.

"19. Now, therefore, you are no more strangers and foreigners; but you are fellow-citizens with the saints, and the domestics of God;

"20. Built upon the foundation of the apostles and prophets, Jesus Christ Himself being the chief corner-stone;

"21. In whom all the building framed together, groweth into a holy temple in the Lord;

"22. In whom you also are built together into a habitation of God in the Spirit."

The Archbishop delivered a very eloquent sermon on this occasion, saying, among other things, that " he could not neglect this opportunity to congratulate the brethren of the Catholic Church of Western New York, on the completion of this beautiful edifice. The work had been accomplished in spite of difficulties that would have discouraged one less devoted than the honored Bishop of Buffalo. It was a triumph of architectural beauty. The evidences of genius, apart from religion, were all

---

* Rt. Revs. McCloskey and O'Loughlin.
† Rt. Rev. John Hughes.

around, but they are devoted forever in the service of God. This beautiful cathedral, so perfect in proportion, so complete in every part, the ornaments that embellish it, all are consecrated. No man can mistake this for a court room, or a senate chamber. It is a house built for God, and to be His forever."

In the afternoon, grand Pontifical vespers were celebrated, and the *Bishop of Milwaukee preached in the German language.

In the evening, service again was held, at which the †Bishop of Louisville preached a most eloquent and impressive sermon.

Bishop Timon also took occasion to remark that the immense stained window *now* in the rear of the cathedral, was *then* at Münich on exhibition, where crowds, from all parts of Europe, flocked to see its beautiful and perfect workmanship, and which was said to be the most magnificent stained glass window in America. The entire cost of the cathedral, when the towers should be completed, *at that time* was estimated would reach one hundred and fifty thousand dollars. On Monday, Sept. 24th, 1855, Bishop Timon convened the first Diocesan Synod of his clergy in St. Joseph's cathedral. Bishop Young, of Erie, and a numerous body of the clergy, assisted in the solemn and important ceremonies. On the Sunday following, at ten o'clock A. M., the clergy moved in procession from the Episcopal residence to the front door of the cathedral, repeating the sacred Psalms as they proceeded, with religious pomp, through the streets. Whilst the Bishop was vesting, the clergy sung the *Tierce;* the venerable ceremonies of the Pontifical high mass were carefully executed, the clergy receiving communion at the hands of the Bishop. After mass the Diocesan Synod was solemnly opened, with all those ancient, mysterious rites by which the Church marks her deep conviction of a Divine, Adorable Presence, in official reunion of the consecrated ministers of the " Body of Christ " in His " Body, the Church," for the salvation of souls. Next followed the solemn chant of the Litanies, invoking all the saints of God to pray for the assembled patrons and their flocks; invoking

---

* Rt. Rev. Bishop Henni.
† Rt. Rev. Martin John Spalding.

the Son of God to be merciful to His people, and hear the prayers of the Church and the singing of the sacred hymn of the Holy Ghost, to beg His help and His holy inspirations upon the people. The Bishop sang the Pontifical vespers. Several private sessions of the synod were held at stated intervals, merging, finally, into one grand and solemn session. Only a few decrees were passed, and in a pastoral letter afterwards, Bishop Timon took occasion to speak of them, and also of the affairs of his diocese, from which we gather that three thousand dollars of debt still hung over the cathedral. He had in vain tried to borrow money to meet this sum, and now appealed to his people to make the combined effort at least to reduce it. He also contrasted the state of the diocese when he first assumed charge of it, with its (then) present progressing condition, and humbly thanked God for His many blessings, both temporal and spiritual. On another subject he said:

"In the cup of life, God ever mixes bitter and sweet; He is good, goodness itself, goodness infinite and unbounded. But we are on trial; life is a battle, wounds and bruises, weariness and sorrow, must be felt, but He comforts His soldiers; He binds up every wound, He often fills with joy in the midst of tribulation. Such was it with us, dearly beloved, when, on the occasion of the *Triduan*, or retreat, in honor of the Immaculate Conception of Mary, the congregation of St. Louis, under the powerful and most touching preaching of the Rev. Father Weninger, S. J., unanimously accepted the regulations which we had ordained, and by which there is best reason to hope that such difficulties as have existed between Bishops and the trustees of that church, will never more occur; this consolation, then deeply felt, has more than once been renewed in our hearts, by the proofs of a truly Catholic spirit, which the congregation has since frequently given."

Bishop Timon by no means was pleased to think that as soon as the building was erected, and ready for Divine worship, that his cathedral would be entirely finished. His high aspiration for the glory of God and religion, as well as his own tastes for the gratification of the human ear, led him to make a crowning effort for his beautiful church. In the delightful music that may be heard at times sweeping over the city, when played by skilled and musical fingers, will be found a living witness of the effort he made, but which he did not live to realize. Without doubt, the carillon of bells that swings within the tower of St. Joseph's cathedral, is the finest on the continent, and ranks third in number in the world. It is to be regretted that the compass of the tower is such as to obstruct the melody that dwells in rich and magnificent chords in the carillon, although this difficulty could be some what obviated, by widening or increasing the number of the apertures in the tower, so far as not to endanger the strength of the latter.

ST. JOSEPH'S CARILLON.

BY CHARLES G. DEUTHER.

Forth from a choir of harmonizing tongues,
  A multitude of chorded strains arise;
The silver bells, like perfumed censers swung,
  Evolve their tribute praises to the skies.

On every hand, 't is magic art conspires,
  And wakes a sleeping world to prayer and God;
'T is music calling with her wonted fires
  To christians in the paths their fathers trod.

Upward on soaring wing the anthem swells,
  Whilst naught but echo rifts the stilly air;
From limpid throats of three and forty bells,
  Ceaseless peals the Sabbath morning's prayer.

How eloquent these soul-subduing strains,
  Whose echoes kiss the ambient wave afar,
Whose music o'er the distant landscape rains,
  As sweet as fall the beams of evening star!

What sense of happy ease pervades the hour,
  What solace to the heart, this Sabbath morn;
More sweet, more rare than perfume of the flower,
  This flood of sacred music, newly born!

O! sacred bells, how soothing to the ear,
  When world and sin we leave afar behind,
To sit and listen to thy tones of cheer,
  And in thy heavenly language comfort find!

There comes an hour in life we least expect,
    When sadness casts a shadow on our joys;
When hopes, like stranded vessels, lie abject,
    And pale adversity our work destroys;

E'en then, in hours most solemn for our years,
    Perchance at night, when all abroad is still,
Thy voice will wake our slumbering, languid ears,
    And with reanimated hope instill.

Then voices from a fairer sky awake,
    And on the waiting zephyrs flood the lea,
Bid sadness from our midst its flight betake,
    Before thy grand prospective jubilee.

When streams of melody invade the air,
    What molten notes in golden waves expand;
As, wedded with the christian's vesper prayer,
    The sacred stillness throbs on every hand.

Within the precincts of that solemn pile,
    Where sombre shadows fitful vigils keep,
'Round fretted arch, and through the long drawn aisle,
    How sweetly do thy whispering echoes sweep!

Ring on, oh bells! ye heralds of that bourne,
    Unknown to mind, unseen by mortal eye;
Your mellow tongues shall solace those who mourn,
    And build a bridge of hope 'tween earth and sky.

BUFFALO, January 20th, 1870.

The intention of Bishop Timon originany embodied a carillon of twenty-eight bells only, and an order for this number was accordingly given. Subsequently, however, through some inducements held out to the Bishop, he concluded to increase the number to forty-three.*

But amidst all this advancement of the church at home, Bishop Timon did not forget the rest of his diocese. All his leisure time was spent in Episcopal visitations, the record of which alone would fill a volume. Among many interesting reminiscences that occurred, none will be more eagerly read than the following:

"On Saturday, the 21st of July, 1855, the Rt. Rev. Dr. Timon reached Elmira, according to previous engagement, and was received at the depot by the Rev. Mr. Boyle. No sooner had the venerable prelate reached his destination and alighted from the carriage, than he bent his way, (as he was wont to do,) to the sanctuary, to pay his respects to the Incarnate Word, and obtain

---

* See appendix to this work for a full description of these bells, etc.

that refreshment which the world cannot give. The Bishop assisted in the confessional in the evening, where crowds continued to flock. The rising of the sun next morning, found the good Bishop again in the confessional, where he remained until nine o'clock. At the half-past ten o'clock mass, the Bishop preached; in the evening he visited the Sunday school, * * * * * * * and never have I heard or seen the words of the great Apostle of the Gentiles, who made himself 'all to all, in order to give all to Christ,' more strikingly realized, than on this occasion; among the children, the Bishop seemed as though he had never been elsewhere, and as if divested for the time being of all Episcopal dignity and authority. Among children he becomes like a child, enters into their feelings, speaks to them in the language of children, adapting himself to their various capacities, calling to his aid the most familiar similes and parables, and from things of earth leads captive their minds to heaven.

"In the evening, at the benediction of the blessed sacrament, he preached again on the conversion of Mary Magdalene. This was one of the most admirable and affecting discourses I have ever heard the Bishop deliver; never have I seen a picture drawn with such appropriate colorings; the Saviour and the sinner placed in such striking contrast, majesty and misery, side by side. Excessive sorrow, blended with most ardent love on the one side, infinite justice outweighed by infinite mercy on the other. For more than an hour the Bishop spoke on this consoling subject, during which a death-like stillness reigned throughout the church, save now and again, when the sigh or sob of some penitent soul was heard in sympathy, perchance for Magdalene, or, *like her*, yearning to do homage at the feet of an offended Saviour."

In the interim, the decrees passed at the Provincial Synod, held in the Fall of 1854, had been submitted to the Pope for approval. The latter, in reply, sent a letter to all the Bishops of the province, a part of which we copy:

"The letter, subscribed by you all, was delivered to us by our Venerable Brother John, Bishop of Buffalo, whom we received most kindly, and listened to with great pleasure, speaking of your affairs. Certainly, it was no small joy to us to learn more and more from that venerable brother, as well as from your letter, how great piety, love and obedience you bear towards us and this chair of Peter, the centre of Catholic truth and unity. Most gladly we learned with what Episcopal solicitude you provided for the celebration of the first Provincial Synod of New York, whose acts, according to ancient rule, you have sent to us, and asked that we would vouchsafe to approve, or even, where need be, to correct."

The Holy Father expressed his gratification at the new Bishop for Portland, and encouraged all of the Provincial Synod to stimulate their efforts to renewed zeal in the vineyard of Christ and His holy faith, and to this end proposed and encouraged the establishment of an American college at Rome, where the youth may be sent, to receive ecclesiastical education to fit them for the proper discharge of sacred duties in the broad fields of America. Bishop Timon, through diversified cares and perplexities, yielded obedience to the wishes of the Sovereign Pontiff in every respect, particularly in his zeal for the spread of the light of true faith. He continued his visitations to all parts of the diocese, administering confirmation to children and adults, giving lectures, assisting in the confessional, dedicating churches, and laying the corner-stones thereof.

In the Winter of 1856, despite the inclemency of the weather, he visited various parts of his diocese in these exercises of his sacred functions, and such was the attractiveness of his eloquence in the pulpit, whenever it was known among Protestants that he would preach, that they flocked in crowds to listen to his sermons, leaving their own "meeting houses" deserted.

In the Spring of 1856, however, business called Bishop Timon to St. Louis, Mo. From a letter, descriptive of his visit whilst there and at the Barrens, we glean the following:

"Shortly after his arrival at the Cape, he was greeted with expressions of gratitude and respect, by a large number of the citizens, and expressed his surprise and joy at seeing the place, which, twenty years ago, was the field of his apostolic labors, so much improved, and to find the number of Catholics, then small, so much increased. Arriving at St. Vincent's College, (a favorite place of his affections, for he founded it, and by his wise administration, raised it to that flourishing condition in which we see it now, ranking among the first literary institutions of our country, provided with able and efficient professors, and attended by a large number of students from different parts of the Union,) he was received by the inmates of the college with all the love and respect that gratitude and veneration could inspire. He was addressed by some of the students in five different languages, viz., Latin, English, French, Spanish, and German, and replying in his usual happy style, he impressed them at the same time with strong motives or becoming truly pious christians and diligent scholars, whilst to give greater expression to their joy on this occasion, the students had in attendance a band of music, which, at intervals, played appropriate airs.

"On the morning of the 21st ult., (April,) the Bishop left for St. Mary's Seminary, Perry county, at which place his reception by the Superior, professors and students, was no less cordial and respectful than it was at the Cape. On the evening previous to his departure from the seminary, the students and the members from that institution assembled in their hall to partake of some refreshments ordered by the Superior. It might be called a family feast, and was occasionally interrupted by some fine French, English, and German songs by the students. At the close, a French discourse was addressed to the Bishop, thanking him for his visit, and for the benefits conferred on the establishment when he was its Superior, which are truly appreciated by all the members, to which he responded, reminding the students in particular of the great advantages they possess in that secluded place, the nurse of piety and of learning, and exhorting them to make good use of their time and opportunities. On the 25th ult., (April, 1856,) the Bishop left for St. Louis."

On the 23d of August, 1856, there occurred a very interesting event in which Bishop Timon participated. It was the ceremony of laying the corner stone of the Franciscan College at Alleghany, New York. Bishop Timon was assisted by the Bishop of Brooklyn,* and a number of Catholic clergymen.

Lieutenant S. B. Seward and corps, Captain S. W. Johnson, of Company "K," Sixty-fourth Regiment, joined in the religious exercises, at intervals, with the booming of their cannon. Over two thousand persons were present, although the rain fell heavily during the day.

The land on which this college stands contains two hundred acres, whilst the building itself is of the Doric Corinthian style. This land was generously donated by Nicholas Devereux, of Utica, New York, whose memory, for acts of liberality and christian charity, deserves to be handed down to posterity with lasting honor and praise.

During the civil elections of the Fall of 1856, when the spirit of the " Know Nothing party" was still rampant, Bishop Timon issued a pastoral letter, earnestly beseeching his flock on the day of the election to cast their vote and immediately leave the precincts of the polls. Above all, he exhorted them to refrain from the use of intoxicating drinks, and in all things to conduct themselves like well behaved and christian people.

"Remember, dearly beloved," said the Bishop, "that the Almighty, who will call us to a strict account of all our actions, will certainly call each voter to a strict account for this most important act. Vote, then, according to your conscience, and as you will answer to God for it. We take no part in politics; we refrain from expressing an opinion of candidates. Should, indeed, a so called political party denounce the Church of God, and become an almost anti-Catholic persecuting sect, we would be recreant to our duty did we not raise a warning voice. May God, in His mercy, grant that no such party may be perpetuated to tarnish the lustre of the 'Star Spangled Banner.'"

Notwithstanding the foregoing expressed wishes of the Bishop, a daily paper,† after election, took occasion to say in its columns

---

* Right Rev. John O'Loughlin.
† Buffalo *Republic*.

that Bishop Timon "had issued, or caused to be issued, in the churches in this city, precisely similar orders."* Bishop Timon, however, soon silenced this political viper, by placing a copy of the pastoral letter referred to before the editor's attention, which the latter did not dare to publish, but contented himself with merely apologizing for his statements, based upon the misinformation of others.

We now approach the consideration of another circumstance in the "history of past events," in which, as of old, Bishop Timon became a zealous participator in the interests of religion and justice. If we find him in his early missionary career, fearlessly asserting the truths of religion before its enemies; if we see him dissipating, as chaff before the wind, the errors and malice of false prophets and teachers, even within the very circle of their "camp meetings" and assemblies; if, owing to his zeal, we observe the Church militant, struggling under heavy embarrassment, rise up free of its encumbrances, and glittering more beautifully and bright in the refulgence of holy principles; if, with his usual independence of spirit, we see him stamp the impress of his character upon the institutions and works of his brain; so shall we ever find him, in this instance, and even to the day of his holy death, the sacred defender of the faith, as well as of the justice and civil rights of man.

On the 7th of April, 1856, "an act to incorporate the Buffalo Juvenile Asylum," passed the Legislature. By this act the "Children's Aid and Reform Society," of the city of Buffalo, (incorporated in January, 1854, under the general act for "the incorporation of benevolent, charitable, scientific and missionary societies,") was merged into the corporation therein erected. The act further authorized this corporation to procure, within the city of Buffalo, suitable buildings, sites and lands, for the purposes of the corporation, and to enable it to pay for the same, (section 27,) provided that the Common Council may, from time to time, *authorize and direct* the Mayor of the city, "whenever it shall

---

*This paper had accused Archbishop Hughes, of New York, of commanding his people to vote the Buchanan ticket.

be made to appear to the satisfaction of said Mayor, that there has been raised or obtained by, or donated to the corporation created by this act, lands, moneys and securities to the value of at least fifteen thousand dollars, to issue the bonds of said city, bearing interest at seven per cent, payable annually, for such sum or sums, not exceeding in the aggregate forty-five thousand dollars, as to the said Common Council may seem meet."

Besides this pecuniary burden, it would thus necessarily impose upon the shoulders of the people, in an increased taxation of sixty thousand dollars, there were other more serious and grave considerations in the bill that were hidden in the character (charitable, heaven save the mark!) in which it was sought to establish its existence. In the very origin of its existence, its dark purposes were plain to the keen sighted eye of justice and right. It was a *private*, a *close* corporation, *not one* of its "twenty-nine directors" being a Catholic.

Looking at the features of the bill, even at this late day, with a calm and dispassionate eye, it must not be cited to the discredit of a neutral but logical inference, that the existence of this "Asylum" was indirectly intended as another blow at the Catholic Church. Evidence of a grave weight substantiates this opinion, in the fact that in a city where at least one-half, if not three-fourths of the population *were* Catholics, nearly all of whom were citizens and tax-payers, there should be established an institution directly supported by the people, but in which they had no ascertainable or conceivable rights beyond what these twenty-nine directors chose to give them, and that of the board of directors not one of them should be a Catholic. Further, "both the vicious and virtuous children were to meet there, and form an assemblage far too vast (if filled up,) for safety, since they could receive

"*First*. Children whose parents or guardians may surrender to it.

"*Second*. Children from seven to fourteen years of age from the *county poor house*.

"*Third*. Children found in any public house, lane, alley, street, highway or public place in said city.

"*Fourth.* Children found on any wharf, dock, boat or vessel in a state of want.

"*Fifth.* Children being abandoned or improperly exposed, or neglected by his or her parent or parents, or such other persons who may have them in charge.

"*Sixth.* Children soliciting alms without being licensed by the Mayor or City Council.

"*Seventh.* Children in any of the aforesaid places, that are idle and truant and without lawful occupation, or in violation of the ordinances* of said city of Buffalo."

Hence the interest and fears entertained by Bishop Timon for the morals, culture, and future of little children committed to the care of the asylum, (many of whom would be Catholics,) were well founded. In a meeting of the board of directors, held on Monday, December 22d, 1856, at the Common Council rooms, a petition signed by George A. Deuther, Patrick Milton, and others, was read by the Hon. George W. Clinton, secretary of the board, the purport of which was to enquire whether Catholic clergy would be allowed access to the institution, and permitted to afford religious instruction to the children of that faith. This was referred to a committee of five. Bishop Timon being present, expressed his deep interest in the religious character of the institution. He said he was prompted to attend the meeting in order to ascertain whether the object of the petition would be granted, basing his remarks upon the petition on the fact that Catholic clergymen were denied admittance both to the House of Refuge at Rochester, and to the Protestant Orphan Asylum of Buffalo, although a large proportion of Catholic children were in both of these institutions.

He said he was willing to contribute to charities so far as his humble means would permit; but he could not sanction this (asylum,) if Catholic children were to be placed where they would be prejudiced against the religion of their fathers, and come out hostile to it. He also protested against the power vested in the managers, to sunder the relations of parent and child.

---

* Among other ordinances, it was forbidden to walk on the grass in Parks and other public places.

"Yet still the question would come, 'Can you depart from all the wise legislation of our country, by lodging that despotic power in officers whom the law will not permit to judge of any other important affair, not even of a paltry debt that exceeds a limited sum?' In the name of common humanity, I appeal to the respectable and honorable gentlemen around me, to modify powers most despotic, which tear the child from the parent, intrude on the sanctity of the domestic circle, and empower every justice of the peace to have any man, by a summary process, brought before him and tried as to his honor and virtue, or his improvidence and vice, and condemned to lose his child or children, if *that justice of the peace decide that the parent is improvident or vicious.* Born in America, and clinging with fond enthusiasm to the institutions of our free country, I abhor despotism. I hope that under the abused name of benevolence, such disgraceful scenes as have made 'the Soupers' a by-word and a shame not only in Ireland, but also in all Europe, may never dishonor our country. To give shelter or food, as a price for the faith of the poor, is what no generous hearted American can ever brook. If the Catholic be wrong, let him be convinced and converted; but let not the benevolence which may give him increased well being for a few days of mortal life, be the inducement to reject the faith to which his understanding and his remorse-torn heart still clings. Let benevolence form this institute, and, if it be true benevolence, let the child take his faith with him, and refuse him not the food that will nourish that faith.

"For the class of whom the District Attorney* spoke, the grand jury, our judges and our laws in many ways make ample provision; but this scheme embraces very many who do not come under the class of those whom I have just described, and hence why pass despotic laws for them? The Catholics of Buffalo are generally poor, and it is but fair to suppose that a great portion of the children detained in the Juvenile Asylum will be Catholic. If you want to reclaim them efficaciously, must you not appeal to those convictions of truth and right which they received with

---
* Mr. Sawin.

their mother's milk? Is it holy, just or right, to deny them the religious instruction which alone will find an echo in their conscience? Is it, therefore, throwing a firebrand in the midst of this meeting, to ask for fair play and justice? to beg that the sacred rights of parents and the holiness of the domestic circle be respected? Would any one of us wish to be put on trial for our honor, our virtue, or vice, before the same office, on the summary process as that established by this law? The poor man has his feelings as well as the rich, and his honor and virtue, too, are dear to him; his children are his treasure. This law, however, most despotically deals with his honor, his virtue, and his children. Make the law such as it should be, then I will support it, remembering that nothing can be permanent that is not just."

Section 14 provided ten days only in which a parent had time to claim his child from the asylum, and if he failed to do so within that short space of time, he should forfeit all further claims upon it until it should be of age. Should a parent, (Section 15,) however, succeed in getting his child out, and it were again arrested as before, then there was no further redress. These and other sections were contained in the "act" which was so odious and despotic that it was a matter of surprise to find men in favor of it who stood so high in the community for honor, integrity and justice. In the meantime, the people of Buffalo were aroused to a sense of the danger threatened against their liberties, and several enthusiastic meetings were held to take proper action on the subject. A report, modifying the "act incorporating the Juvenile Asylum," and embodying new and more healthy features, was adopted, with resolutions and a petition praying the legislature for relief. Every effort was made to restrain the enforcement of the passage of this odious "act," and at length it was so far repealed and modified as to permit the existence of the asylum, restraining the board of directors from incarcerating a child without notifying the parents of the same, and relieving the city from any taxation whatever for its support. This virtually made the entire undertaking "a dead letter," since it was robbed of its proscriptive features, which was mostly what its originators desired to effect.

---o---

CHAPTER X.

NIAGARA FALLS SEMINARY.—CATHOLIC FUNERALS.—BISHOP TIMON GOES TO ROME.—HIS JOURNEY.—HIS RETURN.—HIS SERMON.—JUBILEE ANNOUNCED.—EFFORTS FOR THE ROMAN COLLEGE.—JUBILEE EXTENDED.—CATHOLIC FUNERALS AGAIN.—ZEAL OF BISHOP TIMON.—WILLIAM B. LECOUTEULX.—ST. PEREGRINUS.

IN 1857, a theological seminary was opened near Niagara City, N. Y., on the American side, under the auspices of the Lazarists, in which Bishop Timon took a great interest. This seminary was subsequently destroyed by fire, but by dint of renewed zeal upon the part of the Bishop, who opened his purse very liberally, it was rebuilt upon a more improved plan. The annual session of the Synod of the clergy of the diocese took place in September of this year, (1857,) and upon the termination of its labors, Bishop Timon issued a pastoral in which, among other things, he referred to "wakes" and Catholic funerals, deprecating the desecration of religious rites and ceremonies, that often occurred upon the death of a departed soul.

In a previous pastoral, the Bishop had required that the faithful should employ the use of a limited number of conveyances at funerals, and now, under pain of excommunication, (the right of absolution being reserved to the Bishop alone,) any scandals at wakes, through debauchery, drunkenness, or other crimes, were entirely prohibited. The subject of Catholic funerals was subsequently more seriously agitated, not only in this but also in other dioceses, owing to the disgrace and discredit which the conduct of certain persons brought upon the Church by their irreverent practices at the funerals of their friends. The prompt and decisive step taken by the Bishop, of course, had its salutary effect, since non-Catholics have little or nothing in this regard to complain of now.

Business of great urgency about this time called Bishop Timon to Rome and other parts of Europe, and accordingly, on Wednesday, May 5, 1858, he sailed from New York in the Cunard steamship "Canada."

Before leaving his diocese, he received marked expressions of love and esteem from his beloved flock in Dunkirk, Buffalo, Rochester, and other places. At Rochester, besides a handsome purse, he was presented with an address, in which was said:

"All churches reared by you through other hands, all houses of learning fostered by your zealous care, all religious institutions encouraged by your teachings, are as living monuments of your solicitude for our future welfare; and when we have passed from earth, and other generations have taken our place, then these institutions, in letters of love, will teach our children of your interest for their good, and their prayers will ascend as precious jewels to deck your crown of glory."

The Bishop's journey was very favorable. He was present at the celebration of the great Festival of St. Peter and Paul, in Rome. Here the Pope gave his apostolical benediction for himself, his clergy, and people. From Rome he went to Paris, where he delivered to the Emperor of France, Napoleon III, a verbal communication of great importance from the Pope himself. From Paris he went to Brussels and along the German States, passing over to Ireland, and thence, by way of England, to his own native shores. This visit was productive of much good to his diocese, both temporal and spiritual.

On Tuesday, September 13, 1858, he reached home, in good health and excellent spirits. His arrival home was the signal for a hearty and generous welcome from his people.

He received a large crowd in front of his Episcopal residence, where he delivered an appropriate address, in which he referred to his recent visit to Rome. On Sunday following, the Bishop delivered a sermon in his cathedral, which was thus substantially noticed in a daily paper: *

---

* From the Buffalo *Courier*.

"A large congregation assembled, in which we recognized many leading citizens of Protestant denominations. The occasion was the first service conducted by the Rt. Rev. Bishop since his return from Rome. The fame of the prelate's eloquence, and respect for his character, attracted the people to listen to his teachings, and extend to him a personal welcome home.

"After the celebration of the mass, the Bishop ascended the pulpit, and, having read a few verses from the first chapter of the Ephesians, proceeded to address the audience upon the subject of his recent journey.

* * * * * * * * *

"He had not accomplished all the objects of his mission; but the success he did achieve he trusted would promote the spiritual well-being of his diocese. He had failed in obtaining a loan with which to pay off the debt of the church, owing to the severity of the times and a want of confidence abroad, aggravated by untoward influences and events. But he had secured numerous valuable relics, which he had hoped would be conducive to spiritual edification and stimulate to religious attainment.

"Among these is the entire body of a sainted martyr of the Church, with the rudely sculptured slab which chronicled the name and the fate of the departed. * * * * *

"The Bishop gave a flattering contrast to the people of his diocese, between the condition of things abroad and that which exists here. He assured the congregation that the lines to them were cast in pleasant places. Whether he regarded circumstances of social, civil and political influence, or those which more immediately affected the religious interests, there was every reason for congratulation. A marked improvement in the state of the Church showed itself in all its surroundings. Their edifices for worship, their numerous religious establishments, their increasing numbers,—all gave tokens of their prosperity and progress. Most of the institutions of the Church were in their infancy; but they were planted on solid and abiding foundation, with every element of expansion to encourage hope of permanency and wide-spread influence. The cathedral (of

Buffalo,) in which they worshiped, was a noble monument of classic taste and elegance. The Bishop had visited most of the celebrated cathedrals of Europe; and though many of them surpass this in size, few, if any, are superior in justness of proportion and beauty of architecture and decoration. He had seen the magnificent cathedral of Cologne. The windows presented to it by King Louis of Bavaria, were the delight and wonder of the beholder; but they were confessedly inferior to those which, in our own cathedral, elevate the pious-minded to contemplation of the birth and suffering and glorification of the Redeemer.

"In many an audience with the Sovereign Pontiff, the Bishop had recounted the piety and ardent zeal of his flock in the service of the Holy Church. * * * * * The Pope, he said, listened with delight to these representations, and charged the Bishop with a special blessing for the good people thus strongly commended to the love and protection of the Church.

"The venerable prelate described the Holy Father in his personal ministration at the altar, with a touching pathos. The saintly benevolence that irradiated the features of the Pontiff, reflected, he said, the impulses of his heart, as he pronounced his benediction upon the congregation of worshipers. We are but channels, said the prelate, of the grace which comes from God. We are but channels, whether Pope, Bishop, or priest, and the grace itself derives no efficacy from any personal sanctity in those by whom it is transmitted. But to the recipient it seems doubly blessed, when it comes to him through a channel of translucent purity, and is administered with tokens of cordial sympathy and love. This character gives a special interest to the heavenly blessing which I am charged to bring you by the earthly head of the Church.

"Bishop Timon said he was obliged to make one important exception to his commendation of those institutions established amongst us by the authority of the State. The exception was to what he pronounced an odious, because a godless school system. He disclaimed being influenced to this belief by religious bigotry. Opinion and practice in Protestant countries in Europe, he avowed, fully bore out the training of children six days in a week with careful exclusion from religious influence. In Protestant Prussia and in other European communities, the sentiment of gratitude was universally expressed, that the system of secular, without admixture of religious instruction, was abandoned. They wanted no more experience of the fruits of a system, which, in their estimation, leads to civil disorder and anarchy, to political persecution and despotism, than what they had already suffered. Opinion, then, had almost universally established the plan of allowing communities of various creeds, respectively, to form schools of their own, in which the religious tenets of the parents were inculcated upon their children, and the State apportioned the tax raised for educational purposes, on the basis of numbers of the system in vogue, and here, he said, that Brownson, Robert Dale Owen, and Fanny Wright, were among the prominent originators and advocates. The Bishop doubted the right of the State to tax the people for an educational system which they conscientiously disapprove. He denied the justice of having to pay for palatial school edifices in which the teaching conflicts with his views of duty. But he recommended acquiescence and obedience to the laws. Good citizenship he regards as a Catholic virtue. He expressed faith, however, in a change in the public sentiment, which he thought certain to remedy the grievance under which the people labor. You all know, he said, the opinion held by Mr. Seward[*] on this subject. And I have been gratified within the past week, to read in the report of a discussion held by Mr. Smith,[†] who is now canvassing the State for the office of Governor, that avows unmeasured hostility to the present odious and oppressive school system. The State of New York appropriates four million of dollars to the support of public schools, and another million, as far as I can learn, is contributed from other sources to this same object. Less than half the amount would accomplish all the educational advantages thereby

---

[*] William H. Seward, afterwards Secretary of State, under the administration of Presidents Lincoln and Johnson.

[†] Hon. Gerrit Smith, Abolition candidate for Governor of the State of New York, in 1858.

acquired, in a much safer and better manner, were it applied in accordance with the wishes of parents. It is to parents that God has committed the training of the children whom he gives them. Neither the State, nor even the Church has a right to take them from that trust. The State may assist, but it is not competent to assume and usurp. Tell me not of sectarian schools. Sect means cut off. A sect is something lapped off, divided from the parent stem. But from what was the Catholic Church? No, it is not a sect, it is the parent stem; it is the Mother Church!

"The persuasive and impressive elocution with which the Bishop urged these peculiar views, and which, indeed, characterized every part of the address, can be appreciated only by those who heard him. The congregation hung upon his words, as on the admonitions of a beloved and venerated parent. A solemn stillness pervaded the audience during the whole discourse, save when, at intervals, a spontaneous universal movement marked the surging of a sympathy that could not be repressed."

On the 13th of October, 1858, Bishop Timon published a pastoral, in which he announced the jubilee granted by the Holy Father, Pope Pius IX. The Bishop, in announcing the joyous circumstance, observed:

"Before the written records of Christianity noted the fact, usages, which the oldest of living men could only remember, traced back the christian jubilee, and urged the Sovereign Pontiff to establish, as a gracious law, what venerable men, bowed down with years, came to seek as a just privilege of mercy, of which, on the bed of death, their dying grandfathers had spoken as fore-appointed to grace the beginning of each christian century. Human life being too short for graces at intervals so distant, the christian jubilee, like the Jewish one, soon took place every fiftieth year; but as even then the life of many was too short for its recurrence, twenty-five years was fixed upon for the regular return of those stars of mercy which brighten the christian sky. Extraordinary jubilees, for particular great reasons, became as comets that might shine more brightly, but irregularly, amidst those fixed epochs of mercy and holy joy."

The good results of religion in this country, and the prospective abundance of a large harvest, began to be felt. The Holy Father, encouraged by the American Bishops, therefore strove to provide for this spiritual abundance, and urged the establishment of an American College at Rome, in which young men could be educated and fitted as priests for the numerous missions of the New World. For this purpose collections throughout the entire province were taken up, and a beginning, though feeble, made, to which Bishop Timon liberally corresponded.

In the meantime, the jubilee already alluded to had been finished. But late in December of the year, by a special permission of the Holy Father, based upon an urgent application of the Bishop, an extension of the jubilee was granted until the close of the month following, January, 1859. This favor, in the plenitude of charity of Pius IX, was granted particularly to give those whose avocations in summer kept them away from home, on the waters, as sailors, an opportunity to reap the benefit of its blessings.

We have already alluded to the steps taken by Bishop Timon for establishing some system and order with regard to Catholic funerals. On the 11th of April, 1859, he issued another pastoral, the principal features of which were, that the burial services over deceased Catholics should be performed at the parochial church to which they belonged. That no more than four carriages and hearse would be permitted to attend the funeral of such deceased. That to any person or persons, violating these ordinances, burial services shall be denied. And finally, he recommended that the friends of the deceased should walk in procession from the house to the church were the funeral service was to be performed.

This new order by the Bishop was gladly and willingly obeyed by his flock, and resulted very materially in putting an end to much disorder and scandal, thitherto prevalent at Catholic funerals among the poorer classes of the diocese. The Bishop himself, very beautifully, observed in a letter to his flock:

"According to those rules, everything in our christian funerals will assume the form of a religious act. The sacred calm, the religious quiet, which then must become habitual in the cemetery, will make it, indeed, a hallowed spot. Soon a monument, or at least a cross, will be placed over the grave, which affectionate hands will deck with flowers. From time to time, dear friends and loving relatives will drive out to bend in prayer over the grave; perhaps bedew the flowers with their tears, but there will be 'joy in their grief;' the holy calm, the religious spirit that breathes around; the emblems of faith and hope that speak from every grave of a better life, will console; the mourners will love to return; in the course of the year many carriages will thus be used without tumult, racing, or scandal; a pilgrimage on foot will be preferred by some; but whether on foot, or in a carriage, all, according to the Scripture demand, 'will be done in order;' all will be done for God's blessing, both for this life and the next."

This zeal for order, peace, and the dignity of faith, by no means measured to the fullest extent the labors of Bishop Timon in his arduous mission. It would require a volume alone to give the details of his tireless efforts in every direction for the promotion of good works and religious institutions. We necessarily avoid the recital of them in the pages of this work, as they belong more properly to a volume especially devoted to the " Missions in Western New York." It will suffice at this period of our writing, to quote an extract from the pages of a paper,* dated June 25th, 1859:

"Our readers may wonder, while reading the appointments under the head 'Episcopal Visitations,' how they can be attended to by a prelate of the advanced age of our zealous and untiring Bishop. Let us state what he accomplished last Sunday: In the *morning*, he officiated at the blessing of St. Mary's Hospital, Rochester; preached at *ten o'clock* service at St. Patrick's; proceeded seven miles, (same day,) to Greece, and officiated at laying the corner-stone for the church of our Lady of Sorrows, and preached an eloquent sermon, and returning to Rochester

---

* Buffalo *Sentinel.*

again, preached in St. Mary's church in the *evening*, (same day.) We venture to say, that not another prelate can go through as much service *as the Bishop of this diocese does week after week.*"

On the 18th of July, 1859, Bishop Timon was called to attend the last moments of William B. Lecouteulx.* a man who, during his lifetime, figured so prominently against the Church, though professing to be a Catholic. It is refreshing, therefore, as we draw towards the close of these pages, to be able to speak more favorably of this misguided man, and to observe that, although he was openly the avowed opponent of the Bishop, the latter did not forget the charity of his sacred character, and administered to him, with his own hands, the holy viaticum.

Among the many relics and sacred things brought by the Bishop from his late visit to Rome, was the entire body of St. Peregrinus, a martyr. It was given to him by Cardinal Franzoni, and was contained in a box, which, with the marble slab that covered the tomb, he brought with him. This martyr suffered death in A. D. 190, and was in a remarkable state of preservation when first exposed to the light. Still it was deemed best to adopt a practice, common in Europe, and which was to keep from exposure to light and air bones, (that now, after so many ages, would rapidly disintegrate.) by making a figure of wax, and placing the skeleton form within the enclosure. The box also contained a vial of a portion of the martyr's blood. Though the vial was unhappily broken, enough remains to show its curious form.

---

* Born in May, 1787, and seventy-two years of age when he died.

CHAPTER XI.

PUBLIC SCHOOL SYSTEM.—BISHOP TIMON'S VIEWS.—BISHOP LYNCH.—PROVINCIAL COUNCIL.—ITS IMPORTANCE.—SIGNIFICATION OF THE BLOOD OF ST. JANAURIUS.—PETER PENCE—PROVIDENCE INSANE ASYLUM.—BISHOP TIMON'S SERMON.—DEAN RICHMOND.

THE agitation of the question of the present State Public School system, is no new issue. It is an undeveloped and unsettled subject, that has provoked the consciences of a large class of people for many years, in the United States particularly. Although frequent efforts have been made through just legislation, to regulate and adjust the objections entertained against the present system of public education, (all to no purpose,) still it will not be inopportune in this connection to review at some length the views advanced by Bishop Timon on this subject, as they will be found not only interesting, but at the same time serve as another powerful instance of the Bishop's astute and keen judgment. As late as November, 1859, he wrote:

"The Church of the living God, as spouse of the Incarnate Word, and mother of His redeemed, has ever 'the mind which was in Christ Jesus.' She wants 'little children' to come to *her*, that she may lead them to *Him*, to consecrate the sweet morning of life to God. Hence, even in the ages most unfavorable, amidst the wildest tumult of war, and the threatened approach of a second barbarian, she made gigantic efforts to instruct and educate youth. She covered the civilized world with seats of learning, from the noble university down to the common school; and when violently despoiled of the stately edifices which she had erected, protesting against the unjust spoliation, she patiently, resignedly, and confidingly set to work, and erected others in their stead. Notwithstanding the unblushing hardihood with which, almost daily, it is falsely stated that Catholic countries are deficient in schools and in school attendance, it is a fact, vouched for by learned Protestants, who have examined the question, that, in proportion to population, *non-Catholic* countries are behind Catholic governments (or countries,) in schools and in school attendance; and that, in this particular, Rome and the Pontifical States are *far* ahead of boasted England.

"But instruction without education may become a curse, not a blessing. If, whilst cultivating the intellect, the heart becomes corrupt, the additional force which learning adds to a wicked nature, increases the power for evil. The proverb that 'ignorance is the mother of crime,' is not true in its commonly received meaning. Ignorance is barren, it cannot be a mother; but allied to false principles in morals or dogma, *that false teaching* begets in fallen nature the crimes which still further degrade it.

"An unlearned man who firmly believes in God, as his first beginning and last end, can be more safely trusted with his neighbor's fortune, honor, or life, than the smart, learned man, who, scarcely believing in God, makes himself the last end of his being.

"We need but examine the dark record of crime, which disgraces our age, to be assured of this truth. Deceptive statistics induce some to believe that a large proportion of crime is committed by the unlearned, but a close examination of details shows that great numbers of the ignorant, who figure as criminals, are punished for *faults* or crimes by no means of the darkest hue, many, perhaps, of which would be overlooked if committed by *the respectable*.

"But suicide, parricide, poisoning of parents or relatives, cold blooded murder under a false code of honor, murder long planned for sordid gain, or dark revenge; forgery, arson, and swindling on a gigantic scale, which destroys public confidence, and brings on a commercial crisis and ruins thousands, are generally perpetrated by the well instructed, intellectual men and women, whom false principles of religion or irreligion have led to substitute self for God, and vice for virtue, and taught to call good evil, and evil good.

"The wisdom of experience coincides with the wisdom of the Bible, and the wisdom of the Church, in assuring us that to make instruction profitable, for true happiness in time, and for boundless happiness in eternity, it must be based on religion, and 'seasoned with the salt of the earth,' that is, seasoned with the doctrines of Him who is 'the truth, the way, and the life.' Certainly, in ancient Greece and Rome, the age of highest mental culture was also the age of corruption and of wide spread crime, which menaced to render human society impossible. God forbid that we should seek by these remarks to disparage learning, or to encourage ignorance. True learning, the highest intellectual courage, leads to the Church, and is her boast, her glory, and her strength. But learning or intellectual culture without religion or virtue, too often increases power for evil, and enables the unprincipled man to heap greater treasures of wrath against the day of wrath.

"Within these later years, from the chair of St. Peter, our beloved and venerated Chief Bishop, the charitable, learned, and holy Pope Pius IX, has frequently raised his saintly voice to warn all parents, throughout the Christian world, of their strict obligation to give their children a Catholic education, to remove them from godless, and to send them to Catholic schools. His honored voice has been re-echoed by Patriarchs, Primates, Archbishops, Bishops and councils, throughout the Christian world. Lately, the truly learned and pious Dr. Cullen, Archbishop of Dublin and Primate of Ireland, has, with all the Archbishops and Bishops of our country, denounced the Irish system of public or national schools, though it is far, very far less oppressive and tyrannical than ours. The Archbishops and Bishops of our country also denounce or deplore the evils of our public school system. We, too, have often protested against the proselytizing, sectarian spirit which often is displayed in its administration. And often we have warned, as now we warn the faithful, not to send their children to 'Godless Schools,' lest they awake, when too late, to conviction of the danger, when their loved offspring will either have lost the faith, or all will to practice the sacred duty of faith, and, with faith, having lost reverence for their Heavenly Father, reverence and obedience to their earthly parents will also depart.

(18)

"In many public schools the Protestant Bible is read; we consider it as much a controversial work as any other. Protestants themselves admit that it is mistranslated, and seek in vain to make a new translation which their different sects can adopt. Their Bible is also mutilated; many of the sacred books are omitted. Can we, without sin, permit our children to read or study as the word of God, a mistranslated, mutilated version of Holy Writ? We have often most earnestly begged that, if our Protestant fellow-citizens persist in using the Bible as a school book, they would, at least, permit our children to make use of *their Catholic* Bible, whilst the Protestant children still retained *their Protestant* Bible; this just request has always been refused. Our Catholic youth, at the wish and will of Protestant superintendents or teachers, must read, or hear each morning read, as the true word of God, a Bible, so mistranslated, so mutilated, as to be, perhaps, the most efficient work of controversy against Catholics.

"In many public schools Protestant prayers, and Protestant hymns, commingle with the reading of the Protestant Bible, and poor Catholic children must assist at such Protestant religious exercises, or be flouted, or punished, whilst too often their favored Protestant school fellows use the effective argument, which at home or from teachers they learned too well, 'no wonder you'd be poor, you go to the Catholic church; no respectable people go there.' Alas! even in the first age of the Church, we learn what power such taunts had, when rich Gentiles used it against christians who were generally poor. No wonder, then, that we consider each public school a proselytizing institution; and that we deeply feel the injustice of making us pay a heavy tax for them, and for libraries, in which some of the works against our faith abound.

'Were Catholics the majority in this country, and did they frame such a school system for Protestants, how awful would be the outcry? Did a Catholic majority tax a Protestant minority for the purchase of school libraries full of books that insult, ridicule, and malign Protestantism, how would not Protestants protest?

Did Catholics tax them for schools in which the Catholic Bible would be read and studied; tax them for Normal schools, in which all the students, educated at great cost to be the future teachers of youth, were Catholics; tax them in order to pay high wages, *almost without exception*, to Catholic teachers, who, in many ways, by word or by gesture, would show their contempt for Protestantism; tax them for splendid school houses, in which poor Protestants could not study without danger of being, by a thousand appliances, made ashamed of the faith of their fathers; oh, were this the case, how the world would ring with Catholic injustice, and Protestant suffering.

"But Catholics have never done this. See, in Lower Canada, the just and liberal system which Catholics have enacted for Protestant schools; see, in Catholic France and Belgium, the fair, just and liberal regulations in favor of Protestant schools; see, in the much maligned Austria, containing a population of about forty millions, with scarcely three or four millions of Protestants, (mostly Lutherans and Calvinists,) how, up to our day, this handful of Protestants have, as regards instruction and conscience, rights for which we, in this land of liberty, would be most grateful. The London *Times* of last September, (13th, 1859,) tells us that these Protestant liberties in Austria have lately been placed in the organic law, with the following clauses:

"'The Protestant schools are, for the future, to be under the direction and inspection of their own ecclesiastical organs.

"'No books can be used in Protestant schools which have not been approved of by the general conference, (Protestant,) and by the ministry for ecclesiastical affairs.

"'If a Protestant school is established at the expense of the State, only Protestant teachers can be employed in it.'

"How ample is this liberty. If, in Austria, Protestants build private schools, (where, of course, the teachers are Protestants,) no one even talks of making laws to force their children to frequent public schools hostile or dangerous to their faith; yet, in different States of our country, people have not only *talked* of this, *but even tried to force it by law*. In Austria, when the school buildings for Protestants are erected by the State, the *teachers must*, by law, be Protestants. There no system of proselytism is found in the schools, no insidious influence to warp the judgment of unsuspecting youth. Oh, may God grant to poor oppressed Catholics in this free country, the liberty of conscience and education which Protestants enjoy in despotic yet Catholic Austria."

What force and reason are embodied in the foregoing extract. What a just rebuke to the bigotry and prejudice that measure out such injustice to a people of a free country.

On Sunday, November 20th, 1859, the interesting ceremony of the consecration of Rt. Rev. J. J. Lynch, as Bishop of Toronto, C. W., took place. A number of Bishops and clergymen assisted at the ceremonies, which were very imposing. Bishop Timon was also present, and preached the consecration sermon, which was very elaborate and evinced a great amount of learning.

In the meantime, in the beginning of the year (January 10th,) 1860, a solemn Provincial Council was held in New York, presided over by Archbishop Hughes, and assisted by the seven suffragan Bishops of the Province. It was the most solemn of any of the Provincial Councils until then convened, from the earnestness of the questions that occupied its attention and judgment. The principal point of interest that was discussed was the (then) present state of affairs in Italy, including the sovereignty of the Holy See. In the first session of the council, it was considered by the Bishops whether their convention was meant simply as a meeting for the purpose of presenting an address to the Holy Father, or whether it should be considered as a Provincial Synod, for the purpose of attaching more weight and authority to the conclusions they might reach and publish. The latter course was finally agreed upon, and when the council was closed, a pastoral, signed by all the Bishops of the dioceses of the Province. including the name of Bishop Timon, was drawn up and published. Copies of this pastoral were sent to every sovereign of Europe, excepting Queen Victoria and Victor

Emmanuel. They were also sent to several Bishops of France, and to all the Bishops of Great Britain and Ireland. As soon as His Holiness, Pope Pius IX, received his copy, he was so pleased with the views and kind sympathies it contained, that he caused it to be "printed at the Propaganda, both in English and Italian,—the only pastoral yet published in Rome by the order of the Pope." Two or three months subsequently, a correspondent of Archbishop Hughes wrote: " You will be glad to hear that the Propaganda has received letters from many parts of Italy, calling for a new edition of the pastoral."

The decided stand of the council was the key-note of an expression of public opinion that echoed from one corner of the country to the other. Laymen as well as clergymen boldly asserted their views, both orally and upon paper. In the bosom of Bishop Timon, the temporal sovereignty of the Holy See awakened an unbounded enthusiasm. In the columns of the Buffalo Sentinel, as leading editorials and in private pastorals, he clearly and earnestly enunciated his sympathy and sentiment on this question. In a note to the editor of the above-mentioned paper, (the Bishop's official organ,) he said: "Oh! that God would raise up among us many Montalemberts, to defend the cause of true liberty, of order, virtue and truth, now warred against, in the person of the Pope." Writing from Naples about the liquefaction of the blood of St. Janaurius,* a correspondent of the Buffalo Courier observed: "What superstition! what credulity! what absurdity! that thousands of men should be gulled by a deception, the mystery of which a little chemistry could unravel." Although it is not an article of faith in the Church, for persons to believe that the process of liquefaction is miraculous, still the circumstance is regarded with considerable reverence by every pious christian in the world. The quoted

---

* In the cathedral at Naples is a vial said to contain a little of the blood of St. Janaurius, in a congealed state. Twice each year the liquefaction of the blood takes place, and is repeated each time eight successive days. The blood of the saint was collected by some pious christian, at the time of his martyrdom, A. D. 305.

extract of the *Courier* correspondent particularly provoked the feelings of Bishop Timon, and in an issue of his official organ he very aptly replied:

"Does the writer not know that the blood and the above process have, under the most favorable circumstances, been often examined by most learned chemists? Does he not know that Sir Humphrey Davy, one of the greatest chemists of this century,* closely examined it, pronounced it miraculous, was converted, and died a Catholic?"

It is no new circumstance to our readers to know that in this century they have witnessed the efforts of unscrupulous, designing men to rob and destroy the temporal possessions and power of the Holy Father at Rome. But in the disposition of Divine Providence the efforts made have been yearly thwarted, and his limited resources provided for by the two hundred million christians from all quarters of the globe. Much money and valuable presents are from time to time donated to the Holy Father. In the Spring of 1860, Bishop Timon remitted to the Pope four thousand three hundred dollars, as the first instalment from the laity of this diocese. This was gratefully acknowledged by the Holy See, in a letter "given at Rome, St. Peter's, the 24th of May, 1860."

The labors of Bishop Timon for his diocese were truly remarkable. During the short period of his Episcopacy, he has raised a barren mission into a vineyard, fruitful with a golden harvest. We have seen how he has traveled miles for means to carry out his purposes. We have seen his zeal more particularly directed to fostering his charitable institutions, and how he has watched over the morning of their infancy with unwearied anxiety and zeal. They have grown well, and taken deep root in the soil of the diocese. Their good influence has been frequently recognized in the laudations from the pens of newspaper writers, both here and abroad.

This much, at least, is true for the fine building erected in September, 1860, and known as the "Providence Insane Asylum,"

---

* "Consolations of a Philosopher on his Travels."—*Sir Humphrey Davy.*

for lunatics. The asylum stands upon a tract of land covering thirty acres, that will yield, on an average, enough each year to feed the cattle attached to the farms, as well as the inmates of the institution itself. The land was bought in 1860, from Dr. Austin Flint, of New York. Immediately after the purchase, Bishop Timon commenced the erection of a commodious brick building, and by his indefatigable zeal, succeeded in finishing it so as to be able to receive patients within a year afterwards. In 1861, he blessed the building with appropriate ceremonies. Visitors in numbers thronged the spacious grounds, on which booths, with refreshments, had been provided; a band of music and various civic societies were in attendance, to give animation to the scene. During the ceremony, Bishop Timon delivered an excellent discourse, in which he bestowed a fulsome tribute to the labors and zeal of those good Sisters engaged in the cause of christian charity. He alluded to similar institutions for lunatics, and illustrated his remarks with a very fine example of humane treatment over brute force, to be employed in the care and nursing of those by misfortune deprived of the proper use of their reason. He said it had been exemplified in France: that once a man confined in an institution for lunatics, with whom brute force had been employed to reduce him to subjection, was, by way of experiment, transferred to the care of Sisters of Charity for treatment. When the vehicle containing the unfortunate man, (who, from the extreme paroxysms of his lunacy, was bound hand and foot,) had arrived at the door of the Sisters' asylum, it was received by the good Superioress herself. She employed all the known arts of persuasion to induce him to enter quietly, and with all the gentleness of a mother over the wounds of a wounded child, tried to gain his confidence. At first he refused point blank to be governed. But, by degrees, the kind treatment of the Sister, to which he had been a stranger for many months, began to assert its influence. Yielding gradually to the impressions made by the good Sister, he finally consented to leave the carriage and follow her, provided the manacles were taken from his hands and feet. The attendants, accustomed to see him often in the most violent fits of insanity, in which he not only threatened his own, but even the lives of those happening to be near him, at first hesitated to consent to this condition. But the Sister, conscious of her control over him, finally prevailed over these objections, and accordingly the handcuffs and shackles were removed. Immediately the man left the carriage with a firm and reliant step, like a child obeyed the direction of the Sister, and calmly entered the house. Very few months afterwards he left the asylum, *entirely restored* to reason, the simple result of *kind* and *humane treatment*.

Since September, 1861, when the first patient was received, over five hundred have already been treated in this "Providence Insane Asylum."

Bishop Timon guarded its infancy with zealous care and a watchful eye, and in every way worked for its success. Money advanced to him liberally to the amount of six thousand dollars, on his good credit, was expended in introducing all the improvements that could be commanded. He himself delivered a lecture for its benefit, from which he realized the sum of four hundred dollars. Nor has the good asylum, under the judicious management of its Superioress, Sister Rosalind, been wanting for kind friends and benefactors. Dean Richmond,[*] in whose praise and honor the pen cannot be too lavish for frequent donations to institutions of charity, presented this asylum with one thousand four hundred dollars, and evinced a deep interest in its success. A firm and warm friend of Bishop Timon, and an admirer of the latter's sincere and indomitable labors for the good of man, be it said to the memory of Mr. Richmond, he indirectly, to a certain extent, strove to aid the progress of good works, although widely differing on religious points of doctrine from some of the objects of his charity.

---

[*] Of Batavia, N. Y., President of the New York Central Railroad.

Dean Richmond, with thy setting sun,
    Full many a lesser orb shall rise,
Fired by the glories thou hast won—
    Most marvelous of destinies!

The world will look, but long in vain,
    Before another star shall dawn,
To lead the bright, illustrious train,
    Whose beacon light is just withdrawn.

Thy memory can ne'er decay;
    Too many hearts enshrine it there;
Nor circling years shall steal away
    The fragrance of the flower fair.

'T was thine to right the cruel wrong,
    To succor want, to comfort grief;
To raise the weak and make him strong,
    And grant distress a sure relief.

Thy ready hand a bounty gave
    For earth's forsaken, famished poor;
And ne'er the suppliant did crave
    Unaided at thy generous door.

And every deed shall have requite;
    "A cup of water," saith the Lord,
If given in the cause of right,
    Brings verily a bright "reward."

The world will mourn thee long and deep,
    But deeper still the sacred woe
Of home, where stricken mourners weep
    Unsoothed, beneath the bitter blow.—ANONYMOUS.

---o---

CHAPTER XII.

FALL OF 1860.—WAR.—BISHOP TIMON'S POSITION.—LINCOLN.—FLAG RAISING.—BISHOP TIMON'S REMARKS.—SECOND PROVINCIAL COUNCIL.—BISHOP TIMON'S SERMONS.—EVIDENCES OF DECLINING HEALTH.—ST. VINCENT'S ASYLUM.—BISHOP TIMON GOES TO ROME AGAIN.—JAPANESE MARTYRS.—GUEST OF THE ARCHBISHOP OF TUAM.—ARRIVES HOME.

IT was in the Fall of 1860. At the November elections, Hon. Abraham Lincoln, of Illinois, had been elected President of the United States. Those who now survive that period will remember the portending shadows that darkened the political horizon of the country. It was an hour full of foreboding, fear, and uncertainty, and an hour, also, in which the patriotism of men was to be tested. Events since then have shown the effects of a civil war between two sections of the country, and pointed out who were devoted to the cause of the Union and the Constitution. Aside from the people in general, Catholic prelates and clergymen testified their devotion to their country in prayers, words of exhortation, and upon the battle field. One in particular, (Rt Rev. John Hughes, Archbishop of New York,) was a representative of the government to some of the courts of Europe. Thus, throughout the length and breadth of the land, of the many who, according to their station in life, contributed their services, Bishop Timon was by no means an exception. As early as December 15th, 1860, whilst the nation was rife with rumors, and States were beginning to efface themselves from the map of the country, he publicly declared his views, at once decided and patriotic: "With all good citizens, we mourn over the dangers which now threaten our beloved country. We, from earliest youth, eagerly listened to the maxim, exaggerated perhaps, but as then in the mouths of all, most assuredly breathing the true spirit of devotion to our noble confederacy, 'United we stand, divided we fall.' Alas! what evils may not lurk in the dark clouds that now thunder forth '*Secession*.' But God, who was with our forefathers, giving success against fearful odds; God, whose Holy Providence has guided our cherished country to wonderful prosperity, giving her a rank among the first powers of the earth, will, we hope and pray, yet speak peace to the storm. He says, 'Ask, and you shall receive.' Let us, then, dearly beloved, ask Him to soothe the angry emotions of many a generous heart, to dispel the clouds that darkly brood over the Union, save us from disunion and strife, and 'give us peace.' To this end we ordain that the collect *Pro Pace* henceforward, and till the feast of St. Joseph, March 14th, be said at mass on all Sundays and festivals; and that the following prayer,* at late mass, during the same time, be recited before the sermon."

---

* The prayer alluded to we omit, as too lengthy for reproduction. Suffice it to say, that among many things, he earnestly prayed that God would, in His wisdom, guide the councils of the nation, and avert the calamities that threatened the disrupture of the glorious Republic

This notice was read in each church, on the Sunday after its reception. But the key note to rebellion and secession had been sounded, and like falling meteors from a troubled firmament, one by one, States sundered their connection with the galaxy of the Union, and plunged themselves into a terrible civil war. Abraham Lincoln had been inaugurated President. His address, full of promise and pacific in its tone, was disregarded, and the strife commenced in dread earnest. An electrical enthusiasm permeated the masses of the people of the North, when the first call for volunteers was telegraphed throughout the land. Flags fluttered from almost every housetop, and men and women were compelled to establish their identity as patriots and Union loving citizens.

Among thousands of others, Bishop Timon also testified his devotion to his country, by unfurling to the Summer air the emblem of the Union, the Star Spangled Banner, which had been kindly donated and raised by some gentlemen over his residence. A number of citizens were assembled in front of his Episcopal residence to witness the event, and congratulate him, as well as themselves, on his firm and prompt response to the requirements of patriotism. As soon as the flag had been raised, the Bishop made his appearance at the door of his residence, and said:

"*Much Respected and Beloved Fellow-Citizens:* Born under our country's honored flag, which you now so kindly raise over my dwelling; having, with enthusiastic love, looked up to that flag from earliest youth, warmly do I thank you for the honor you do me in planting it upon my house; greatly too, do I rejoice in this patriotic display. Yet, the occasion is one in which joy and sorrow strangely mingle. We all grieve at the disruption of our glorious Union; we mourn over drops of blood already shed, and in fear of the torrents that yet may flow during this unwelcome struggle. For you, as for me, all the years that have passed since birth or adoption, that made America our country, have been years, during which the men of the South have been loved and cherished as brothers. At first, our souls recoiled from the thought of waging war against them. Alas! there seems now to be no other alternative. The issue has been forced upon us. Our country calls; with patriotic zeal, with devoted hearts, we should obey her call; yet, still, it is sad, for we fight against brothers, misguided brothers.

"Yet, with the sadness which such thought must bring, there is much to console. And first, how noble is the outburst of a nation's enthusiastic patriotism. As I look around, I see my country's flag from almost every house, consecrated by it as a fortress for patriotism, honor and duty. Each man and each woman seems a soldier. Sublimely grand is this spontaneous outburst of patriotic, generous sentiment. It was thought by some that patriotism had long died away from the American heart, supplanted by the love for money, and by a love for unbridled license. We have had a long peace; in the inaction of prosperity and peace the more generous impulses of our nature seemed to sleep, whilst base weeds, choking up the nobler plants, stifled more and more each generous demonstration. The strife of races, and the enmity of creeds began to dishonor our land. Not long since, a party denounced their Catholic brethren; not long since, a party attacked their adopted fellow-citizens. It was often said the age of patriotism had passed away. But the storm reached us; the sickening air of inaction was purified; and now, we see on every side patriots, generous patriots, rushing to sacrifice even life, if necessary, for country's sake; we see noble and generous patriots who make the greatest sacrifices in order to save or to aid a beloved, imperiled country. We also see Catholics and Protestants united as brothers, in the same military band, to battle together, and mingle their blood in defence of their beloved country. We see Americans, Irish, and Germans, vieing with each other for the post of danger, in defence of a common, much beloved country. Hence, long years of peace had only lulled to sleep the determined patriotism, the generous spirit of our forefathers. The blast of war has awakened to energy the noble and sacred impulses of our nature; the trumpet sound of the coming storm has made those generous sentiments sink their roots deeper in the American heart, whilst it also uprooted the foul weeds of dissension, of party strife, and of religious intolerance

"Our country it is our duty not to question, but to obey. So much the more holy will be the war, as it is not one of passion, but of duty. Those gallant soldiers do not rush to battle through enmity, hatred or revenge. Ah, no! they love their brethren of the South; they mourn over the necessity of arraying themselves in arms against their late beloved fellow-citizens. A very few, the guilty authors of disunion, are blamed, others are pitied as deceived, and are all still loved as brothers. *But the South began the war; the North cannot back out without forfeiting its manhood, its honor, and its glorious future.* So says our lawful government, so say the wise and the good, throughout the length and breadth of our untainted land. This war, then, is not one of hatred or personal enmity; it is a war of duty, of lofty patriotism, of obedience to our country's call. It is a war to preserve the high standing of our beloved country among the nations of the earth. It is a war which, if successful, (as who can doubt,) will be one of benefit to patriotic citizens, in the South as well as in the North. Hence, with our sorrow there is mixed consolation, in evidence of which are the patriotic virtues of our gallant volunteers, some of whom grace by their presence the raising of the stripes and stars over this dwelling. In earlier years, when I loved to seek wisdom from the pages of history, I learned one think which I can never forget. Lately, I have had no time to revise what I then learned. I am a soldier, an officer, having others under my direction. I am a counsellor at law, often, too, an attorney at law, but in a law of wondrous extent, that intertwines itself with the most mysterious fibres of the human heart. I am a physician, having under me a large staff of physicians, all skilled in the care of souls diseased, and also seeking my directions. Such duties now leave me no time to study history, or to follow closely the politics of the day. But from the studies of earlier times, I remember that the wisdom of past ages declared *this* as an axiom. *If war must be waged, let it be waged with* vigor; thus alone can it be rendered less bloody, thus alone can it end speedily in peace. May the uprising of a nation overawe all discord, and make rash and daring men recoil before the consequences. May God give us peace before war, or make that war short. Gallant soldiers, who go to battle for your country, trust in the mercy of Him who is not only *the God of peace*, but also *the Lord God of armies*. If, as I trust, you march and you fight as christian soldiers, God's mercy will be with you. Venerable doctors, great theologians have taught that the soldier's death on the battle field in defence of his country's rights, has special privileges of mercy, prepared by the Lord God of Hosts, who is also the God of mercy, to aid at that moment when mercy is most needed the dying, patriotic soldier. But my prayer to God will be, that this uprising of a great nation may induce misguided men to pause and retrace their steps. Or, if war must come, that its evil time may be short, and will be soon followed by a peace that will be perpetual."

This decided expression of patriotism was well received by persons of all denominations, and quieted the apprehensions of many, that Catholics, and particularly their Bishops and priests, were sympathizers with rebellion.

On the 2d of June, the "Second Provincial Council of the Ecclesiastical Province of New York," convened at the cathedral, and was a very interesting affair in the history of the Church.

The procession formed in front of the Archepiscopal residence in Mulberry street, and moved thence to the cathedral. Among the distinguished prelates present, were the Archbishop of New York, Right Rev. John Hughes; the Bishops of Hartford, Portland, Newark, Brooklyn, Buffalo, Boston and Albany; and the Bishops of Guadalajara, and San Luis Potosi, Mexico.

At the conclusion of mass, Bishop Timon delivered the sermon. It was very elaborate in its reasonings, and very forcible in its hypothesis. He spoke of other creeds, and by comparison with the Catholic Church, made the latter stand more prominent and in bolder relief:

"When Luther and Calvin separated from the ancient Church, they excused that rending of Christ's mystical body on the grounds that gross immorality prevailed, that rapacity and grasping after riches were universal, and that not only were morals corrupt, but that faith had become affected, that errors of doctrine had crept in, and the purity of the ancient faith had been obscured and tarnished. Such were the grounds on which they based their justification. Faith, as they alleged, had not been preserved inviolate, and so highly did they estimate that theological virtue, that they declared faith without good works sufficient for salvation, and proved their belief in the inefficacy of good works, by discarding them altogether. Indeed, as one of their own writers observed, they taught that if man believed firmly, he might sin boldly, and be sure of heaven notwithstanding. Look at the descendants of these men now, and mark the reverse of this doctrine. Faith, considered the one thing necessary then, is now deemed of no account, and morality is in the fashion. Let a man, they say, believe what he pleases, so long as he does not believe what the ancient Church teaches, or believe nothing if he likes that better; but let him live a good moral life, keep up appearances, pay a due regard to the proprieties of life, and commit none of those acts that make humanity shudder, and he will be saved. How strange it sounds to hear the descendants of those who, three centuries ago, preached the all-sufficiency of faith, now teach that salvation can well be gained without it. And yet, both these extremes look to the Bible as their guide and rule of faith. Both refer to the Sacred Volume as their authority and inspiration. I turn to the Bible and read: 'Without faith it is impossible to please God,' and, 'the just man liveth by faith;' but I also read, 'faith without good works is dead,' and I know that St. Peter, speaking of the Epistles of St. Paul, said, 'there were many things in them difficult to be understood, which the unlearned and the unstable wrested to their own destruction.' The Bible cannot decide apparently conflicting texts, and besides, the Bible, as a rule of faith, is imperfect, as I learn from its own pages; much of it has been lost. How do I know but that part which has been lost contained matter that it was necessary for me to know. It might have unfolded something to me of which I was ignorant, or it might have elucidated something which is obscure. In this view of the case, another important consideration is the length of time that elapsed before the Bible was written. If it had been so essential to salvation, would the world have been left so long without it?

"Generations passed away in the saving faith of the Jewish Church, before one line of it was written. Four hundred and thirty years after the establishment of that Church, Moses first committed the sacred deposit of truth to writing. Before that time written testimony was not necessary; and we find that in each epoch of the world, God chose different means of preserving alive in the human heart the remembrance of His works and ways. Before the flood, the knowledge of God was preserved by transmission; the highest human testimony runs through that period, the life of one man, (Methuselah) connecting Adam with Noah. Methuselah had talked with Adam, and heard from him in all its freshness the history of the creation; he was two hundred and forty-three years old when Adam died, and two hundred and sixty-nine years old when Noah was born. After that event he lived six hundred and two years, and died, we may say, on the eve of the deluge. In this antediluvian period, therefore, we find the life of one man connecting its two extremes, linking the deluge with the creation, conversing with Adam and Noah, and transmitting from the first to the second founder of the human family, the knowledge of God's marvelous mercy and power. Throughout this history we have no idolatry, for the sins and vices of the antediluvians arose not from pride of intellect, but from corruption of heart; and during this period we have no written records.

"In the second epoch, we find idolatry and the knowledge of the true God, side by side, but for a long time unmixed; gradually the true and the false become blended together, and in this confusion of right and wrong, something more trustworthy than mere human testimony is required. Those who have traveled down the Mississippi, must have observed for what a distance it preserves the purity of its waters uncontaminated after its junction with the Missouri. Side by side they run together for miles, and boats cross and recross from one to the other, and yet the difference is as marked as if they were in different regions. But gradually they commingle, and then the pure bright waters lose their identity, and the amalgamation is complete. In the same way, as we come down the stream of time, we find true and false religion flowing side by side together, but separate, then gradually blending and becoming one.

"In this epoch, it is not an individual nor a family that is set apart to preserve the truth of revelation inviolate, but a whole nation, governed by law imposed by God Himself; a true theocracy, a nation whose march through time was a succession of stupendous miracles, a focus, towards which all the scattered rays of primitive truth converged, and from which the refulgent rays of revealed truth diverged."

It is now in the Spring of 1862, a period in the Bishop's life when the splendid exhibition of his talents seemed to wane. At the advanced age of sixty-six, and suffering somewhat from the infirmities of age, owing to the austerities and labor of his youth, the Bishop now began to reveal symptoms of decline. By the advice of his physician, he was compelled to use gentle stimulants, to recuperate the wasting vitality of his body. This prescription was particularly odious to him, on account of his strict, temperate and abstemious habits, and, although compelled to obey his physician, he nevertheless endeavored to avoid as much as possible the full amount prescribed. Though the winter of age "crept on apace," and wasting vitality forbade him the freedom of exercise and labor to the extent he had in earlier years enjoyed, he, by no means, ceased to watch carefully for the welfare of his beloved flock. About this time, a petition to defray the expenses of the free school attached to St. Vincent's Orphan Asylum, was laid before the Common Council of the city. It was referred by that body to the usual committee. Majority and minority reports were made to the council, in which the minority was disposed that the prayer of the petition should be granted.

After some debate and enquiry through sub-committees, the report was finally adopted. Subsequently, in April, Bishop Timon was called to Rome. He sailed from New York on Wednesday, April 23d, 1862, in company with several other Bishops. Before leaving, he was presented with a handsome purse of money by the members of the Young Men's Catholic Association, of Buffalo, New York, accompanied with a neat address. Bishop Timon arrived in Rome on the 14th of May following, where he was *graciously received and tenderly embraced by the Holy Father.*

The object of the Bishop's visit was to assist at the canonization of the Japanese martyrs, or, as a correspondent expressed it, "Our glorious Pius IX invites the Catholic Bishops of the whole world to the Eternal City, as he is about to place diadems of heavenly radiance on the heads of the *twenty-six* martyrs[*] of Japan."

The ceremonies on this occasion were beyond description. In these ceremonies our Bishop took an active part. A sumptuous dinner was prepared in the library of the Vatican, at which all the Bishops with the Pope were present. After the solemnities were entirely over, most of the Bishops returned home by the way of Ireland, where, among many others, Bishop Timon was well received by His Grace the Archbishop of Tuam. He was the guest of the latter, and during his stay improved his time in visiting cathedrals, convents, nunneries and schools. At length, after an absence of nearly four months, Bishop Timon, on the 7th of August, 1862, reached Buffalo. Here, as upon former occasions, a demonstration was made to receive him, as he alighted from the cars in the depot. An immense procession greeted him, composed of the various civic societies in full regalia. Even non-Catholic citizens joined in the welcome tendered

---

[*] These martyrs suffered death by crucifixion, on the 5th of February, 1597, outside the walls of Nagassa, in Japan.

to the aged and holy man. At his residence appropriate remarks ensued, and a happy exchange of "welcome" lent sunshine to the joyous hour.

Bishop Timon, in this visit to Europe, acquired still further information and knowledge of the religious houses as they were conducted on the continent, hoping to add some of their features to his own institutions; but the gradual decline of life, and the foreshadowings of death, were too overpowering to admit of an application, and he, therefore, reluctantly laid aside those pious intentions.

---o---

CHAPTER XIII.

Public School Text Books.—Bishop Timon Lectures at the Central School.—Correspondence with the Sanitary Commission.—Anonymous Correspondence.—Its Authors Guilty Wretches.—Incident.—One Cause of the Bishop's Death.—Depressed Spirits.—Lectures at Dansville.—Catches the Erysipelas.—Decline of Life, but does not Expect to Die Soon.—His Last Sermon.—Confined to the House.—Predicts his Death.—Death of Bishop Timon.

Although the premonitions of death were continually reminding him that his hour was near at hand, still Bishop Timon strove to discourage this unwelcome idea, and endeavored to exert anew the gradually wasting energies of his physical frame for God's greater glory and honor. His devotions were more frequent and longer protracted than before; his intellect, keen though pliant, grasped with such circumstances as it could combat, whilst his eager eye was constantly alert lest the wary foe of religion should invade the soil over which he held spiritual supremacy. Thus, at the Central School of Buffalo, a text book* on Moral Philosophy had been introduced for the advanced pupils. None could receive a graduate's diploma from this school unless he had studied this text book, which, upon examination, was found to be so fraught with contradictory statements, as to be unworthy of the name. A copy of this work was shown to Bishop Timon, who took special

---

* By Prof. Laurence P. Hicock, D. D.

time to peruse and criticize it. In the words of the Bishop, the author of this text book was proven to be "christian and anti-christian; theist and atheist; pantheistic and a believer in a personal God." In the columns of the organ of his diocese—the *Sentinel*—under date of January 17, 1863, he published his views at some length, reviewing several chapters, and showing the flagrant inconsistencies of the author's (im)moral philosophy.

Thus, with pen and voice, he labored for the rescue of christian principles and the preservation of the holy faith. In May of this same year, he published another lengthy article on "Public School Text Books," in which he exposed the indirect insinuations of bigotry, contained therein, against the Catholic Church, and unveiled the immoral expressions* so contaminating to the plastic mind of the child. By dint of a continued demand for their removal from the public schools, it ultimately was brought before the attention of the City Council, whose action compelled the superintendent to substitute other text books of less objectionable character. Here and there, in the public newspapers of the day, and personally from the pulpit, did the Bishop labor for his flock and principles of true religion. In the Fall of 1863, he accepted an invitation to lecture before the scholars of the Buffalo Central School, and chose for his subject the "Deity." To the author of this work, (a pupil of the above school at that time,) was given the honor and pleasure of waiting on Bishop Timon, and escorting him to the Central School. As we left the house together, we entered the cathedral, in order, as the Bishop remarked, "to ask God's goodness to bless the efforts he might make in the midst of an audience of dissenting religious views."

I watched him as he bent before the altar and bowed his aged and venerable head, and observed the devotion with which he prayed; and as he finished his prayer, he arose to go, a sweet

---

* "Do not blush if the Dutch dunce is drunk."—Page 51.
"If they communicate the story that this man's concupiscence destroyed our connubial love, I will declare it confutable."—Page 174.
"The Bishop is a bibbler and a bigot."—Page 73.
"The clergy in a certain Church, though fervent, are not perfect."—Page 68.
—*Parker & Watson's Text Book.*

and heavenly smile illumining his countenance. It made a deep impression on me at the time, and afterwards, as he began to deliver his lecture before the young men and women of the school, the same smile revisited his countenance, but this time more vividly and strong; his voice, still firm though flexible, grew by degrees more eloquent, until, towards the close of his remarks, he dispelled the unfavorable reception he at first received, and dissipated the fears, the gibes, the sneers of contempt which, though in a suppressed manner, could be plainly seen in the countenances of a few of the scholars. Both teachers and pupils were dumbfounded at the display of knowledge he evinced, and listened with avidity to the magnificent similes he employed in endeavoring to make them comprehend the "Deity." His discourse was listened to for nearly an hour, during which he made a most favorable impression.

On previous pages of this work, we have spoken of the patriotic interest which Bishop Timon took in the welfare of the country during its recent struggle for the restoration of the Union. The following correspondence, illustrative of our remarks, will speak for itself:

"BUFFALO, May 18, 1864.

"*Madam:* The Sovereign Pontiff, Pope Pius IX, has, through His Eminence Cardinal Barnabo, notified me that, with the deepest sorrow and the most fraternal interest, he has heard of the number of gallant soldiers wounded in our many battles, and that he desires me to give, in his name, and out of his private purse, five hundred dollars, as some aid to alleviate their sufferings.

"Your truly providentially organized society has done very much to aid our wounded soldiers; hence it seems to me that there can be no better means of accomplishing the kind and paternal wish of His Holiness, than to hand over to you this check for five hundred dollars, with my humble and fervent prayers that God's blessing may not only rest on your gallant wounded soldiers, but also on the honored members of your Commission, who aid them so generously.

"Accept the expressions of respect and esteem with which I have the honor to be

"Your most obedient, humble servant,

"✠ JOHN, *Bishop of Buffalo.*

"MRS. HORATIO SEYMOUR,
"*President B. U. S. Sanitary Commission.*"

"GENERAL AID SOCIETY FOR THE ARMY,
"BUFFALO, May 19, 1864.

"RT. REV. JOHN TIMON,

"*Dear Sir:* It is with no ordinary feelings we acknowledge the receipt, at your hands, of five hundred dollars from the Sovereign Pontiff, Pope Pius IX, for the relief of our wounded soldiers. Large contributions have been received from foreign countries for this humane object. We are deeply touched by such evidences of interest in our present struggle for national life, and the endorsement of this national channel for our charities, which we believe to be the most direct, humane and efficient one through which the good will of a christian people can be conveyed to the wounded patriots in field or hospital.

"Please present our thanks to His Holiness, and accept for your part in this munificent act, the grateful acknowledgments of the society. With sentiments of the highest regard,

"Yours, truly,

"MRS. HORATIO SEYMOUR, *President.*"

At this point in our present writing, a circumstance of a very delicate and painful nature commands a careful and concise explanation. We allude to it with regret, though in justice to the memory of the deceased Bishop, we can not pass it by in silence. In the Spring of the year 1864, Bishop Timon received an anonymous correspondence in the form of printed circulars, the contents of which were scandalous, and betrayed, in language too evident to be denied, a malicious and villainous disposition, as well as a disappointed ambition. The most foul-mouthed loafer on the street corner would blush to be even accused of using such language to one of his equals.

The correspondence was a confused mass of vituperation, from beginning to end, in which the guilty authors, (like thieves in the dark,) under a blank signature, endeavored to stab at the life of a good and pious prelate, whose shoe-laces they were unworthy to untie.

They evidently possessed neither the moral courage of men, much less the principles of good christians, to openly face their victim. They accused him of cruelty, of avarice, of injustice, and numerous other faults, all in highly colored terms, that were entirely false, if we judge him merely from the good uses to which he put all the monies, no matter from what source they were collected. As for cruelty towards any person, it was not in the nature of Bishop Timon to be cruel, as all well disposed people who knew and loved him, will testify. In point of injustice, if any priest felt chastisement at his hands, it was either because he deserved it, or else, if he did not deserve it, no man than Bishop Timon was readier to retract, and make amends for an offence given. A little incident will explain:

On one occasion, a priest had contemplated leaving the diocese, because he had been reprimanded in a very gentle way by the Bishop, for a slight dereliction of duty, in which, however, we are free to confess, Bishop Timon was acting from misinformation. No sooner, though, had he discovered his error, and (non-intentional) *injustice* to the priest, than he immediately sent for the latter and invited him to dinner. At the dinner table, in order to show him full honor, he placed the priest at the *head of the table*, in his own seat, and during the meal conversed with him more particularly than with the others at the table. After dinner, as usual, all adjourned to the library for their accustomed half-hour recreation. They had just entered the library, and were commencing to enjoy themselves, when Bishop Timon, as if to save from embarrassment the feelings of the pious priest, suddenly observed:

"By the way, my dear child, I have something important to tell you. Please, let us adjourn to my room." And, taking the arm of the priest, they went to the Bishop's room. Here they found Bishop Young, of Erie, who was making a retreat at the Bishop's residence.

Without further ceremony, Bishop Timon turned to the priest, and adverted to the unhappy circumstance that had taken place, in which he (the Bishop) had been inadvertently mistaken. *He then threw himself on his knees before the reverend gentleman, in the presence of Bishop Young,* and humbly asked to be forgiven. The good priest could not refrain from tears, and said such apologies were not suited for him to make, for he was already forgiven. Such was a sample of Bishop Timon's *cruelty* and *injustice!*

But, whilst we know that the character of Bishop Timon is *such* in the hearts and veneration of his people and generous minded men, that it needs no vindication from our pen in this particular, since the bullet intended to blacken his name shot wide of its mark, we still are forced to allude to this circumstance as having an important connection with his life. We confidently declare from the opinions of well informed men, who knew Bishop Timon intimately and well, that he was never the same after he received this anonymous correspondence, until the day of his death, and indirectly it was one of the causes that hastened the early termination of his life. This printed defamation of his character completely unnerved him. All the difficulties he had ever met with in his whole career as a servant of Christ, even the imminent dangers to his personal safety, failed in every instance to affect him. But in this case it was far different. He published a disclaimer to these aspersions of his conduct and administration, which nearly all of the priests of his diocese signed. At close of the diocesan synod, held in September, 1864, he turned to his priests, and in a voice full of emotion and tears, and on bended knees at the foot of his throne, asked every one present if he had in any manner treated them unjustly, for which he had not yet atoned, and if so, he fervently asked to be forgiven, even as he forgave all who had borne false **witness** against him.

During the subsequent four remaining years of his life, he frequently referred to this unfavorable document, and asked himself if he really **did** deserve, in the least particular, any of the accusations contained therein. It affected him mentally more than bodily, and he endeavored by renewed devotions, **by** prayer and fasting, to prepare for the hour when the Bridegroom should come. He knew his own frailty, and, therefore, increased his austerities and penances. We pass over to the well merited contempt of posterity the authors of this infamous libel, since they deserve **no** better mention for their conduct. Though he felt himself daily declining in health, he continued to discharge the usual routine **of duty** throughout the diocese, such as Episcopal visitations, sermons, lectures, and a variety of interesting correspondence.

In 1866, he lectured in Dansville, and during the delivery of his lecture was obliged to be seated. The Rochester *Union* referring to it, observed in substance:

"Bishop Timon lectured last Sunday evening at Dansville, but was obliged to be seated during the delivery of the lecture. **As** usual, it was one of the good Bishop's happiest efforts, although suffering so much from ill health. But from all appearances, it seems, the Bishop is resolved to die in the harness."

Gradually, however, the infirmities of age made a serious **raid** upon his vitality, and compelled him to confine himself **to his** house. His career as a public man, therefore, ends here, and as we depict in **sad and** solemn diction the last moments of this truly christian prelate, **let us pause** to admire his virtues and drink "deep draughts **of wisdom**" from the lesson of his self sacrificing and charitable life. In an unfavorable hour, his heart bursting with zeal for the **wants and wishes** of his beloved flock, he contracted a fatal disease, which, as the *immediate* cause of his death served to destroy rapidly what little vitality remained **after the rude shock** he **had received from the** anonymous **correspondence referred to, which might** appropriately be called the remote cause of his early demise. This disease was Erysipelas. He was called to the bedside of one of those "angels of mercy," a dying Sister of Charity, to administer to her the last sacraments of the Church. This happened two or three years prior to his death, and it is thought that, whilst in the act of hearing the Sister's confession, he contracted the sickness of which the Sister herself was dying. The Bishop took medical advice to rid himself of the malady, and visited Avon Springs, New York, and other places that he thought would benefit his condition. But whatever efforts he did put forth, were entirely insufficient to save him. His worthy physician, James P. White, M. D., in whose skill Bishop Timon had unbounded confidence, prescribed faithfully and skillfully for him. He forbade him to be so severe in his religious discipline, such as fasting and excessive labor, since an invalid in his condition needed repose and refreshment to recover. But his piety and religious fervor made him forget the warning injunctions of his friend and medical adviser. In fact, though depressed in health, Bishop Timon did not expect to die so soon. About a month before his holy death, he contemplated making another visit to Europe, in June following, partly on business and partly for his health, and had even named for the Vicar General of his diocese, during his absence, Rev. William Gleason. But his days were numbered. During the holy season of Lent, prior to his death, he actually increased his mortifications and self-denials, so that, on Palm Sunday, when he entered the pulpit of his cathedral to pronounce the last sermon he should ever deliver to his people, he was obliged to be seated. On that day he felt for the first time the symptoms of his immediate demise. He spoke feelingly and sad of his position then, and knew he had but a few hours to live. He asked his people to pray for him, exhorting them, as usual, to think of themselves and eternity. His remarks were sad and funereal, and when he rose, almost exhausted, to leave the pulpit, there was scarcely a face in the congregation but was suffused with tears.

He returned to his room, where he principally busied himself in preparing for a happy death. During the whole day he was compelled to lie down, whilst kind and willing friends gathered around to pray and comfort him. Still, it was not definitely thought that his hour was near. Though weighed down with the cares and perplexities of his station, (for, amid all his sickness, he ever anxiously thought of his duties, and Episcopal obligations,) and suffering from the pains of his bodily ailments, he bore all afflictions with fortitude, forbearance and christian resignation. During the day he felt himself gradually sinking, and found but little aid in stimulants. Early on Monday morning of Holy Week, he arose as usual, though with difficulty, and, according to rule, assembled with his priests for morning prayer. Generally, towards the close of the prayer, it was customary for the Bishop to ask the assembled priests to pray in particular for some pious object or purpose, in which all readily joined. But on this morning he asked them to join with him in prayer for a happy death, as he felt his end was near. All turned to him with commingled apprehension and surprise, as if to ask the meaning of this strange request. Alas! his prediction verified their fears about thirty-six hours later. He then went to his room, and with great efforts reached his bed, which he never left again alive. His physician was duly summoned, but he could not arrest the progress of dissolution that was rapidly going on. It being evident that the Bishop was dying, Bishop Lynch, of Toronto, and Farrell, of Hamilton, were telegraphed for, who arrived a few hours before he died, and administered the last rites of the Church, according to the custom on the death of a Bishop. In the meantime, the news of the Bishop's serious indisposition, spread like wildfire throughout the city and diocese. The air was rife with conflicting rumors, and a gloom of sorrow hung like a shadow on the countenances of all. We do not exaggerate in this particular, for Bishop Timon's name in the city was a household word. Protestants vied with Catholics in their respect and esteem for him, whom they regarded not as a sectarian, but as a great and good man, as a christian prelate, as a humanitarian in the community in which he lived, and as a citizen, with whose memory were linked some of the earliest reminiscences of the locality in which he lived.

But during all this state of uneasiness on the part of his people, Bishop Timon was dying. He continually ejaculated, "Lord, into Thy hands I commend my spirit;" "Jesus, Mary and Joseph." He held the crucifix in his hands, which he occasionally raised to his lips, at the same time joining in the prayers that were continually said around his bedside by his pious clergymen and friends. At intervals he would address some particular individual in the room, exhorting him to some particular duty towards the Church, or gave his last requests with regard to certain unsettled affairs. He lingered all day and during the night of Monday, without apparent serious change in his condition, his mental faculties still in good order. Early on Tuesday morning, however, a rapid decline set in, and as the day wore on he was expected to die every minute. His physician sat near his bedside as he died. At length evening dropped her shadows over the scene, and he drew near his last. The prayers for the dead were said, and as the weary watchers and mourners prayed for a happy eternity for his soul, all that was immortal of John Timon, the first and well-beloved Bishop of the diocese of Buffalo, took to flight. He expired on Tuesday evening, at forty minutes after eight o'clock, April 16th, 1867.

Thus passed away from the diocese of Buffalo, a man endowed with faculties of the most remarkable order.

It will be the purpose of the closing pages of this work, to deal a little with the character of this prelate, and bring out, in bold relief, the beautiful virtues he possessed, as well as relate the pious practices he indulged in, but of which his deep humility and retiring modesty refrained from making any public display. He loved to worship God in silence and in solitude. He sought consolation and spiritual happiness in prayer and other practices of devotion. He would be found often, (when at home,) in the church, making the stations of the cross; or when wanted on some occasions where pleasure would be the leading feature of an evening's entertainment, such as festivals or suppers, he frequently absented himself and sought refuge in his cathedral, where, in the deep shadow of one of the pillars that support the superstructure of his beautiful church, he buried himself from the world and its vanities, and offered up to his Creator the spirit of self-denial and continence. We could write pages on the character of the subject of this memoir. We loved the subject itself when amongst us, and we are candid when we say a secret impulse of reverence and of duty impels us to build a monument of praise such as is due to the memory of Bishop Timon. However, under distinct headings, we will consider more appropriately the further development of his character.

---o---

CHAPTER XIV.

BISHOP TIMON'S BODY EMBALMED.—HIS RESIDENCE DRAPED IN MOURNING.—NINETY THOUSAND PERSONS VISIT HIS REMAINS.—THE FUNERAL.—PROCESSION.—THE BODY DEPOSITED IN A VAULT OF THE CATHEDRAL.—BISHOP TIMON'S CHARACTERISTICS.—HIS HABITS.—LETTER FROM FATHER SMARIUS, S. J.

IMMEDIATELY after death his body was embalmed, and placed in a richly mounted coffin. The lower parlors of his residence were magnificently draped in mourning, relieved by beautiful rosettes, from which large festoons hung suspended in graceful though sombre profusion from the ceilings and sides of the walls. The taste exhibited in the adornment of this room was governed by the style that was used on the occasion of the death of Emperor Alexander I. of Russia. The gentleman who superintended the work was a Russian* himself, and a most intimate friend as well as warm admirer of Bishop Timon.

Here, beneath this stately canopy of funeral honor, were the remains laid. By a preconcerted plan, arrangements were so made as to enable all who desired to take the "last view" of their Bishop, to do so without difficulty.

---

* George A. Deuther.

During the whole week, (it being Holy Week,) a continuous stream of people, both from this city and from abroad, passed through the room to pay their respects to the deceased. It is estimated that over ninety thousand persons availed themselves of this opportunity to see him.

At length the solemn hour for his funeral arrived. Early on Monday, April 22d, every civic society in the cities of Buffalo, Rochester, and other places, congregated in immense numbers on the squares and streets of the city. A large catafalque, drawn by six gray horses, was prepared, upon which the coffin was to be laid in the funeral procession through the city. From an estimated opinion, the procession was nearly three miles in length. The little orphans, who had experienced his kindness and charity, trod the streets ankle deep in mud, clad in their thin habiliments, vieing with the stalwart and robust members of the various civic organizations in doing honor to their beloved Bishop. The pupils of the various parochial schools also joined the ranks; acolytes in full dress, priests in numbers, with the various Bishops and Archbishops of the Province, as well as from abroad, followed, the Bishops seated in carriages. Thus, in splendid order, the procession slowly and mournfully meandered through the principal streets of the city, until it finally returned to the cathedral. Here the solemn obsequies of the dead were performed over the corpse, and amid the tears and grief of thousands the mortal remains of Bishop Timon were deposited in a vault beneath the floor of the sanctuary, near the high altar. The slab concealing the entrance to the resting place of the illustrious dead was then replaced, and closed with cement and mortar.

The inscription on the plate of the coffin read:

RT. REV. JOHN TIMON, D. D., C. M.,
First Bishop of Buffalo,
DIED APRIL 16TH, 1867,
Aged 72 years.
R. I. P.

Both Archbishops Kenrick, of St. Louis, Mo., and McCloskey, of New York, pronounced panegyrics at the funeral services of the dead Bishop.

The city was unusually thronged with visitors, whilst flags hung at half-mast throughout the city. The Common Council passed appropriate resolutions to the memory of the deceased, whilst from all parts of the country came words of condolence and sympathy from an honest though non-Catholic press.

Bishop Timon was a remarkable man. He was a self-made man. In stature he was not tall, his average height being but a little over five feet. His hair, at the time of his death, was iron gray, and worn combed back behind his ears. To the casual observer, his eyes seemed very small; but this was not the case. Owing to an accident that occurred to him on the Mississippi river, when only a young man, as well as constant application to study and correspondence afterwards, his vision became quite indistinct, and he was obliged to keep his eyelids partly closed, as he could not bear the full rays of light.

The accident above referred to consisted in this, that when he was a young man, the Mississippi river overflowed its banks at a certain locality where there was a convent of Sisters. The lower portions of the building were inundated, driving the inmates to the upper stories and to the roof. Among many who volunteered to go and rescue them from their perilous position, was young Mr. Timon. It was a very hot, sultry day in August, and the sun, glinting askance the bright water of the river, reflected very sharply and severely upon the eyes of Mr. Timon. He succeeded, however, in saving all the Sisters in his small boat, and with them returned to St. Louis. But he lost the temporary use of his eyesight. It was only by being kept in a darkened room, and proper treatment administered to his eyes, that he recovered a partial use of his sight. The phrenological characteristics that predominated largely in Bishop Timon, were secretiveness, benevolence, veneration, combativeness, casuality and comparison. He possessed other traits of character, though less developed, and to a great extent had learned to keep them under self-control. If, at times, the vehemence of his nature overstepped boundary lines, it was quickly arrested before serious injury either to himself or others had been done. This peculiarity was particularly noticeable when unforeseen obstacles thwarted his pious purposes. On such occasions his temper would sometimes attempt to assert its superiority, but the discipline under which he governed himself was such that he finally, though gradually, succeeded in curbing its vehemence. He was a rigorous Churchman and an exact disciplinarian. Nothing displeased him so much as disobedience to the laws and discipline of the Church, as we have seen in the case of St. Louis church. He was likewise jealous of the temporal rights of the Church and the Pope. In the columns of his organ he assiduously wielded his pen in defence of the Popes and their temporal sovereignty. Even Brownson, the able reviewer, came in for a share of the good Bishop's criticisms on several subjects, in his treatment of which the Bishop seemed to find statements and inferences in conflict with theology or other sciences.

If he lacked in any thing, it might have been individuality. This was, in some instances, exemplified in the conduct of priests he ordained, who afterwards gave much trouble. But in his zeal to extend, as rapidly as possible, the benefits of religion through all parts of his diocese, necessity seemed to excuse him for not exercising more precaution in his selection of persons to be ordained. After returning from frequent Episcopal visitations, and disengaged from the consideration of any particular business at home, he studiously occupied himself either by storing his memory with knowledge from valuable books, or in acquiring a further acquaintaince with chemistry, theology or philosophy. He was a man of continual labor. He was proficient in four languages, and during his frequent travels abroad had become very familiar with two or three other foreign tongues. He knew English, Latin, French and German well. At the advanced age of fifty, he undertook and mastered a sufficient acquaintance with Italian, Spanish, and a few of the dialects of the German tongue, so as to enable him to travel through those countries with ease. Often, when the rest of the household had retired for the night, has the Bishop been seen after midnight, seated at his table buried in a mass of papers and books, writing away, at times nodding over his labor, overcome with the stupor of fatigue, and then suddenly arousing, as though from a reverie, to renew with refreshed vigor, the pursuits of his brain and pen.

He was the first to rise in the morning, "and often," said a student, "have I been awakened by him as early as three o'clock in the morning, to rise and go to the dark and cold cathedral to assist at his morning mass. After mass would be over, he returned to the house, and, without refreshment, left, satchel in hand, to take the first morning train to some part of his diocese. To see him going down the steps of his house and through the streets, *knee deep* in snow, as though it were mere play, filled me with indescribable astonishment, for he was then past sixty years of age, and needed care and rest." And thus often, unannounced and unexpected, would he arrive at some mission, to the surprise of both priest and congregation. At such times he was sure to observe every circumstance likely to favor or disfavor the conduct of the priest in the administration of the affairs of the parish or mission.

If he observed anything that was discreditable, he frequently said nothing at the time. But later, when the circumstance of the Bishop's call had almost been forgotten, perhaps a month, or two months afterwards, something was sure to happen. Hence, the Bishop made frequent changes from mission to mission. Another motive of the Bishop in removing and displacing his priests, besides mal-administration of the spiritual or temporal affairs of a mission, was to test their vocation. At other times, when a priest complained how hard was his position, or, as it really happened, that his life was threatened by impious men, because he would not conform to their views, the Bishop simply silenced their murmurs by quoting appropriate texts from Scripture, or in vehement tones would exclaim: "Why do you complain? Why did you become priests, if you cannot bear the responsibilities?

Do you suffer more than I do. A true soldier, when he enlists in defence of his country, bears and suffers everything rather than yield to the foe. Will you be less courageous in defence of the truths of holy religion, and the interests of those committed to your care? Go! and do not come again until you have conquered." Though severe, the Bishop always tried to discriminate justly, and had many ways of rebuking or reproving another, besides an indiscreet use of the tongue.

On one occasion, a certain priest, since fallen from his vocation, imagined that his character had been vilified before Bishop Timon by a layman. Filled with this idea, he dared to approach the Bishop in order to retort on the good name of his supposed vilifier, and, in the course of the conversation, adroitly sought to inform the Bishop that this gentleman was a man that could not be trusted, that he was a Free Mason, etc., etc. The Bishop, as though encouraging the information, listened eagerly to all the priest had to say of him, and whilst the latter was still speaking, wrote a letter to the poor layman to come and see him immediately. Without interrupting the conversation, he touched a little bell, to which a seminarian responded. In an undertone he directed the latter to take his private carriage and deliver the letter to the layman, and, if possible, bring him instantly to the house.

Twenty minutes had scarcely elapsed, when, to the dismay of the priest, the layman, of whom he had ceased speaking, entered the room.

The Bishop, however, not wishing to provoke any enmity between the two, simply rose, and, taking from his private desk a small box, containing a precious relic, a little piece of which had become loose, he turned to the layman, and said:

"My esteemed friend, here is a small box, containing a precious relic, a piece of which has become slightly detached, as you see, and I sent for you to take it home, and repair it, as best you know how. It is very valuable to me, so valuable, that I would not part with it for any sum of money. I thought of no one whom I could *trust* with greater confidence than you, and I know you will do me the kindness to fix it. That will do my child." The circumstance suggests its own moral.

When traveling, whether by rail or water, no one ever found him idle. Either he occupied himself in reading his breviary, or in saying the rosary; at other times he perused some pious book, or engaged with others in conversation, during which he never failed to make a most profound impression. On the cars he has frequently been seen kneeling in his seat, engaged in devout prayer. Conductors and railroad men knew him well, and saluted him with high respect. In his travels to Europe, during the long and weary sea voyages, he devoted certain hours in the day to religious profit and instruction, to which he cordially invited all to be present. In 1862, he went to Europe, and on board ship preached most eloquent sermons to the passengers, most of whom were Protestants. His charity to the sick on board was unceasing; forgetful of himself, mindful only of others, especially the poor and friendless, he called on each individually, and assisted and revived all by the sweetest words of encouragement and consolation. One instance, in particular, deserves mention, in its resemblance to the life and deeds of the great St. Vincent de Paul. Finding among the passengers a little infant boy, three months old, whose father, mother and nurse were lying sick, he took the child and carried it around the vessel in his arms, trying to please and amuse it. Finally, he asked a Sister of Mercy, accompanying him to Ireland, to take charge of it, which she did with pleasure. Father Burlando, in a private correspondence, observes:

"Bishop Timon was very remarkable for kindness to others whilst among us, on all occasions caring little for himself. If he was traveling with some of his confreres, and happened to put up at some place on the way for the night, he was always sure to choose the worst room, or the most uncomfortable bed. He looked at the wants of everybody else, but his own. I well remember the attention he paid to me once, when traveling with him from the Barrens to Cape Girardeau. It was a very cold day in the month of February. Before starting, he, with his own hands, and truly fatherly feelings, adjusted the clothes about me, and carefully fixed the wrappers around me, that I might not be inconvenienced by cold in riding, (as I was then quite inexpert in the mode of traveling,) whilst he, however, entirely overlooked his own comfort."

When he was building a certain charitable institution in this city, he one day threw himself on his hands and knees, to draw a rough plan of the building on the floor. In doing so, the slippers became detached from the heels of his feet, and exposed his stockings, which were very badly worn. His humility was such, that the remark of the Sister present, who observed this poverty, and said: "Oh! Bishop, how much your stockings need mending," did not in the least disconcert him, for he quietly continued on and merely replied, that "it were better to have holes in one's stockings, than sins on one's soul."

Bishop Timon's favorable characteristics were well known in Europe. The Pope, it seems, placed deep confidence in his integrity, and esteemed him highly, if we may judge by the warm and ardent receptions he received. On one of his late visits to Europe, Pope Pius IX sent him as a Papal courier from the court of Rome to the throne of France, to Napoleon, with important *verbal* despatches. Among many of the high dignitaries of the Germanic race, his name was a synonym for piety, zeal, and benevolence. Hence, on reading an account in one of the Paris papers, of the labors of Bishop Timon in his diocese, and the struggles and embarrassments he suffered in order to succeed, a certain Germanic prince, generously and voluntarily, opened his purse, and sent him a handsome sum of money as a donation for such pious purposes as the Bishop saw proper.

Father Smarius writes:

"SEMINARY OF THE SACRED HEART,
"ROCHESTER, N. Y., July 6th, 1869.

"CHARLES G. DEUTHER, ESQ.,

"*Respected Sir:* Your letter came to hand on the eve of my departure from Chicago to this place. Allow me to inform you that my acquaintance with the late lamented Bishop Timon was confined to the three last years of his saintly life. I never was among the Indians as a missionary, and only once as a Visitor, and long after Bishop Timon's missionary days. None would more readily and cheerfully add his mite to the general fund of biographical knowledge, which you are gathering together in honor of the blessed man of God, whose memory shall live for generations among the people whom his zeal converted to, or strengthened in the faith, whom the examples of his rare virtues led to justice and holiness of life. Never shall I forget the days of the missions for the laity and of the retreats for the clergy, which I had the pleasure to conduct in the cathedral of Buffalo, during the three or four years previous to his holy demise. The first to rise in the morning and to ring the bell for meditation and for prayer, he would totter from door to door along the corridors of the Episcopal residence, with a lighted candle in his hand, to see whether all had responded to the call of the bell, and betaken themselves to the spot marked out for the performance of that sacred and wholesome duty. So great was his own love for that holy exercise, that, but a year previous to his death, when, on account of his increasing weakness and multiplied infirmities, he could scarcely stand up or kneel in prayer and meditation, he would, despite all persuasions to the contrary, be the first to reach, and the last to quit the chapel and its sanctuary, where we assembled to commune with God in contemplation. And then, that last general confession, (last as he called it, for he seemed to have had a presentiment of his not far distant dissolution,) how fervent the zeal, how intense the piety, with which he prepared the ways of the Lord, who was coming less as a judge than as a bridegroom to welcome His servant to the heavenly nuptials. And then, that more than fatherly heart, that forgiving kindness to repentant sinners, even such as had again and again deservedly incurred his displeasure, and the penalties of ecclesiastical censures or excommunications. 'Father,' he would say, 'I leave this case in Your hands, I give You all power, only save his soul.' And then, that simple, childlike humility which seemed wounded by even the performance of acts which the excellence and dignity of the Episcopacy naturally force from its subjects and inferiors. How often have I seen him fall on his aged knees, face to face with one or other of my clerical brethren, who had fallen on their's to receive his saintly blessing. May God send the Church of America many such devoted pastors.

"Your obedient servant,
"C. F. SMARIUS, S. J."

———o———

CHAPTER XV

REVIEW OF THE BISHOP'S CHARACTER.—HIS SPIRIT OF PRAYER.—HIS HABITUAL PEACE OF MIND.—HIS HUMILITY.

THE SPIRIT OF RIGHT REV. JOHN TIMON. *

1. *His Spirit of Prayer.*—Bishop Timon lived as a Lazarist from the hour that he joined the community, until his saintly death. He rose every morning, (when at home,) at five o'clock. Half an hour was then given to dress. If the seminarians forgot to ring the bell at the appointed time in the morning, he himself rang a little bell, which he had ready for this purpose near his bed. At the second sound of the bell, all the household, priests, seminarians, even including the servants, assembled in one room. The Bishop, kneeling at the side of a table, then recited the morning prayer; after this, his Vicar General read the meditation, with the usual points and stops; this meditation usually ended with a prayer from the Bishop himself. The morning exercise concluded with the Angelus, during the recital of which a seminarian rang a bell three times.

At six o'clock A. M. the Bishop began his mass, at which he was assisted by two seminarians, sometimes by his Vicar General,

---

* For the information contained in this chapter, I am gratefully indebted to the Rev. Geo. Pax, formerly Secretary to the Bishop.

and at other times by a deacon and subdeacon. He went to confession regularly every week to his Vicar General, and generally after the hours of meditation, **when** he would rise and invite his Vicar General to follow him **to his room.** He recited those prayers with profound gravity **and punctuality.** After saying **his mass, he often** heard another **before leaving** the sanctuary, **usually the mass** of his Vicar General. Speaking once in synod about the honoraries of the mass, he observed that, although he **often read such** masses for the intention of those persons who **ordered them,** nevertheless he offered up the Holy Sacrifice frequently **for such** priests who, by their irregular conduct, **mostly needed it.**

He went to breakfast **at 8 A. M., to** dinner at 12¼ P. M., and **to supper at 7** P. M. During the hour of breakfast, a seminarian or a priest read chapters from the "Imitation of Christ," of which little book the Bishop was very fond. He was accustomed **to say** that, after night prayers, and **when** the business of the day would be so very **distracting as** not to enable him to sleep, he nourished his **soul and** calmed his mind by reading a few pages from this **charming little volume.** Before conferences, he ordered passages from the same work to be read.

During dinner hour, however, " Bancroft's History of the United **States,**" or similar works, were read, and whenever he met with remarks **in the** book against religion, or when the reader made a fault in pronunciation, the Bishop immediately turned about to criticize and correct. He even appointed persons to read, **whose** familiarity with the English language was **not** complete, in order **to** correct and **improve their** mistakes. **On these points he was** very rigid, particularly when guests were at the table. **He once** very playfully observed to Bishop Domenec,* of Pittsburgh: **"Do** you remember when **I** gave you your first **lesson in** English, how I pulled **your** hair?" In these corrections, however, he was truly like a father. Often, after having corrected a reader very strongly, he would say: "Now you pronounce better, and if you continue to listen, you will improve, and read well in a very short

---

* He was a Spaniard.

time." These corrections were likewise made at the supper hour. After dinner, the "Martyrology" was read, and then followed the usual prayers of the breviary. On the eve of certain feasts, he ordained Butler's feasts and fasts to be read, according to the festival, upon which he made historical remarks from time to time.

From these rules of his household he never deviated when on visits to priests, so far as it was possible. At eight o'clock P. M., he generally attended night prayers, and then spent the greater part of the night in reading, writing, studying and praying. Night prayers were said in the same room in which the morning exercises were held. Before retiring to his room for the night, he gave his orders to his priests for the next day's duties. Besides his usual office of the breviary, he daily recited his beads. In this pious exercise he might be seen, beads in hand, walking up and down the graveled walks of his garden, or making a solemn round of the aisles of his cathedral. When returning from Episcopal visitations of his diocese, he went regularly to the prayer room, even though he came a little while before the hour for rising.

Religious communities, such as Sisters of Charity, the Passionists, of Dunkirk, and others, were often astonished to find the Bishop already in the prayer room when they entered it for their accustomed morning prayers. They often recount strange but edifying stories about such visits, and say they were never positive not to have the Bishop next morning at their prayers. Thus he watched over every religious community in his diocese.

On one of his visits to Europe, Bishop Timon called upon the Rev. Mr. Pax,* at his parish of Dubling, in the diocese of Mertz, France. This reverend gentleman received him in a most magnificent manner, and entertained him in conversation, mostly about the affairs of St. Louis church, until very late at night. Both then retired. Early next morning, however, to the intense surprise of Father Pax, Bishop Timon was already in the church,

---

* Former parish priest of St. Louis church, who was so shamefully abused by the trustees, and compelled to leave at the peril of his life.

and had been there before daybreak. As soon as the congregation had come together, Bishop Timon suddenly left his seat, went to the sacristy and asked Father Pax to hear his confession. The acolytes of the mass were told to leave the sacristy. But the Bishop said, "No! I will go to confession where every body goes." Father Pax was confused. The Bishop insisted. Thus he went to confession, at the usual confessional, to the good parish priest, in the presence of the whole congregation, greatly to their edification. Bishop Timon held Father Pax in high esteem, and observed that "in all his relations with St. Louis church, that congregation could find no fault with him as their parish priest." In a letter to Father Pax, dated January 15th, 1867, in which he exhibited his presentiment of death, the Bishop wrote: "Please to add to your kind prayers that when the Lord will call the poor old Bishop of Buffalo to judgment, he may be assisted by sacraments and holy helps, and thus meet, in hope, his Judge."

His devotion to prayer was sometimes unusual. In the year 1864, in the beginning of one of the private sessions of the synod, as he was reading the passion of our Lord out of the Scripture, he stopped at once and commenced to shed tears, so that a priest had to continue the lecture. Frequent sighs could be heard as he recited his prayers, especially at the memento of his mass, if some serious trouble weighed heavily on his mind. Nothing troubled him so much as the disorders of some unfortunate clergymen. "It is better," he said, "to deal with ninety-nine bad congregations than with one clergyman who deliberately disobeys the injunctions of his Bishop and superior." Bishop Timon never gave any important advice or decision at once; he always said, "Let me pray first," or "Come about this time or that time, and I will, in the meantime, reflect in holy prayer what, before God, will be best to do."

Sometimes he made a short retreat of a few days at his house, just as religious do. Silence was then observed. After dinner he took a short recreation of about half an hour. "Pray for me," was the usual way he dismissed a visitor or a friend. He was a continual example of prayer to his priests and people. In traveling, he carried with him copies of the litanies of the "Blessed Virgin" and of the "Holy Name of Jesus," and other pious prayers. These he recited immediately after his breviary or his beads. He was known to always recite the "Itinerarium" of the breviary in the beginning of a journey. In fact this prayer he knew by heart, so that if, on any occasion, he was disturbed in reciting it by a pious clergyman, who was unaware of the interruption he caused, he was enabled to readily continue his recitation. Indeed, amid all the turmoils and troubles of a long and laborious life, Bishop Timon was able to maintain the spirit of prayer.

2. *His habitual peace of mind.*—Although Bishop Timon was naturally of a lively and even quick-tempered disposition, he rarely manifested either dejection or anxiety. He was prepared for contradiction and disappointment. He sought himself so little, that he seldom experienced much pain from disappointments. Nay, his will was kept in such constant subjection, that amidst all his trials his first impulse was to bless the hand that sent them.

Once he unfortunately was thrown from a buggy, whilst riding with Rev. Mr. Quigly from one mission to another, owing to a fright which the horse received. When he arrived home, he exhibited a bruised hand, eye and cheek, and though suffering inconvenience as well as pain, he never murmured in the least. In fact, he never complained. He even seemed strange in his patience. Once a priest came to him and said that he had a difficulty in his mission, that threatened to be serious to himself. The answer was simply, "Our Lord says: The kingdom of heaven suffers violence, and only the violent will carry it away. Our holy state of priesthood makes no exception to this general rule."

Sometimes, in answer to complaints, he opened the Bible without saying a word, except to quote appropriate texts, most of which he knew by heart. In reply to another, who came with many complaints about the bad spirit of the missions, the Bishop promptly stood up and said:

"Why did you become a priest? answer!" The priest did not answer, being afraid of the serious tone of his Bishop. He asked him again, and getting no reply, he said, "Know this, then, that you became a priest to suffer, to be persecuted, according to the example laid down by our Lord Jesus Christ."

To another he said: "Well, then, take my seat and be Bishop for a few days, and I will go to your church for a week as pastor. At the end of that time we will see who will have suffered the most."

Another priest complained of threats against his life, and that he stood in danger of dying in his mission. "Well, then," replied the Bishop, "you will die in a good cause."

In defending the interests of poor Catholic orphans, before a large assemblage of citizens, he boldly said: "I want the Catholic orphans for my asylum. I will take care of them at half price. I will not allow decisions to be made for Catholic orphans." Some bigot present said: "Shut up; what do we care for an old Catholic Bishop?" But the Bishop was not confused, and immediately said, "I will not keep silence here, for I am an American citizen, and as such have a right to exhibit my claims."

His maxims of charity and peace were: "If I have to choose between being too *severe* or too *lax*, I prefer to be too *lax;* because I want to be judged by Almighty God rather with mercy than with severity." (Good and great maxims, indeed.) He always wished to be informed when others went astray, that he might remedy the evil in time. He was always astonished to be the last who knew any thing about an evil or a scandal.

He was in habitual peace of mind, come what might, and was one of those men spoken of in the "Imitation of Christ," who are prompt to promote the peace of others.

3. *His Humility.*—From what has already been said, it must be concluded that his virtues were solidly founded on humility. When he first came to Buffalo, a great procession led him to St. Louis church. It was thought he was in the carriage, but the night being dark and rainy he could not be readily distinguished. To the surprise of many, however, he was found,

carpet-bag in hand, walking *after* the procession. His humility was grave and dignified, yet simple and natural, because it was sincere. He possessed no affected politeness.

In the last synod held the year before his holy death, he said to his priests: " My life is drawing to a close. I feel this sensibly. I have but a short time to live, and *this will be the last time that I shall see my venerable clergy together again.* When I think of what my diocese was when I came to Buffalo, and what it is now, I have reason to congratulate my venerable clergy for their generosity, zeal and sacrifices, which with God's blessings and graces helped to accomplish great works. We were laboring together with God's grace and help. But as I have soon to appear before my Judge, I here acknowledge that, having naturally a hasty and quick temper, I did my best to subdue and repress it. I have reason to think that in this way I might have offended some of the venerable priests here present. If this has been the case, I am free to say that I have acted from no bad or malicious motives. If I have offended any one of you, I humbly kneel at his feet and beg pardon for my shortcoming. Pray, therefore, for me, dearly beloved clergy, as I have soon to appear before the throne of Him who is our Master and Lord."

"I hope not soon," exclaimed Father McCool.

"Yes, my child," replied the Bishop, "I feel that my time is come."

He was so weak then that he could scarcely stand, much less ascend the altar without being helped. Priests told him not to sing Pontifical high mass, but he would not be dissuaded from doing so. At the distribution of Holy Communion, he trembled so much from weakness that Father Gleason, V. G., had to receive the Ciborium from his hands, and finish the distribution of the Bread of Life. A short time before he died, he wished to see a certain rector of a German parish personally, and sent for him to come and see him. But he waited in vain for the gentleman's (?) pleasure, and turning to a friend in the room, (the Bishop was obliged almost constantly to lay on a lounge, from debility and pain,) he said: " I have sent twice already for him, stating that I wanted to see him badly; but he does not come. Now, Mr. ——, I have to gather my last strength to go in my buggy and drive to see the reverend gentleman." He pronounced these words without excitement, however, although touched by the circumstance. He was very much attached to the seminarians. In the seminaries of Europe that he had chanced to visit, he was often seen standing in the midst of a group of seminarians, recounting incidents and explaining the geographical situation not only of America, but even of parts of Europe itself, with which he supposed it likely his young hearers were not entirely familiar. He has been seen frequently playing not only with the seminarians, but even with the children behind the cathedral, on the ground where now stands the Christian Brothers' School. And we have it on good authority that when visiting the Orphan Asylum, some of the boys were so well acquainted with him as to mount upon his back, whilst he went upon all fours playing and enjoying himself in their sports. This humility really endeared him to all. On such occasions he was very pleasant and very kind. When at home, he went into the confessional usually every Saturday, but after an hour or more, a fit of coughing would compel him to leave. If unable to hear confessions himself, he never neglected to observe that his priests were on time attending to their duty. Nay, the humility of Bishop Timon was once put to a greater test. At East Eden, where he was adjusting, or trying to adjust, some difficulties that had occurred there, a German Catholic (perhaps half drunk) spat in his face. But like his Divine Saviour, he suffered this insult meekly, and wiped off the spittle without saying a word of reproach. (Oh, admirable example of patience and humility!) Bishop Timon used to say, "As long as a priest is humble and obedient to his Bishop, he can easily rise again should he be so unfortunate as to fall into faults; for after faults have been committed, he can do penance and make due reparation. But a proud priest never can."

This idea he entertained and pushed farther than any other Bishop we ever read or heard of, so much so, at least, that he took pleasure in breaking and curbing the proud sentiments of such priests who made use of religion as a cloak for their pride. Hence, with one or two honorable exceptions, he made frequent changes among his Vicar Generals, in whom he thought he found more or less pride. These changes he justified upon the maxims already quoted, and also from a confidence that God resists the proud, and gives His grace the to humble. "Pride," said he, "always comes before the fall." Perhaps no Bishop was more strict than Timon about Church discipline and ceremonies. He has left his throne in the cathedral, and, dressed in full Pontificals, gone to the railing of the sanctuary and separated children given to too much talking during Divine service. In the observation of the Rubrics, his vigilant eye could detect the slightest deviation from the rule, and although a priest, deacon or subdeacon committed a fault during the service, he instantly sent another priest or went himself, to correct the mistake. Singing possessed a peculiar charm for him. He had no cultivated voice, though he sang very strong and clear. He, particularly, favored the Gregorian chant.

In his dress he was especially plain and humble. His housekeeper told him once that he needed new shirts. But he said: "The old ones are good enough for the old Bishop yet." In Church ornaments, however, he was more precise. These could not be fine or excellent enough.

An unfortunate circumstance once occurred at the cathedral. A clergyman* preached one Sunday very eloquently from the pulpit of the cathedral. After he had finished, the Bishop went up to the pulpit himself, and said that, although Father —— had preached very eloquently, he had uttered a heresy. This he came to prove, and he proved it. Of course, it was highly offensive to the priest's feelings to be criticized, so much so that he could not suppress his feelings in the presence of the Bishop after mass. But before night, the Bishop and he were never better friends.

---

* Rev. Mr. ——, an English gentleman, and convert to the Church.

Our pen would scarcely ever weary in recounting the mass of incident that lies before us, descriptive of his character. As will be seen, we have narrated the most simple details we could reach, in order to depict more graphically a portrait of his real interior virtues. But Bishop Timon is now dead and gone. His memory and the sweet odor of his sanctity is all that linger here after him in the hearts of the people. Generations to come will hear of him and his deeds, and as they read this plain narrative of his life, will breathe a prayer that his lot may be with the just.

FINIS.

APPENDIX.

APPENDIX.

ACCOUNTS OF THE CARILLON.

As everybody with a particle of curiosity in his or her composition is of course anxious to know all about the progress being made in the work of hanging and adjusting the bells and machinery of the new automatic *carillon* at the cathedral, we give below the information gleaned during a late visit.

From the tower floor we ascended the stairs leading to the organ loft and turning to the right mounted another flight and a ladder, which brought us to the first floor occupied or to be occupied by the machinery. This is lighted by the smaller arched windows seen below the lofty barred ones of the belfry proper, which are intended rather to let sound out than to admit light. On this floor will be placed the cylinder and communications, analagous to that of a Swiss music box or ordinary barrel organ, and occupying alone a space of six by twelve feet horizontally and seven in height. This will connect by means of simple and delicately adjusted machinery with every bell in the tower, so that when the motive is applied any of the set tunes in its *reportoire* is rung out with beautiful and unfailing accuracy. To some likings this mechanical way of producing the music would rather "take the poetry out of it," but to reassure these we must say that upon this same floor will also be a key-board, connecting by like apparatus with a set of hammers distinct from those of the automaton.

A beautiful clock, also of European make, has arrived, and will occupy a corner of this room, connecting by rods with the dials, nearly fifty feet above.

From this floor a ladder leads to the beginning of a labyrinthine framework, in and upon which are hung the bells, and upon leaving which the inquisitive mind had better take good heed to its steps, and if not encased in an ordinarily steady head, content itself with the moderate altitude already attained. Passing the two larger bells which hang side by side with just room to swing clear of each other and the walls, we mount by the frame to the next range. It is proper here to explain that, except at the bottom, this frame does not touch the sides of the tower and, therefore, cannot transmit the shock and vibration it sustains to anything around it. It was at first intended to build the structure upon two immense beams originally built into the walls where its base rests, but upon test one of these was found quite unsound. Both were sawed off and in their stead two others were placed with the ends resting not in the wall, but upon firmly secured projecting stones, and braced from near the ends to a point some six feet lower, where like projections occur, so that the strain and pressure, instead of being out at any point, is directly downward and safely distributed.

The rest of the journey to the dial openings, slightly above which hang the highest of the small bells, is accomplished by clambering up the transverse bars of the large belfry windows. Reaching a point where the lower tier of stationary bells is below the level of the feet, we find a narrow planking upon which we stand while the obliging manager of the work explains its various details, visible and projected.

From the joists or beams on which we stand rises on either side a perpendicular framework, connected from centre to centre by crossbeams, on which hang the first thirty-seven bells of the *carillon*. These are all sounded by means of the hammers and key board or automaton, and do not swing. The smallest five are distributed in the intervals between the large ones. Still below this frame work is another of the same height, but entirely taken up by the six remaining bells, which, of course, increase in size and weight in a rapid ratio from those just above.

From the collar of each of these on the side nearest us, or facing the rear of the tower depend three hammers, their handles fastened to a projecting yoke by means of cast steel straps or springs, and their faces resting at a distance of about two inches from the rim of the bell.

HOW THEY ARE PLAYED.

A long tongue-shaped spring bolted to the yoke at the same place droops between each and its striking point so as to catch a projection, and while allowing the hammer to fall with sufficient force to reach the bell, is still strong enough to prevent a repeating stroke. The hammers are drawn back by wires running from a ring in their heads to the parallel beams next the new wall, where they will connect by means of the usual bell-hangers' apparatus for turning an angle, with others running to the cylinder. This triple set of hammers is necessary when the same note is to be repeated sooner than the vibration of the first hammer would permit it to be used again with safety and certainty. At the cylinder the wires are fastened to a row of levers, which rest upon its surface until in its revolutions they are caught by the pegs and drawn with force enough to spring the hammers. The hammer connecting with the key-board bangs inside the bell, and is drawn against its rim by a wire passing just beneath it. This wire connects on the outside with a small stop which, when the key is released and the hammers fall back, is drawn or sprung against the bell, and checks its vibration, so that a note may be held or discontinued at will as by a similar contrivance in the piano forte. This arrangement, however, only applies to the larger bells in the lower lines, the small ones above being struck by hammers fastened to the beams beneath.

Our inspection of these satisfactorily concluded, we descend by means of our rather awkward ladder to the next floor supports below. Here on a level with our heads are the tongues of the four next in size. These are provided with levers at the point where they are balanced, so that a man standing by each on one of the beams on which it is balanced may set it in motion with his foot. They are also played by means of the above described contrivances, the hammers being fastened in such a manner that the bells swing clear of them when used in the ordinary way. Still ten or twelve feet below are the final pair, the two monsters which swing side by side, and whose boom and terrible swing suffice to affect with sentiments approaching to awe the beholder who looks down upon them in motion for the first time. To see and hear these six in full swing underneath one for five minutes, will materially add to the cautiousness with which he retraces the road he has just seen blocked and terrible with their rush and awful clangor. We know that in the path of one of these, when in motion, fate would be simple annihilation. Fancy being struck by nearly five thousand pounds of metal in a space where it barely has room to swing; and we think shudderingly of a tale we once read, in which a stranger crawling curiously among the cobwebbed lofts of an European cathedral, found himself suddenly driven to the wall by the first swing of a monstrous bell; how he crouched to avoid it, and how, for what seemed an age to him, this ponderous thunderer passed and repassed him with a booming rush of wind that struck him like a mountain wave, and but for a death-like grip upon the timber where he lay, would have sucked him like a fly into its track, to be crushed as easily; how he was found more dead than alive and unable to help himself from the spot, and his dark hair streaked with silvery gray, as a proof of the mental agony crowded into that long half hour.

But we are down at the ladder-top again and will say good-bye to our new friends for a season. We shall continue the acquaintance at some future time when their organization is complete, and we will end this with a few facts about these and

OTHER BELLS.

The only other *carillon* in America is in the church of Notre Dame Du Lac, at Montreal, and numbers twenty-four bells. There are but two in existence comparing with ours, as Buffalonians will proudly call it, those of Notre Dame, at Chalons sur Marne, France, and St. Jaques De Chatellerant, Vienna, the first of fifty-six bells, the largest weighing 5,590 lbs., and the latter of fifty bells, the largest weighing 4,400 lbs. The former is the most complete in the world, the latter has only seven bells more than ours, and the largest weighs six hundred and sixty-eight and one-quarter pounds *less* than our own. So that probably, all things considered, we may dispute the right to the title of "second best in the world" with this one.

The cost of ours, including everything when ready for use, cannot vary much either way from the sum of one hundred thousand dollars.

The manufacturer, Mr. Ernst Bollee, includes in his catalogue the following description of noted bells in various parts of the world, from which it may be seen that our claim to the possession of the second best carillon ever made is not without good foundation:

CARILLONS DES EGLISES DE:

N. D. De Chalons-Sur-Marne, carillon composé de 56 cl., tonique, 2.723 kil.
Les six plus grosses servent aussi de cloches paroissiales. Cylindre mécanique, clavier à main. Ce carillon est le plus complet du monde.

Cathédrale de Buffalo (Etats-Unis d'Amérique.) Carillon composé de 43 cloches, tonique 2.122 kil.
Les six plus grosses servent aussi de cloches paroissiales. Cylindre mécanique, clavier à main.

Chatenay (Isére.) Carillon de M. l'abbé Combalot, 19 cloches.

Saint-Jaques de Chatellerault (Vienne.) Carillon composé de 50 cl., tonique 2,000 kil.

Les six plus grosses servent aussi de cloches paroissiales. Cylindre mécanique clavier à main.

N. D. Du Lac (Amerique,) Carillon à cylindre et clavier; 24 cl., g., 5,795 kil.

Nantes (Sainte-Croix.) Carillon de la ville, 12 cloches.

The foundry is at Mans, in the Department of Sarthe, North Western France. The composition used is 775 parts red copper and 225 of tin.

In a very short time this magnificent instrument will begin to take its part in the daily life of our city, sending abroad its concord of sweet sounds and setting to music the hours as they pass, adding a solace to labor and a charm to rest. The spire above them points to the heaven of all our creeds; they are consecrated to the worship of the one God. And when the solemn sounds of those grand services dedicated to His worship float over the turmoil of the day, or out upon the silence of night, may they take up with them the aspirations of all faiths in one prayer to the Eternal Father.—*Buffalo Express.*

Yesterday was made musically memorable in this city, and in the country at large, for that matter, by the consecration of the new Chime of Bells of St. Joseph's Cathedral, the largest Carillon on the American continent, and one of the most magnificent in the world. Our first notion of the magnitude of this chime was derived from a letter written by one of the editors of the *Courier* while in Paris during the Grand Exposition; and now that we have had an opportunity of seeing the bells arrayed in all their glory, we can the better appreciate the enthusiasm of our correspondent.

The late Bishop Timon contracted for the chime with Bollee & Son, of France, a firm of bell founders who are probably unrivaled in the world. The firm was ordered to contribute to the Paris Exposition; they had just completed these bells, and without hesitancy they added them to the stock in trade of that exhibition, subsequently writing an apologetic letter to those in authority here, for their detention. They remained in Paris for five months, during which time they were operated, and the founders were complimented with a medal. They will soon be elevated to their places, and while they swing in the tower of St. Joseph's, the name of the revered Timon will be indissolubly associated with them. A grander earthly monument could scarcely be raised to the memory of any man.

HIGH MASS.

Pontificial High Mass was commenced at 10 o'clock, the celebrant being the Rt. Rev. Bishop Ryan, who was assisted by the following clerical gentlemen:

Assistant Priest—Very Rev. W. Gleason, V. G.

Deacons of Honor—Revs. M. Creedon and J. Durthaller, S. J.

Deacon of the Mass—Rev. J. J. Bloomer.

Sub-Deacon of the Mass—Rev. J. Fitzpatrick.

First Master of Ceremonies—Rev. W. J. McNab.
Second Master of Ceremonies—Rev. J. Rogers.
Third Master of Ceremonies—M. J. McGrath.

SERMON BY RT. REV. BISHOP McQUADE.

Bishop McQuade, of Rochester, ascended the pulpit, and announced his text: The last Psalm of David, (ch. 160:)

Praise ye the Lord. Praise God in His sanctuary; praise Him in the firmament of His power.

Praise Him for His mighty acts; praise Him according to His mighty excellence.

Praise Him with the sound of the trumpet; praise Him with the psaltery and harp.

Praise Him with the timbrel and dance; praise Him with stringed instruments and organs.

Praise Him upon the loud cymbals; praise Him upon the high sounding cymbals.

Let everything that hath breath praise the Lord. Praise ye the Lord.

The Right Reverend Bishop then proceeded, in substance, to state that, as in those days the people were called upon to praise the Lord with instruments of sound, so you are to-day gathered to witness the consecration of these bells to give praise to the Lord. Such a ceremony, and one as imposing as this, has never been known in the land, and it may be surmised that not many now present will ever again witness that which is to take place this morning. These bells are to be blessed—to be consecrated—because the work given to them is a sacred one. This temple so grand, so vast, so magnificent; that organ so loud-spoken in its harmony; yonder sanctuary with its altars, and its ministers; all these tell of God, tell of heaven, and proclaim the praise of the Lord, and the people who gather in these walls, make use of these things to praise the Lord, His knowledge and His grandeur. There stands the minister at the altar, where up to heaven go his praise and thanksgiving; join with him, all ye people who are in the church, even as does the music from yonder choir

These bells raised aloft to the tower of the church, domineering over the city, will take up the words of praise, the words of glory, and carry them heavenward; and thus, you see, to consecrate them is the holy work of religion. To-day they are consecrated to God, and in thus giving them to God the church blesses them as she blesses everything she gives to God. In "the blessing of the bells," or their baptism, the word is not correctly used, but it is understood by the people, because the ceremonies used are similar to those used at the baptism of a child. The baptism or washing of the bells is made similar to the baptism of children. The sponsors are, generally speaking, the donors of the bell itself. It is therefore an honor bestowed on them for the work they have done. The Psalms are recited. Holy water is then poured on them, and afterwards seven crosses are made with the finger dipped in holy oil with which the bells are anointed. These seven crosses signify the seven gifts of the Holy Ghost, that by the ringing of the bells the people may hear them. Then the bells are anointed with chrysm three times in the form of three crosses, to represent the virtues of faith, hope, and charity. Thus truth and religion are to be spread over the city, to incite the people to prayer and worship.

The burning censers filled with incense and myrrh, are to be placed under the bells, signifying by their odor how delightful to the christian, how fragrant in the sight of God, are the works with which man honor Him. The Bishop who consecrates the bells then strikes them three times, and after him the sponsors do the same.

Praise ye now the Lord, who reigns above. Sound aloud His praises. Make known how pleasant it is in the busy hour of life, to praise the Lord, remind the people of God's praises, that the world might know where is the work of God. In the first ages of Christianity the services of religion and sacred rites were attended to; in many places was generally found some retired spot—as in pagan Rome, in the Vatican and the Catacombs. In those they did not dare to proclaim publicly the Divine service, and trusty messengers were sent to the faithful to tell them of the services of the Lord.

In the time of Constantine the Great, when he became a christian, they made use of a trumpet to summon the faithful to prayer and worship. But afterwards, in the fifth century, when bells were invented and brought into use, they were the mediums by which the hour of prayer and worship were rung out to the people.

The first idea of bells is a useful one. It is to ring out the hour of service, and to call the people to church. But, as in the course of time convents and monasteries began to spread on every hand, the civilized world became musical with the sound of the bells. In those days religion was not an affair of Sunday, but of every day and of every hour of the day. Religion was not confined to the recital of a few short prayers. In those days religion made life for the people. This may be strange to say in the nineteenth century. But in those days religion did not interfere with man's duties, his business and his country. The more he attended to his church, the more he worshiped God, he became a better man and a better citizen. In those days the bells gladly rung out when the young couple came to the church to be given in happy wedlock. In those days the bells solemnly rung out and sent up a prayer to heaven for mercy over the soul of the departed christian. It was like ringing from heaven to earth, for a people to know that the bells were ringing for them.

But 300 years ago came a change, a sad change. In that land from which many of us have come, where the people no longer have a voice, where the king, the lords and powerful men, disabusing their power in their lust and indulgence, men who had forgotten their God—these men took possession of the church, and robbed its sanctuaries, and its altars of their gold, their crosses and ornaments, robbed the towers of their bells that had sung for a thousand years the praises of God—this they did in the name of law. They used the bells for their own purposes. Some were scattered over Europe. Others were sent to be cast over again. To-day, however, they were trying to restore, trying to repair what they have undone; but which they could never do. They who would banish churches, convents, monasteries, etc., would if they could banish religion, banish God himself. But the

Church of God to-day is stronger, is greater, and is rising in beauty. We build churches not for man merely or for meeting houses, but we build them for God. Thus, what was a hut yesterday, is to-day a church, and to-morrow will be a cathedral.

Men there are who would be astonished to hear this; who would be astounded, even, that we build churches, hospitals, convents, and ask how we can do this. And we say that it is the christian faith within us, which is the secret of our power, by which we have done these works, and mean to continue. We are told to beware; that the government may even confiscate these, as was done 300 years ago. But little know these men that we are the American people, and that it is only a few prejudiced bigots who preach such insignificant impudence. Well, then, we have built the cathedral, and into its towers will go the bells, and when over the city, in the stillness of night or of evening, their sweet music is pealing; or in the morning the *Angelus* rings out; or at noon, these bells tell Catholics it is time to think of Christ, of virtue, and with bowed heads lift aloft their thoughts to the Creator, oh, it would be a sacred tribute to the Bishop now departed, and who lies in yonder sanctuary, on the return of the anniversary of his death, to then join your voices to the voices of the bells. These bells, indeed, would help to remind man of his duty, and make this city a christian city.

Praise ye the Lord in all His works. Praise Him in all things beautiful. Praise Him ye mountains and valleys. Praise Him ye works of man. To the end of time, while this cathedral shall last, let these bells give praise to the Lord, for to the Lord belongs honor and praise.

BLESSING THE BELLS, ETC.

At the conclusion of the sermon, Bishop Ryan, aided by the officiating Bishops and clergy, proceeded to bless the water with which the bells were to be baptized. Then, accompanied by Bishop Farrell, of Hamilton, Ont., and Bishop McQuade, of Rochester, he left the sanctuary, and washing three or four of the smaller bells, inside and out, the work was taken up by the priests. The ceremony of anointing with holy oil was next in order, the three Bishops named joining in the service. While the holy oil was being applied, incense was allowed to burn beneath each bell; and during the entire ceremony the Psalms of David were sung by the choir. The sponsors or their representatives were present; and we should have stated before, that a card appended to a number of the bells gave the names of the sponsors to each respectively. The ceremony was entirely in Latin, but the significance of each outward feature of the ceremony has been so far explained by Bishop McQuade as to relieve us from the duty of referring to them specifically. The ceremonies were concluded with the Gospel prescribed by the Roman Pontifical, which was rendered by the choir. From the beginning of the High Mass to the close of the consecration, the warmest interest was manifested by all present.

Archbishop Lynch, of Toronto, was in attendance during the earlier exercises, but was called away by a pressing engagement in Canada, and did not participate in the ceremony of consecration. Among the clerical gentlemen who assisted, we may mention Rev. J. Early, Vicar General of Rochester, and Revs. Hughes, Stewart, English, Gregg and De Pegge, of the same place; the Very Rev. Laurent, Superior of St. Michael's College, Toronto; then there were in attendance nearly all the clergy of the diocese, many of whose names will appear as sponsors to the bells.

THE SPONSORS.

In giving the names of the sponsors, we mention the bells in the order of their size, beginning with the largest, albeit it is possible, in view of the difficulty of procuring the names, that in two or three instances, among the smaller bells, we have changed sponsors. This, however, is immaterial, and the following is the list:

FIRST BELL—Cathedral Parish: Sponsors—Messrs. Falvey, Devlin, Macnamara, Chas. Darcy, Sheehan, Flanigan, Crowley, Jas. Mooney, Cronyn, M. D., Owen Smith, Ashton, Nellany, Edward Byrne, Chas. Muldoon.

SECOND BELL—St. Joseph's Cathedral: Sponsors—Messrs McCoole, T. Doyle, Dennis Egan, John A. Walsh, Jas. Dolan, Mackay. M. D., Chace, M. D., E. H. Hickey, Ryan, Justice of the Peace, John Powers, Lovett, Edward Powers.

THIRD BELL—St. Louis church, Buffalo: Sponsors—Rev. Joseph Sorg, pastor; Michael Lettau, Mrs. Ann M. Born, Jacob Davis, Anthony Diebold, Gerhardt Lang, John Ordner, Miss Magdalen Ordner, Nicholas Ottenot, Peter Rosar, Arnold Weppner, Jacob Weppner, Anthony Werle, Peter Wax, Jacob Barthel, John Zoll, Nicholas Henry, Nicholas Loesch, Martin Fisher, Michael Lang, John Welter, Louis Jacobs, Martin Ehresmann, Edward Jehle.

FOURTH—St. Bridget's church: Sponsor—Reverend Father O'Connor.

FIFTH—Cathedral: Messrs. Jeremiah Kavanagh, J. Kelly, N. Baker, T. Durkin.

SIXTH—Cathedral: Mrs. A. McDougal, Mrs. Captain Robinson, Mrs. J. Devlin, Miss Jennie Holland, Miss Healy, Miss Anne Cumming.

SEVENTH—Hornellsville: Rev. M. Creedon.

EIGHTH—Elmira: Revs. Bede and Hopkins.

NINTH—Batavia: Rev. T. Cunningham.

TENTH—St. Michael's church: The Jesuit Fathers and Mr. Hæffner.

ELEVENTH—E and K, two priests.

TWELFTH—St. Mary's church: Rev. Hesperlein, rector, and members of societies attached to the church.

THIRTEENTH—Le Roy: Rev. D. Moore.

FOURTEENTH—Corning: Rev. P. Colgan.

FIFTEENTH—Java: Rev. Jos. V. Donoghue.

SIXTEENTH—Church of the Holy Angels: John McManus and Mr. Dolan.

SEVENTEENTH—Lancaster: Rev. F. N. Sestor.

EIGHTEENTH—Seminary of Our Lady of Angels: Rev. Mr. Flynn.

NINETEENTH—Suspension Bridge: Rev. J. V. Brennan.

TWENTIETH—Owego: Rev. F. Clark.

TWENTY-FIRST—Addition: Rev. P. Bradley.

TWENTY-SECOND—Gardenville: Rev. C. Wagner.

TWENTY-THIRD—Ellicottville: Rev. J. Rogers.

TWENTY-FOURTH—Albion: Rev. J. Castaldi.

Twenty-Fifth—Watkins: Rev. J. McManus.
Twenty-Sixth—Bath: Rev. M. Darcy.
Twenty-Seventh—China: Rev. J. Fitzpatrick.
Twenty-Eighth—St. Francis Xavier church, Black Rock: Rev. H. Feldman.
Twenty-Ninth—St. John Baptist's church, Lockport: Rev. Hiram McCollum.
Thirtieth—St. Paul's church, Lockport: Rev. J. O'Mara.
Thirty-First—St. John Baptist's church, Black Rock: Rev. P. Mazurot.
Thirty-Second—Portage: Rev. F. Cook.
Thirty-Third—Salamanca: Rev. C. D. McMullen.
Thirty-Fourth—Medina: Rev. M. McDowell.
Thirty-Fifth—Tonawanda: Rev. L. Vanderpoel.
Thirty-Sixth—Belmont: Rev. J. H. Leddy.
Thirty-Seventh—Newfane: Rev. M. O'Dwyer.
Thirty-Eighth—Greenwood: Rev. J. J. Bloomer.
Thirty-Ninth—Collins: Rev. Chas. Wensierski.
Fortieth—Transit: Rev. H. Bochman.
Forty-First—Niagara Falls: Rev. P. Cannon.
Forty-Second—Names of sponsors missing.
Forty-Third—Children's Bell—Sponsors—Katy Shields. Lizzie Broczel, Rebecca Lynch, Kate Grady, David Hanley, Robert Sheehan, John Sullivan, Michael Carroll.

THE BELLS AND THEIR INSCRIPTIONS.

As we have already stated, there are forty-three bells in the chime. The compass of the Carillon is four octaves, semi-tones running from the second octave up to the bass but not through the bass; or to speak technically, the bass octave is diatonic and the others referred to, chromatic. The quality of tone, so far as it could be tested yesterday, proved to be all that could be desired. Four of the bells will swing in the tower and all will be arranged so as to be played through a key board. The largest bell weighs over 4,000 lbs., and the smallest in the neighborhood of 25 lbs., and each bell bears the imprint of the founder, as follows:

"Bollee, Pere and Fils, Foundereurs Accordeurs. Au Mans, (Sarthe.)
Construction de Grands Carillons."

The bells are splendid castings and the ornamentation is singularly chaste and delicate. Flowers, leaves, cherubs, Christ heads, saints and other designs, are artistically brought out; while the Latin inscriptions on thirty-five have considerable prominence.

Beginning with the first or largest bell the inscriptions are as follows, and we leave our readers to decipher them at their leisure:

1. "Deo Uni et Trino Laus et Gloria Sempiterna."
2. "Laudate Dominum Omnes Gentes."
3. "Gloria in Excelsis."
4. "Maria Purissima Sine Labe Concepta Ora Pro Nobis."
5. "Sta. Maria Ave Maria Dominus Tecum."
6. "Maria Immaculata Nunc et Hora Mortis, Maria Sanctissima Ora Pro Nobis."

7. "Joseph Protector, Ste. Joseph, Esto Semper Propitius Nobis, Benefactoribusque Nobis."
8. "Joseph S. V. M. In Morte Nostra Joseph, Sponse Maria Ora Pro Nobis."
9. "Stus. Joannes Timon Ep. Buff. Pax. Requies Aeterna Benefactoribus."
10. "Stus. Michael, Agminaque Angelorum Futura Damina Pellite."
11. "Stus. Gabriel Ut Hoste Antiquos Pellat Angelus Fortis Veniat Gabriel."
12. "Stus. Raphael Adsite e Cœlo Raphael Ut Omnes Sanet Aegrotos."
13. "Stus. Patritius Sempiternas Ste. Patrii Landes Sono."
14. "S. S. Angeli Custodes Custodes Hominum Psallimus Angelos."
15. "Stus. Joannes Ad Amorem Divinum Plebem Voco."
16. "Stus. Petrus Laudo Deum Verum."
17. "Stus. Paulus Dissipo Ventos."
18. "Stus. Vincentius A Paulo Festa Decoro."
19. "Stus. Phillippus Neri Sabbata Pango."
20. "Stus. Bonifacius Excito Lentos."
21. "Nicolaus Defunctos Ploro."
22. "Stus. Rochus Pestem Fugo."
23. "Sta. Elizabetha Fulgura Frango In Nomine Domini."
24. "Stus. Joannes Baptista Funera Plango, Sed Spero, Semperoque Sperabo."
25. "Sta. Teresia Mortuos Deploro. Et Pro Eis Ore."
26. "Sta. Celia Staeque Omnes Laudate Deum In Hymnis Et Organis."
27. "Sta. Rosa Simana Sal. Fac Due Rempublican Et Benedic Populo Ino In Pace."
28. "Omnes Sancti Clamant Sancti Gaudemus Gaudentibus."
29. "Stus. Franciscus Ass. Plorant Sancti Dolemus Dolentibus."
30. "Sta. Familia In Terra Pax Hominibus."
31. "Angeli Omnes Huc Custos Igitur Pervigil Adrola."
32. "Stus. Pernardus Congrego Clerum."
33. "Ernest Bollee Ad Buffalo Me Misit."
34. "Stus. Franciscus Sal Paco Cruentos."
35. "Stus. Elias Pax Vobis."

CONCLUSION.

Now that the reader has fully digested these inscriptions, he will be ready to learn that this superb chime of bells, which cost about $25,000, will be placed in the tower as soon as possible, and their first melodies will ring out on the air some time in August. Mr. Louis Lemeunier, from Bollee's Foundry, who operated the bells for the benefit of the Great Exposition, is in the city, and will superintend their mounting.

We might indulge in an extended commentary on this superb acquisition, if time and space permitted it, but we defer remark till another time, contenting ourselves for the present with congratulating the St. Joseph's Cathedral parish over their enrichment and the people of the city generally over theirs, for like the rain and the sunshine, the music of these bells will gladden or make sad all alike. We repeat, we have now one of the largest chimes of bells in the world, and this is something to be proud of truly! That the parish will want some aid towards the liquidation of the debt incurred by the purchase, is evident from some remarks made by Bishop Ryan yesterday, at the conclusion of High Mass; and we hope that when an appeal is made the response will be generous.

We shall probably have more to say of the bells anon; meanwhile we hope they will do something toward responding to the prayer of Tennyson, and

> "Ring out false pride in place and blood,
> The civic slander and the spite;
> Ring in the love of truth and right,
> Ring in the common love of good;
> Ring out old shapes of foul disease,
> Ring out the narrowing lust of gold;
> Ring out the thousand wars of old,
> Ring in the thousand years of peace."

—Buffalo Courier.

EXTRACTS FROM BISHOP TIMON'S CONFERENCE SERMONS.

Conference by Rt. Rev. John Timon, at Convent of Mercy, Buffalo, N. Y. Feast of St. Mary Magdalene, July 22, 1859.

Multiplied duties and incessant occupations have, for a long time, deprived me of the pleasure of given you an instruction. Indeed, I have been laboring almost without intermission; it was only about one o'clock this morning that I reached home. Many, very many conversions, more perhaps, than I ever witnessed before on like occasions, have taken place, and it seems as if God had prepared unusual graces for his people. All we want are more good priests, and good religious, to carry on the great work of salvation; money is but a trifle in so holy an undertaking; it will come when God pleases, plenty of it, but holiness of life is the great thing. Although I have been unable to see you, my very dear Sisters, I have been thinking about you, and have arranged for your spiritual retreat, which will commence on Sunday evening. A Redemptorist Father, of this city, will conduct it; he will be here about half-past eight each morning, and at four each evening, and will, I trust, enable you to make good meditations.

Now my dearly loved Sisters, give to God whatever remains of your lives. It cannot be much for any of us, for me it must be very short, and for some of you it may be no longer. Offer your holy Communions on Sunday to obtain the grace to make this retreat well, that the ensuing time, like the past, may find you spreading the good odor of Jesus Christ, laboring for the salvation of souls purchased with the blood of God, drawing by that sweet fragrance many stray sheep to the fold, announcing the glad tidings of salvation to all with whom you come in contact.

On this day, as you are aware, we celebrate the touching and beautiful festival of St. Mary Magdalene. O how I love to think of that holy penitent! The great, rich, noble lady is not ashamed to lay aside her ornaments and cast herself at the feet of Jesus Christ. When wounded with love, nothing can stop her. She tramples under foot human pride and human respect; she turns to the service of love what had been before employed in the service of the devil, and casting herself at the feet of her Lord, washes them with her tears and wipes them with her hair. I myself have visited Marseilles, and learned the traditions respecting this holy penitent. I have inspected the cells occupied by her sainted brother Lazarus, first Bishop of that see, and the grotto in which the Magdalene lived her austere life of penance, on bread and water, or worse fare, making loving reparation for the sins and follies of her early days. These traditions I believe as firmly as any I know, and they are as well authenticated as any outside of Holy Writ.

O how consoling to think of this holy woman! Her name will be handed down to the remotest generations as the model, the encouragement of all who truly repent of their sins. How I love to reflect on these glorious examples, gems of the christian year! These holy souls who, like Mary, chose that *better part* which can never be taken from them. You, like her, have chosen to dwell at the foot of the altar, to contemplate your God like Mary, and yet serve Him in His members, the poor, like blessed Martha.

With you, contemplation is mixed with action, and you leave the sweetness of God's blessed presence in the ever Adorable Sacrament, only to serve Him in the poor, the sick, the ignorant, the wretched, whom it is your privilege to relieve, console, instruct and succor. The devil, as you know, goes about like a roaring lion, seeking the souls of men, but he loves to catch a religious more than all. Therefore he will often strive to convince you that he is right and God wrong, to make you relish worldly amusements, to be ashamed of the meekness and humility of Jesus Christ. I have seen persons tempted till they did what every one but themselves knew was wrong. They would swear they were right; they would swear things were necessary which every one else saw were *not* necessary; they would work themselves into a fever, and by sympathy the sickness of the mind soon passed into the body. God in His mercy tries to win back the poor deluded souls, and at last their eyes are opened, they see their folly and repent. But there is no fear of all this for you, guarded as you are by your blessed rules. St. Vincent de Paul used frequently to say to the Priests of the Mission and the Daughters of Charity, in his spiritual conferences: *Keep your rules, and your rules will keep you.* Whether teaching, instructing, serving the sick in the hospitals, comforting the prisoners, *keep your rules*, and you shall do great things for God.

See what a hard rule blessed Magdalene made for herself, and how rigorously she kept it. Your rules are laid down for you by God, and among all the rules with which I am acquainted, I know of none more beautiful than that which He has given you. In this country, some houses must struggle for years before anything like rule can be established in them, but it has not been so in this, thank God; your difficulties are few; the spirit that animates you, one and all, is the Spirit of God. It is no matter who commands, all who have charge over you, directly or indirectly, superiors, general or subordinate superiors, all speak to you on the part of God whose will is that you obey. The Order of Servites, or Servants of Mary, founded by St. Philip Beniti, for many years obeyed a woman. It would not be much to obey

God's voice, for He could crush you to the earth by His power, should you dare to rebel, but when you obey a poor creature, one of yourselves, for God's sake, then you merit grace and glory.

I thank God, my beloved children, that there is no present necessity why I should speak on this subject; your good Superior has informed me more than once, that she herself is continually edified and spurred on to perfection by the example of the docility and zeal you constantly show, and your cheerful resignation to all the labors and privations you have had to undergo. May God preserve and increase among you the spirit of charity, and patience, and sacrifice, so essential to your holy calling, that you may continue to draw souls to Him; and after the lapse of ages, when you shall be seated on your heavenly thrones, your accidental glory will continually increase by the accession of new souls, who will thank you, under God, for their salvation.

Yes, many will be saved through the instrumentality of the Sisters of Mercy, who will bless the good religious who founded this house, which to them was a means of salvation, wherein they first learned to know and love God. Your words, but still more, your example, will, as heretofore, bring blessings to your poor children, and new graces to yourselves in time, and glories for eternity. Cherish, then, your glorious calling; may these good works, fostered by your care, be your joy in this life, and your glory when time shall be no more. This is my daily prayer for you, my beloved children.

Conference by Rt. Rev. John Timon, at Convent of Mercy, Buffalo, N. Y. Feast of Holy Innocents, 1858.

So numerous and so glorious, my dearly loved Sisters, are the sacred mysteries proposed at this holy season for our consideration that I scarcely know which to choose for a subject of instruction for you, who have, no doubt, considered them, one and all, and who are secluded from the world, and released from the most burdensome of your ordinary occupations that you may be able to pass this holy time in greater recollection and spiritual joy. But there is one touching practice ordained by your holy rules which meets with my especial approbation, and it is precisely to this that I mean to call your attention during this short instruction. Holy persons in every age have tried to mark the progress of time with salutary exercises, thanking God for the graces of each year as it rolls by, and begging an increase of grace for the future. Now, this you have particular facilities for doing, since your rules oblige you to pass the last three days of every year in holy retreat, reflecting how you have advanced God's glory and your own perfection during the year which has almost passed, and looking forward to the New Year, which is coming, and during which you may make ample reparation for any little negligences of the past. The festival of Christmas has just been celebrated, and I trust, as you doubtless have been faithful in making the necessary preparation, God has given you to feel something of the deep sentiments of spiritual joy which that ever blessed day is calculated to awaken in the heart of man. It is a season of "glad tidings and great joy;" one of the two greatest festivals of the year If the feast of any

Saint occur during the Octave of Easter or Corpus Christi, or any other great festival, the mass of that Saint is not said; it is sent on to another time, except in case of some privileged Saint. But the very day after Christmas, we celebrate the feast of St. Stephen; the next day, St. John Evangelist; the next, Holy Innocents; the next, St. Thomas of Canterbury, and so on, even on Christmas Day itself, we commemorate, at the second mass, the glorious Virgin and Martyr, St. Anastasia. The Saints have asked the reason of this, and have answered that the Nativity is a mystery which excites to promptitude, and makes us exert ourselves at once in honor of that Adorable Babe who, in the manger of Bethlehem, began to labor for our salvation, or rather, who labored for that end in His mother's womb. Therefore, on Christmas and the days following, the Church honors her Infant God by commemorating His Saints, the fruit of His coming. You, my dear children, have, in your peculiar way, to imitate the wise conduct of the Church in this respect.

You have, I trust, tried to prepare in your hearts, a dwelling worthy of the ever Blessed Babe of Bethlehem; you have knelt by His crib, with St. Joseph and the shepherds, you have clasped Him to your heart, like Mary, His Immaculate Mother. You have thanked Him for the sufferings He endured in that comfortless stable, as a poor shivering Infant, for your salvation.

You will now endeavor more than ever to imitate Him, in one thing especially. The Gospel tells us that He *"increased in wisdom and age and grace before God and man.* This is exactly what He requires of us. He seemed to grow in wisdom, to set us an example. He wishes to grow in our hearts by an increase of every virtue. He wishes that by our increased mildness, patience, gentleness, sweetness and charity, all may perceive that He has grown in our hearts. Now, then, dearest children, strive to profit by those days of grace which you are to pass in holy retreat.

All good people make useful reflections towards the end of the year. Since I have been in this diocese, every year I have had public devotions on New Years' Eve, and on Friday there will be devotions in the cathedral, to remind even poor sinners of the solemn duty of thanking God for the past year's benefits, and preparing to spend the coming year in a manner calculated to glorify God and edify the Church. Now, then, enter into this holy solitude with a firm purpose of correcting anything that may be defective in you. Look at the past, it is now vanished forever. Say to yourselves: Now, what good would it have done me had I broken silence on such an occasion, had I murmured, or yielded to anger, or performed my spiritual exercises carelessly? and in the end, what can it profit any of us to gain the whole world and lose our immortal soul?

Thank God for the many blessings and graces He has conferred on you during this year; thank Him for the crosses and trials He has sent you; all were meant for your good, all entered into the designs of God's adorable Providence in your regard, and if you had not made a good retreat, the fault would have been your own. And then, look forward to the future, and look forward hopefully, joyfully. See what occasions you are likely to fall in, make good resolutions, and beg from your Infant Lord and Saviour the grace to put them in execution.

Then will God Himself speak and act by you and with you. Then will the Spirit of God be united to you and dwell in your inmost heart; and whether you speak words of consolation to the poor and sick whom you visit, or mildly reprove the sinner, or praise your children kindly, your words will be blessed by God, and rendered fruitful for His glory, His greater glory, and the salvation of those whom you are bound by your holy rules to instruct and edify.

Pray, my beloved children, especially during these days of holy retirement, for all these spiritual blessings, and in your fervent prayers, do not forget my many necessities.

INSTRUCTION GIVEN TOWARDS THE CLOSE OF A RETREAT.

You are now, my beloved Sisters, drawing near the end of your holy retreat. You have, I know, tried to profit well of all the graces given you, and to put yourselves in that state in which you desire that death should find you. Now, then, turn to good account the time which remains. Holy writers who treat of these things tell us that the most precious days of retreat are perhaps those after confession, for the best of us must feel some anxiety until we have settled our accounts with God, and repaired anything that may have been defective in our past confessions. But this is the time to resolve for the future, and believe me, dear children, the difficulties are chiefly imaginary. Many people say to me: "O, it is very hard to curb our passions!" Yes, I answer, but it is harder *not* to curb them. We are much happier, even as regards this world, when we control them. And then, think of the happiness of the next world, when we shall see God, and possess peace, joy, love, bliss unutterable, for eternity. We are now but *some beginning of the creature*, as St. Paul expresses it, but then we shall be perfect. Hence holy Job sighed for that great change. Spiritual writers have tried to give us some idea of the glories prepared for us, by metaphors and similes. One of the best they used is that of iron, borrowed from Holy Scripture. Iron cast into the furnace soon becomes red, and assumes all the properties of fire; its lines of dimension alone still prove that it is not fire, but iron, so thoroughly penetrated with fire as to become almost one with it. So, when we shall be plunged in the ocean of God's dazzling beauty, and infinite perfections, we should become almost one with Him by the most perfect union. And this for so little—merely for curbing our evil inclinations for a while.

Suppose some great, some supernatural personage were to say to you: "Here is my horse, hold him for five minutes, and I'll make you a King for a hundred years. It is very easy to manage him if you only mind; don't let go the reins, watch him, it is very little trouble. But if you don't be careful, if you let him slip away, I shall punish you severely!" Oh, if such a man had the misfortune to let the horse run off, how grieved he would be! Oh! he would exclaim, what a glorious opportunity I have lost! Had I been a little more vigilant just for five minutes, I should be a great king; and now I have lost riches and a kingdom, and am punished besides! Oh, what a fool I was! It is so with us, beloved children: our passions may be compared to a restive horse of which we have got charge; they will take us to heaven or to hell, according as we govern them well or ill. If we curb and check them when they incline us to evil, they will lead us to heaven; if we give them free rein, they will take us to hell. Passions are talents to be regulated and tamed, for God's glory. People who have not strong passions never do much good; in fact they can do neither harm nor good, on a large scale. St. Francis Xavier had his passions, so had St. Ignatius; you need only recall their lives to see how they subdued them, and how much they increased their glory in heaven. Others had passions as well, but they would not curb them. Some had a passion for drink; well they got drunk, and died in that state, and went to hell. Others had passions for other crimes, and they indulged them, and died in the act, and they too, went to hell. And though their passions gave them no real pleasure, still they preferred a base gratification to God's pleasure, and they received their reward. When people tell me it is hard to gain heaven, I reply that it is harder to gain hell, for if we are trying to gain heaven, we have peace in this world, and look for bliss in the world to come. Beg of God, my dearly loved children, to make you thoroughly comprehend all this. In some form, you will have to teach it to others. O don't neglect to impress it well on yourselves! You must always be able to say to those under your charge what St. Paul said to his converts: "*Be ye followers of me as I am of Christ.*" See, then, whether you do not fall short of the examples given you by the saints. Have you as yet subdued *all* your passions? Your holy vows are directed precisely against those passions to which poor fallen nature is most prone. O, be careful to observe them faithfully. Ah! my Sisters, I have known novices so touchy that they could not brook the least correction, and I have seen them afterwards the wives of men who treated them brutally, and would strike them whenever they dared to remonstrate. I have seen those who would wear only the finest and neatest, and murmur if an old garment were given them, and I have afterwards met them in rags. I have known young men who could not bear to obey even the rules of the Seminary to which they belonged, who would not take the mildest reproof, and I have seen them in after years crouch before the tyrants who ruled them. I wish I could make some people think of this; it would make them do more cheerfully for God what others are obliged to do for taskmasters. But you, my children, continue as you have been, or rather, aim at still greater perfection, remembering that the more perfectly you conquer self and become all for God, the greater shall be your merit in this life and your glory in the next. Pray for me, dear Sisters, that I may practice what I preach to you.

N. B.—The word "Conference" is used in a European or rather a Continental sense. Conferences are familiar instructions, possessing neither "the dignity of sermons nor the formality of the lectures."

www.ingramcontent.com/pod-product-compliance
Lightning Source LLC
Chambersburg PA
CBHW031853220426
43663CB00006B/608